GARDENWALKS SERIES

GARDENWALKS

IN THE SOUTHEAST

*Beautiful Gardens from
Washington, D.C., to the Gulf Coast*

MARINA HARRISON *and* LUCY D. ROSENFELD

INSIDERS' GUIDE®

GUILFORD, CONNECTICUT
AN IMPRINT OF THE GLOBE PEQUOT PRESS

Garden admission fees and hours are subject to change. We recommend that you contact establishments before traveling to obtain current information.

To buy books in quantity for corporate use or incentives, call **(800) 962–0973, ext. 4551,** or e-mail **premiums@GlobePequot.com.**

INSIDERS' GUIDE®

Cover photo of Vizcaya Museum and Gardens (Miami, FL)
Text design by Diane Gleba Hall
Illustrations by Ted Enik and Carole Drong
Maps by Mary Ballachino © Morris Book Publishing, LLC

Library of Congress Cataloging-in-Publication Data
Harrison, Marina, 1939–
    Gardenwalks in the southeast : beautiful gardens from Washington, D.C., to the Gulf Coast / Marina Harrison and Lucy D. Rosenfeld.—1st Globe Pequot ed.
        p. cm. — (Gardenwalks series)
    ISBN 0-7627-3667-4
    1. Gardens—Southern States—Guidebooks. 2. Southern States—Guidebooks. I. Rosenfeld, Lucy D., 1939– II. Title. III. Series.

    SB466.U65S645 2006
    712.0975—dc22   2005054540

Manufactured in the United States of America
First Edition/First Printing

Contents

Help Us Keep This Guide Up to Date

Every effort has been made by the authors and editors to make this guide as accurate and useful as possible. However, many things can change after a guide is published—establishments close, phone numbers change, facilities come under new management, etc.

We would love to hear from you concerning your experiences with this guide and how you feel it could be improved and kept up to date. While we may not be able to respond to all comments and suggestions, we'll take them to heart and we'll also make certain to share them with the authors. Please send your comments and suggestions to the following address:

The Globe Pequot Press
Reader Response/Editorial Department
P.O. Box 480
Guilford, CT 06437

Or you may e-mail us at: editorial@GlobePequot.com

Thanks for your input, and happy travels!

Preface

$\mathscr{T}$HIS BOOK invites garden lovers to join us in a search for beautiful and interesting sights. While we don't pretend to be horticulturists, botanists, or even to have very green thumbs ourselves, we do know an aesthetic treat when we see one.

As you may know from our previous guidebooks, we are inveterate walkers and connoisseurs of exceptional art and scenery. The gardens we have selected in the Southeast provide both natural and aesthetic pleasures. We describe in some detail our favorite gardens, which reflect the melting-pot aspects of our nation, ranging in style from the most eccentric personal expressions to the traditional formal elegance found in European and Asian forms. Nor have we overlooked natural and wildflower preserves, which some people consider the best gardens of all. Also included are sculpture and architectural gardens; conservatories and indoor gardens; specialty gardens; colonial and plantation gardens; gardens for the disabled;

Asian gardens; and gardens with great views, whose very settings make them special.

Every garden in this book is open to the public on a more or less regular basis in season; we have not included gardens open only one day a year. While we cannot—in a useful, portable guide—fully describe every choice garden, we have given a thumbnail sketch of those you should not miss as you travel around the Southeast.

We have spent wonderful days visiting every sort of garden in every season, on beautiful sunny days as well as in pouring rain. Wherever we have gone, we have been given enthusiastic and helpful suggestions. Many people have directed us to gardens we might have overlooked, and others have recommended books and garden tours and have even led us to hard-to-find places themselves.

Gardens are by definition fragile. As living environments they are subject to the whims and changes of nature—and nurture. As we wrote this book, all the gardens we describe were in good condition and welcomed visitors. We hope you will find them as pleasing and carefully tended as we have.

How to Use This Book

*O*UR READERS use our guidebooks in a variety of ways. Some plan a trip to an area and consult the map at the beginning of the relevant state to find the sites they will visit. Others choose gardens with a specific theme or style, using the feature called "Choosing an Outing" found within each chapter. Some of our readers simply make a special trip just to visit a single garden whose write-up has caught their fancy. And then there are those who enjoy experiencing the gardens just by reading about them in the comfort of their home!

However you use this book, you'll find that it holds many helpful features. At the beginning of the book, the "Garden Styles" chapter introduces the garden styles that you'll read about in the garden descriptions. At the end of the book there's a helpful glossary plus an index of all the gardens.

Within each chapter, gardenwalks are organized alphabetically by town. Details about admission fees, open hours, tours, and driving directions are placed immediately following the garden descriptions. Sidebars appear throughout each chapter to identify nearby places of interest, give a sampling of garden shows, and help you choose an outing by theme or garden style—in other words, to make your gardenwalks experience more enjoyable.

When is the best time to visit the gardens of the Southeast? Most gardens are at their prime during the growing season, but some gardens are beautiful no matter when you visit; their architectural structure can be appreciated even off-season. In our write-ups we often give recommendations for the best time to see a certain feature, but be aware that most gardens are designed to offer a sequence of blooms. Bulbs and azaleas, for example, bloom in early spring, while roses and peonies bloom later. Due to weather variations, bloom time can change from year to year. If you are traveling to see a particular plant at its peak, we recommend phoning individual gardens for that year's timetable.

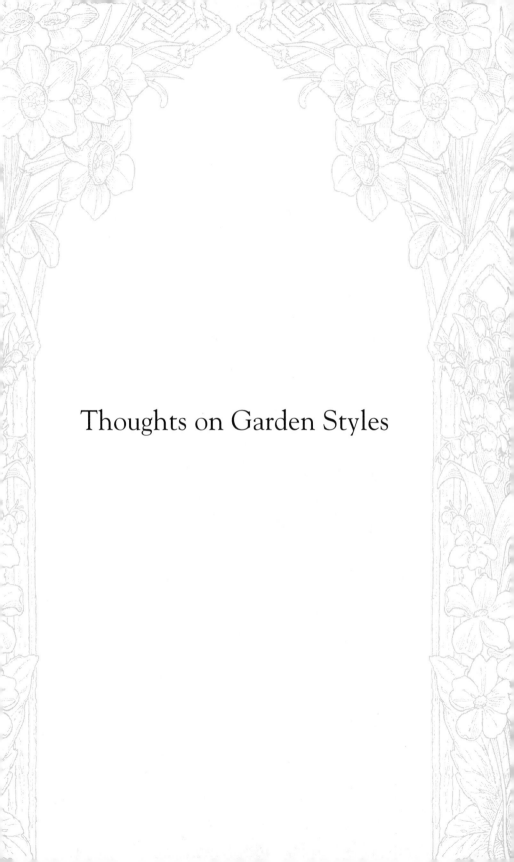

Thoughts on Garden Styles

Formal and Informal Gardens

> "Romanticism" is an idea which needed a Classical mind
> to have it.
>
> —J. F. SHADE (1898–1959)

*A*MONG THE fundamental questions that have defined landscape design in America and other Western countries is the issue of formal versus naturalistic gardens. Should a garden focus on structure and architecture or on its plantings? Should it be arranged in geometric patterns, or in a flowing, more random manner reflecting a natural landscape?

The formal approach has its cultural roots in the traditions of Italy and France. Formal gardens in the Italian and French style share important similarities. Both are regarded as architectural extensions of the house; both emphasize structure, symmetry, and classical motifs, such as statues and balustraded terraces; and in both, plants are considered subordinate to the overall design.

The first Italian gardens (as we know them today) appeared during the Renaissance, especially in the regions surrounding Florence and Rome, where some of the most important patrons, sculptors, and architects lived and worked. Villas were built as rural retreats from the city, much like their predecessors in antiquity. Their gardens, linking the house to the surrounding countryside, were designed to be ideal sites for contemplating and experiencing nature. At carefully chosen sites, viewers were invited to enjoy sweeping vistas of the formal layout and the countryside beyond.

The ideal Italian Renaissance garden—elegant, proportioned, and symmetrical—represented a harmonious balance between

3

nature and architecture. Here nature was tamed and ordered into neatly clipped evergreens of laurel, box, and yew shaped into elaborate mazes and borders. Stone and marble forms—colonnaded stairways, terraces, and statues depicting allegorical and mythological characters—were essential elements of this style. So too was water. The Villa d'Este at Tivoli, with its spectacular fountains, cascades, and basins—and amazing waterpowered mechanisms—is one of the most magnificent Renaissance gardens of all.

The Medici family of Florence helped introduce Italian garden designs to France, as did migrating Italian artisans and gardeners. The formal gardens of seventeenth-century France represented a new interpretation of these ideals. To a substantially greater degree than Italian gardens, these totally controlled landscapes symbolized humanity's mastery of the natural world.

Essential to French formal gardens were ornamental garden beds (parterres) fashioned from exquisitely shaped boxwood and yew. These intricate geometric compartments with squares, circles, and ovals were flawless in their symmetrical designs. They could be viewed from the formal reception rooms of the house overlooking them or along an orderly grid of walkways. Sometimes complementing them were rows of small trees or shrubs shaped into topiary forms. (Topiaries in Italy tended to represent whimsical creatures, while those in France were strictly geometric and abstract.)

Gardens with the Best Views in the Southeast

FLORIDA
Bok Tower Gardens

GEORGIA
Rock City Gardens

NORTH CAROLINA
Biltmore Estate
Cape Fear Botanical Garden
Sarah P. Duke Gardens

SOUTH CAROLINA
Middleton Place

VIRGINIA
Mount Vernon
River Farm

Versailles, the great masterpiece of André Le Nôtre, is certainly the most noted garden in the French style. Everything in it was laid out to symbolize the triumph of humanity (more specifically, the Sun King) over nature, from its majestic proportions and perspectives, to the central axis leading to broad vistas, to the grand canals, fountains, and heroic statues.

In contrast to the formality and symmetry of the continental garden, the English arcadian landscape was a dramatic return to nature. Influenced by romantic landscape painting and the glory of ancient ruins, English garden designers in the eighteenth century sought to re-create a sense of nature's free, wild beauty. Instead of the classical elegance of geometric perspective, orderly planting beds, walkways, and rectangular reflecting pools, the English garden turned to poetic disorder, to free-form designs, even to reconstructed ruins and grottoes—in short, to the garden as a metaphor for romantic poetry and art. Its aim was the "picturesque."

"All gardening is landscape painting," remarked the first great English landscape designer, William Kent. It was Capability Brown and Humphry Repton, however, who created the arcadian landscapes of the great English country houses. In their designs the garden became landscape, a rolling vista that combined hills and fields, clumps of trees, rushing water, poetic lakes, and everywhere distant views. The flower garden was replaced by the beauties of landscape. There are "three aspects of landscape gardening," wrote William Shenstone, "the sublime, the beautiful, and the melancholy or pensive."

The "English garden" as we know it evolved from these poetic landscapes. The flower garden near the house made a comeback in the nineteenth century, replacing the vast green lawns just beyond the door. With a new emphasis on color and an abundance of what appeared to be (though not at all) disordered plantings in mixed species, the glorious flower beds that we think of as English became

Major Gardens of the Southeast

popular. This style of informal "cottage garden" swept into fashion and could be seen everywhere—from the terraces of grand houses of Britain to Monet's gardens at Giverny. The return of flower gardens and the Victorian interest in the exotic and the extravagant led to increasing use of imported plants, rare flowers, and "the gardenesque"—a deliberately near-chaotic approach to landscape.

To Americans, gifted with spectacular landscapes of a "natural paradise," most thoughts of French formality seemed irrelevant. As Americans first moved beyond their careful, colonial-style gardens into the realm of larger pleasure gardens, many were surely influenced by the English style. Americans with large estates, as well as those planning the first public parks, tried to incorporate natural landscape wonders into their own garden designs. Picturesque gardens were nestled into areas like the magnificent Palisades along the Hudson River, their dramatic settings adding to both design and ambience.

As the great era of wealth in the late nineteenth century brought increased travel abroad, America's new rich familiarized themselves with the elegant French and Italian landscape. Castles rivaling those of Europe were constructed in places like Newport and Philadelphia. Surrounding them were great formal gardens, patterned after Versailles or other grand continental wonders. To the owners of the American palaces, the French garden seemed the epitome of grandeur, the free-form English garden a less elegant option.

As you visit gardens today, you'll find distinct examples of both continental formality and the English picturesque. But in many cases, particularly in gardens designed in the more recent past, you'll see a mixture of styles and influences that is typical of so many of our contemporary arts. Borrowing liberally from the varied ideas of the past, today's gardens might include formality and fountains as well as free-form planting beds and abstract contemporary sculpture. Exotic plantings, so prized by Victorians, might grow alongside a traditional Roman wall, or a geometric reflecting pool might be edged with contemporary tile. The postmodern emphasis on using elements from diverse sources has not escaped the world of landscape design. Thus the debate between English informality and continental formality has all but passed into garden history, like the artificial grotto, the ha-ha, and the topiary maze.

The Colonial Garden

Let every house be placed if the Person pleases in the middle of its plot so that there may be found on each side for Gardens or Orchards, or fields, so that it may be a green Country Town . . . and will always be wholesome.
— WILLIAM PENN

$\mathcal{C}$OLONIAL GARDENS are an important part of America's cultural heritage, and one of its most delightful. Scattered about from New England to the South, they represent a particular time in our history. Whether authentic seventeenth- and eighteenth-century gardens, replicas, or simply newer interpretations of a basic style, they all share certain characteristics, with some variation. More formal than not (without being necessarily "grand"), they are ordered, geometric, and often symmetrical. Most are enclosed and intimate. Their organized structure reflects the needs and perspectives of a culture that prized order, balance, and economy.

The early settlers had a pragmatic approach to gardening, whether they were facing the harsh winters of Massachusetts or the milder climate of Virginia. First, it was essential to enclose each

household compound to keep out animals, wild or domestic. Within a fence or stone wall was a well-planned arrangement that emphasized function, rather than aesthetics, without compromising overall harmony and charm. The location of the house, its outbuildings and connecting "yards," and planted areas were carefully sited for best drainage and exposure. Each had its specific purpose. Between the house and outbuildings was the "dooryard," where animals were shorn, soap made, or wool dyed. This rustic spot was hardly a place for much greenery, except for a few shade trees (which were also useful as places to attach pulleys to lift heavy objects).

Each family maintained a basic garden and orchard to serve its needs. These formal plantings were often wedged in small areas between the house, yards, sheds, barns, meadows, and pastures. At first, necessity dictated planting vegetables and fruit shrubs and trees rather than flowers. (During the eighteenth century, gardens became less utilitarian and often included decorative plants as well as edibles.) Orchards contained large fruit trees, such as apples, but pears, peaches, apricots, and plums were arranged in borders or espaliers closer to the house. Herbs used for cooking were planted in simple, rectangular plots next to the house or were sometimes mixed in with other plants. Physicians sometimes kept a "physic garden," or botanic garden, to provide the proper curative herbs for their patients.

On large colonial southern plantations, it was especially essential to create kitchen gardens and orchards, as the plantations were often isolated from towns and villages. Given a more agreeable climate than that found in New England, plentiful varieties of English plants thrived there. According to Robert Beverly, who in 1705 wrote *History of the Present State of Virginia*, "A Kitchen-Garden don't thrive better or faster in any part of the Universe than there. They have all the Culinary Plants that grow in England, and in far greater perfection, than in England."

Most colonial gardens were arranged in neat, rectangular blocks bordered by boxwood (especially in the South) or other decorative plants. Separating these geometric, cultivated areas were brick or stone paths. The more elaborate gardens might also include a central azalea path aligned with the main door of the house and leading to a vista, stone bench, or statue. On either side of the walk were raised plots (for better drainage), usually arranged in symmetrical fashion. While vegetables and small fruits were kept in designated areas, ornamental plants surrounded the more important walkways. Sometimes edible plants and flowers were mixed in together, creating formal geometric designs.

In Virginia and other parts of the South, colonial—or plantation—gardens tended to be larger and more elaborate than in the North. With the large-scale introduction of slavery into the southern colonies, manor houses were built, surrounded by often grand landscaped settings. The Virginia Tidewater plantations were particularly picturesque. Poised on rolling terrain high above rivers or canals, they enjoyed sweeping views over the surrounding landscape. While manor houses were usually set so as to command the best vistas, the gardens themselves were often located on descending terraces, in a theatrical arrangement reminiscent of Renaissance Italian and seventeenth-century English gardens. A large, enclosed, rectangular garden near the house featured vegetables and herbs planted in symmetrical patterns. Other terraces might include a bowling green (popular in mid-seventeenth-century English gardens), boxwood parterres with flowers or vegetables, and fruit orchards. There would also be English-style parklands, complete with grazing animals, adding to the bucolic character of the site. Among the greatest of such plantation gardens is the Governor's Place in Williamsburg, famous for its elegant eighteenth-century gardens (and a popular tourist attraction to this day). Another is Gunston Hall Plantation, an example of a well-designed twentieth-century re-creation that features a stately arrangement of boxwoods growing in neat, geometric hedges.

Thomas Jefferson, who along with George Washington was one of the most famous colonial gardeners of all, had an abiding interest in horticulture, garden design, and botany—and a fundamental belief that the strength of the country lay in its agrarian society. He surrounded his extraordinary estate, Monticello, with vegetable plots (where he conducted various experiments), flower beds, and orchards. Monticello and Washington's Mount Vernon are examples of the colonial style at its grandest; but, still, they were created in basically the same spirit as the simplest colonial garden, emphasizing the order, harmony, and balance of pleasure and usefulness.

The Walled Garden

A Garden is my sister, my spouse; a spring shut up, a fountain sealed. Thy plants are an orchard of pomegranates with pleasant fruits.

—SONG OF SOLOMON

THROUGHOUT HISTORY gardens have been seen as different, idealized worlds in which we create an orderly and beautiful environment cut off from tumultuous reality. Thus, of course, they must be enclosed. Most gardens, in fact, are surrounded in some way—separated from the wild, the urban, the public, the unknown. In this way gardens are like beautifully framed paintings. Such divisions between the wild and intrusive, and the cultivated and the private, create the sense of specialness and secrecy that characterizes an enclosed space. The "secret garden" is a concept that is undeniably inviting.

Artificial boundaries for gardens—when they are not naturally surrounded by geographical borders—are most often created by walls, hedges, or fences. Whether the border is formed by high box-wood hedges or medieval stone walls, trellis fences, or rows of ever-greens, the "framing" of the garden is found all over the world and throughout garden history.

The walled garden is the most private, for walls—whether of stone or hedge—can be high and impenetrable. Their origins are long in the past, when they kept out human and animal intruders and protected those within. In many cultures the enclosed garden, designed for both useful growing and pleasing contemplation, was a practical or an aesthetic choice. But the enclosed gardens of some civilizations—such as Egyptian and medieval Christian—were also metaphors for religious belief. (Walled gardens of the Middle Ages, for example, were thought to symbolize freedom and beauty with precisely set boundaries.)

Beautiful enclosed gardens can be seen in paintings from Egypt-ian and Roman walls, in Persian miniatures, and in the cloisters of medieval buildings. Trellis-fenced gardens appear in Renaissance art; the great classical gardens of France and England used both hedges and fences to enclose parts of their elaborate landscape designs. Box-wood, evergreen, and other living borders were common in gardens ranging from ancient Rome to colonial America, their carefully tended shapes creating dense hedgerows and geometric patterns.

Many of these garden boundaries were not just utilitarian borders to surround the plantings but were integral parts of the gar-den design. Medieval walls featured carvings, patterned stonework, delicate espaliered trees or climbing plants, and carved stone blossoms reflecting the blooms within the garden. Some of the thick hedge bor-ders of the most complex European gardens were cut into topiary designs, making the garden "walls" fantastic in shape and illusion.

American enclosed gardens date to colonial times, when their walls kept out the frightening wilderness. Many early American gardens have high brick walls and matching paths whose subtle

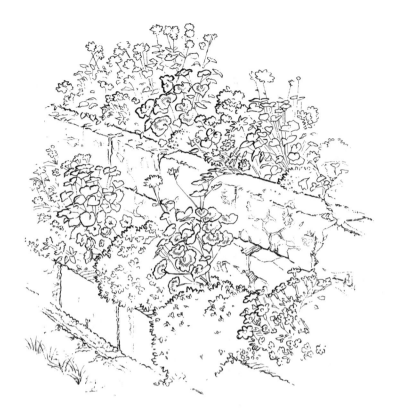

deep red contrasts delightfully with the dark shiny greens of ivy and boxwood. Versions in the United States of European cloisters and Victorian "cottages" included walled gardens. Our great nineteenth-century estates feature many enclosed garden areas, in which marble and granite not only provide a backdrop for plantings and sculpture but create both color and texture in themselves. Espaliered fruit trees, climbing roses, ivies, wisteria, and trumpet vines are among the many popular plantings that can be seen covering the walls of enclosed gardens.

Today the walled garden is often in the middle of a city. Urban gardeners use stone or brick walls in imaginative and contemporary ways, sometimes combining sculpture, falling water, and environmental design. Some of the smallest but most appealing walled gardens today are the "vest-pocket" parks in our cities.

Clearly, the concept of the enclosed garden is still valid; its plantings and design may be symbolic or practical or purely aesthetic, but the walled garden remains the special, magical space, serene and cut off from the world outside.

The Topiary Garden

And all these [flowers] by the skill of your Gardener, so comelily and orderly placed in your borders and squares and so intermingled, that one looking thereon, cannot but wonder to see, what Nature, corrected by Art, can do.

— WILLIAM LAWSON
A New Orchard and Garden, 1618

TOPIARY, the ancient art of shaping plants into living sculptures, has brought charm, whimsy, and surprise to many a garden over the centuries. The term comes from the Latin *toparius*, referring to a gardener who specializes in carving plants, for it is such a gardener who, with the skill and vision of an artist, can transform an ordinary landscape into a delightful living tableau, adding both elegance and fun to the landscape. Because of its many possibilities of expression, topiary art has appealed to gardeners of all kinds, including the most eccentric, who find it an amusing outlet for their imaginations.

The topiary tradition comes with a wealth of sculpted plant shapes and designs. Shrubs and trees are pruned, clipped, cut, coaxed, and styled (sometimes on wire frames) into fanciful animals, mythological creatures, or elegant geometric forms. Yew, privet, hemlock, boxwood, and ivy—to name some of the most popular plants used—can be fashioned into peacocks, roosters, dragons, and centaurs, as well as pyramids, globes, arches, and decorative scalloped hedges. Some topiary gardens feature entire sequential scenes:

for example, a leafy foxhunt or a flotilla of ships. Others are created on an intimate scale and might include potted topiary that can be moved about or brought indoors.

Topiary gardens are not limited to green sculptures, however. There are also espalier gardens, knot gardens, parterres, and mazes. The espalier is a plant trained into an open, flat pattern to create a two-dimensional effect. The branches of shrubs and trees—often fruit trees such as pear, peach, and apple trees—are bent and pruned into intricate, delicate motifs to adorn walls and other vertical surfaces.

Knot gardens are level beds whose designs are made from the intertwining patterns of herbs and hedges. Today's versions some-times include flowers and pebbles as well.

The parterre (French for "on the ground") is a variation of the knot garden. Usually on a larger scale, its designs are more fluid, with arabesques, open scrolls, or fleurs-de-lis. Patterns are created by using carefully clipped dwarf hedges, flowers, grass, and colored stones.

The maze—one of the more delightful topiary forms—is like a lifesize puzzle. It is made of a network of connecting hedges and paths intended to amuse through surprise and confusion. In its

Mazes and Topiaries

Another form of topiary garden developed in France in the Middle Ages: mazes. They were inspired by the medieval belief that a penitent soul might crawl on his hands and knees to imitate the path of early travail and thus gain heavenly grace.

earlier forms in eighteenth-century Europe, the maze sometimes included hidden water games and sprays that were meant to catch the unsuspecting visitor by surprise, or well-hidden lovers' benches at the very center.

The history of topiary gardens shows us that though they were highly popular from Roman times until the eighteenth century, they are much more rare in contemporary gardens (though in European gardens of the past you will find many restored topiaries).

The earliest recorded topiary garden seems to have come about in ancient Rome. Around A.D. 100 the younger Pliny drew a distinction between the beauties of nature—beloved by the Romans— and the beauties of a cultivated garden. Pliny wrote long letters describing the gardens he had laid out at his Tuscan estate. Distinguishing between art and nature, he commented that the beauty of the landscape was owing to nature, while the beauty of his garden was owed to "art."

In describing in detail his plantings and garden design, Pliny indicated that his gardeners had employed what we know of today as topiary gardens. His paths, he wrote, were lined with boxwood hedges "and in between grass plots with box trees cut into all kinds of different shapes, some of them being letters spelling out the name of the owner or of the gardener who did the work." Interspersed with these topiary delights were white marble statues, obelisks, pillars, and seating areas.

A friend of emperor Augustus named C. Matius was responsible for the invention of the topiary garden. Matius, according to Pliny's uncle, had invented the cutting of trees into various shapes around 5 B.C. (Don't be surprised by the sophistication of ancient Roman gardeners; they had been grafting fruit trees, for example, for generations by the time Pliny made his gardens!)

We next hear of the topiary garden in medieval times, when the Flemish in particular favored small clipped evergreens (box or yew, as today) trained into tiers. (You can see a somewhat later example of the Flemish topiary in Pieter Brueghel's painting *Spring*.) But unlike the Romans, the Flemish apparently only clipped their evergreens in simple ways, rather than in the elaborate designs described by Pliny.

French medieval gardeners developed the espalier in their walled cities, where there was little room for orchards. The fact that espaliers required little space and that they bore their fruit early and abundantly was a great asset during those harsh times. Later espaliers became popular as purely ornamental features in French gardens.

Topiary art came thoroughly into fashion in the Italian Renaissance, when all of the arts and their illusionary qualities were so admired, and when so many classical and ancient styles were revived. A Renaissance gentleman named Leon Battista Alberti described the principles of garden design in the fifteenth century. Among his many pieces of advice (on a wide range of architectural and landscaping subjects) was to select sites with "a view of cities, land and sea, a spreading plain, and the known peaks of the hills and mountains." He recommended cool shell-covered grottoes, groves of fruit trees, and box-bordered paths and topiary work. "The gardeners of ancient times," he said, "flattered their patrons by writing their names in letters formed in box and other odorous herbs." We can see examples of the elaborate gardens of the fifteenth and sixteenth centuries, such as those described by Alberti, in engravings and paintings from France and Italy and England.

In fact, in Queen Elizabeth the First's England of the sixteenth century, topiary designs, knot gardens, and mazes became quite fashionable at the palaces and castles of the aristocracy. At Sudely Castle in Gloucestershire, topiary yew hedges included small, door-like openings for sheltering during England's sudden and frequent rainstorms, and Elizabeth's hunting lodge had both a knot garden and flat-cut hedges that are said to have been used for drying "linen, cloathes and yarne"! Among the designs used in Elizabethan gardens were "cockle shells," "beestes," "men armed in the field, ready to give battle," "swift-running grey-hounds," "pretty pyramides," and "little turrets with bellies." Later English gardens featured "outdoor rooms" in which the lawn was the carpet and the topiary the furniture.

France became a center of formal gardens under the Bourbon kings. In the seventeenth century the art of topiary was apparently de rigueur in the great formal settings of the French châteaus. Extravaganzas of all kinds characterized French baroque court life; not the least of them were the elaborate pavilions and topiary designs. These included living plant decorations in the shapes of animals and people, sailing ships, and birds, as well as complex arrangements based on medieval dance patterns, parterres, three-part patterns, crisscrossed walks, mazes, and other features to enter-tain the lords and ladies who strolled through them.

But the craze for topiary gardens came to an end. In 1728 a French garden architect and writer (Alexandre Le Blond) wrote dis-paragingly, "At present nobody gives into these trifles [topiary gardens] in France, how well soever they may be kept. . . . We choose rather a plain regularity less clutter'd and confus'd, which indeed looks much more noble and great." Rousseau's dedication to the principles of naturalism and informality and "the simple life" added to the dislike for the artificial topiary design. Instead a new emphasis on natural beauty replaced the intricate formal gardens of the baroque.

Visits to stately homes of Britain and châteaus of France will still often include historic topiary gardens and mazes. But in the United States, where we do not have the tradition in our past, they are more of a rarity. However, we have found several for your enjoyment. Read on!

The Conservatory Garden

There is an inherent wonderful fascination in being able, in the middle of winter, to open the window of a salon and feel a balmy spring breeze instead of the raw December or January air. It may be raining outside, or the snow may be falling in soft flakes from a black sky, but one opens the glass doors and finds oneself in an earthly paradise that makes fun of the wintry showers.

— PRINCESS MATHILDE DE BONAPARTE, 1869

THE IDEA OF collecting, nurturing, and displaying plants in an enclosed, controlled environment is an ancient one. The first greenhouses may have been built by the Romans to protect the exotic plants they found during their military campaigns in distant lands. The emperor Nero's *specularium* (for so this type of Roman structure was called) contained his much-loved cucumbers, which he could thus enjoy throughout the year. Over the course of human history, plants have been gathered, arranged, and housed for many reasons—from the most pragmatic to aesthetic, spiritual, scientific, or even whimsical. And their artificial habitats—from the specularium to the conservatory—have evolved considerably.

The earliest indoor gardens functioned both as places to display plants and to store and protect them from the sometimes harsh European winters. Ornamental plants were admired and often regarded as trophies won during victorious battles. (The taste for unusual flora existed at least as far back as ancient Egypt, when royal gardeners were routinely sent to other countries to gather rare species.) Crusaders and later many explorers came home with unfamiliar varieties, which required careful tending in controlled environments.

In sixteenth-century England and France, it became fashionable to maintain decorative citrus trees, and orangeries came into being. In the elegant estates of the time, these winter gardens were de rigueur. During the coldest months, orange and lemon trees in large tubs were placed in neat rows inside glass-walled chambers, mostly for show. Some were on a very grand scale; indeed, the 9,000-square-foot orangerie at Heidelberg Castle in 1619 included more than 400 trees, many of which were at least 25 feet high!

But the real "botanic" gardens filled with rare plants—both indoor and outdoor—came into being as a result of a new interest in the spiritual and scientific dimensions of the plant kingdom. The Garden of Eden was actually the inspiration for the botanic gardens of the sixteenth century. After the discovery of the New World's natural life, the first notion arose of a *hortus inclusis,* a gathering of all the plants that had been dispersed from that Biblical paradise. Exotic plants brought back from voyages around the world formed the basis for the first botanic gardens at Leiden, Padua, and Montpellier. In the next century, others were started in Paris, London, and Uppsala, Sweden.

Most of these early gardens were arranged in squares, divided into quadrants representing the four corners of the earth (in those days that meant Asia, Africa, Europe, and America). The quadrants were then divided into parterres, with grass walks dividing them. Each plant was carefully labeled; the botanic garden became a living encyclopedia of Creation. (It was believed, in fact, that the visitor who spent time contemplating in such a place might regain his or her lost innocence and even gain insight into the "mind of God.")

By the seventeenth century, theologians upset this easy method of finding paradise. (They looked at zoos—established for the same reason—and saw no peaceable kingdoms ensuing.) Some great thinkers believed that the natural wilderness was closer to the original than these highly organized settings. And there were problems of a more practical nature: Which climate did the Garden of Eden have? Plants from so many different climes could not grow in the same place at the same temperature. The botanic garden as a place of science was created; it featured indoor and outdoor areas devoted to climatic differences, propagation, and the survival of species.

In their capacity as laboratories for scientific study, botanic gardens and, particularly, greenhouses, became places to grow plants for medicinal purposes. During the seventeenth and eighteenth centuries, botanists traveled to the New World on merchant ships to identify and gather species of possible medicinal or other scientific value. John Bartram, among the most famous of these botanists, discovered many valuable tropical plants in his scientific expeditions abroad. (He was, by the way, a member of Capt. James Cook's scientific expedition in 1772.)

The emphasis on greenhouses and imported rarities from all over the world also had an artistic effect: the concept of a museum of plants. The early botanic garden became a collection of exotic and fascinating individual plants, set out for easy enjoyment and identification, rather than a larger, overall form of environmental or artistic beauty. (As we will see, these diverse aims have been admirably united in the botanic gardens of today.)

One of the first great botanical gardens in the United States was in New York City, where Rockefeller Center is today; the Elgin Botanic Garden was started in 1801. A huge area with a conservatory featured scientifically identified plants. The garden—then in "the wilds" of upper Manhattan—was surrounded by a belt of trees and a great stone wall. Needless to say, it did not survive the city's expansion.

But in 1824 a Belgian horticulturalist named André Parmentier came to New York and built the Brooklyn Botanic Garden. One of its most popular aspects was a tower from which visitors could see

The Genesis of Botanic Gardens

The Garden of Eden was the inspiration for the botanic gardens of the sixteenth century. Each plant was labeled, and the resulting collection was thought of as an encyclopedia of creation. It was believed that the visitor who spent time contemplating in such a place might regain his or her innocence and gain insight into the mind of God.

the gardens and surrounding area with a bird's-eye view. Parmentier's wonderful gardens still exist today and can be visited.

Another such enterprise was begun only twenty-nine years after Washington, D.C., became the capital of the United States (in 1820), when a group of amateur scientists founded a similar enterprise there. Although the garden lasted for only about eighteen years before it ran out of funds, the idea of a national botanic garden was taken up again in 1842.

Plans for a new garden were encouraged by the 1838–42 commercial expedition of Capt. Charles Wilkes (the model for Captain Ahab, by the way). He had circumnavigated the globe with 440 men and six ships (one of which must have been needed just to carry home the 10,000 plant variety seeds, dried samples, and live plants he collected from all over the world!). A federally funded national botanic garden was finally built in 1842. In 1849 it was moved to its present location and it can be visited today in all its splendor.

As indoor gardens have had a variety of functions over the ages, so too have they evolved stylistically. The earliest greenhouses contained little glass; indeed, it is likely that Romans used sheets of mica instead to allow the sun to filter in. With improved technology, particularly during the industrial age, greenhouses became all-glass structures and took on new shapes. While eighteenth-century orangeries and conservatories had had extensive windows but conventional roofs, in the nineteenth century they began to be built with domed roofs. Theorists had discovered that the form of roof best suited for the admission of the sun's rays was hemispherical. Because of the development of iron frames and glazed roofs, it was now possible to build greenhouses that looked like what we now think of as "conservatories" (and what we imagine when we inevitably read about them in Victorian novels). These elegant and fanciful structures culminated with Sir Joseph Paxton's famous Crystal Palace, inaugurated as the main attraction at the First International

Exhibition in London's Hyde Park in 1851. Greeted with great enthusiasm, its enormous success helped stimulate the building of conservatories everywhere, including in America. More elaborate than greenhouses, conservatories contained plants primarily chosen for their showy effect.

The Water Garden

Any garden ornament or piece of architecture mirrored in water receives an addition to its dignity by the repetition and continuation of upright line.

—GERTRUDE JEKYLL, 1901

*W*ATER HAS embellished gardens around the world since the earliest civilizations. It has been used in gardens not only for practical reasons but also for pure pleasure and decoration. The effects of water on the senses are varied and fascinating: Water can delight, charm, soothe, cool, stimulate, and excite. Through its magical powers of illusion and reflection, it can create an environment of mystery and even surprise. Natural sources of water—streams, brooks, or waterfalls—as well as artful canals, pools, or fountains have been focal points in gardens over the ages.

The Egyptians were among the first who recognized the importance of decorative water in garden design. Ancient tomb paintings depict gardens with rectangular pools, water lilies, lotus, and papyrus. Not only were these basins of water practical—they were used to irrigate the surroundings—but they were also refreshingly appealing in the parched lands.

The pleasure-loving Romans copied these early models in their own gardens, adding more sophisticated elements, such as elaborate fountains and canals. The fabled garden of Pliny the Younger included (according to his nephew) "a semicircular bench of white marble shaded with a vine which is trained on four small pillars of marble. Water, gushing through several little pipes from under this bench . . . falls onto a stone cistern underneath, from whence it is received into a fine polished marble basin, so artfully contrived that it is always full without overflowing." It seems that at mealtime, plates of food were placed on the water so they could float from one person to the next.

Water, revered by the Persians as the essence of life, was the chief element in their paradise gardens. These magnificent enclosed oases with fountains, tiled pools, and intricate water channels provided a delicious respite in a torrid climate. Formal and geometric, they usually included rows of stately cypress trees and scented roses, irrigated by underground tunnels.

Water gardens reached some of their highest levels of artistry in those created by the Moors of medieval Spain. Such magnificent and lavish gardens as those in the Alhambra were intricately planned by some of the most sophisticated designers of all time. These masterful hydraulic engineers/artists used ingenious techniques to channel precious water from distant mountain springs

through elaborate tunnels to palaces and courtyards. The gardens were thus filled with the sight and sound of water continuously flowing (and recycled) through fountains, marbled channels, and basins.

The rest of Europe (which during the Middle Ages had confined its gardens to relatively modest cloisters with small wells and fountains) saw a rebirth of the water garden during the Renaissance, especially in Italy. Along with a renewed interest in antiquities came a fascination with science and the study of such basic elements as water; water became a central focus of Italian villa gardens. Amid the waters of elegant fountains and graceful pools, and even inside mysterious grottoes, Italian designers placed statues depicting mythological characters—ranging from river gods and gorgons to Venus and Neptune surrounded by nymphs and dolphins. Amazing waterpowered machines and animated ornaments graced some villa gardens: The fabled Villa d'Este, one of the most dazzling water gardens of all time (it still delights visitors today), displayed spectacular aquatic fireworks in addition to its other exquisite garden features.

Fountains were used most lavishly in seveneenth-century French gardens. At Versailles, for example, the master designer André Le Nôtre (along with an army of artists and engineers) channeled water through myriad dams, falls, pools, cascades, and an especially long canal (where mock naval battles were occasionally held to amuse the courtiers). Le Nôtre's designs for Versailles became a standard by which numerous other formal gardens were (and are still) measured.

Romantic English gardens used water in a less artificial way. Instead of the grand geometric, formal pools, and fountains of the French, they featured meandering streams and rivers surrounded by naturalistic plantings and graceful garden paths. Some of the great Capability Brown's designs called for picturesque garden lakes, created by dammed streams and massive excavations.

Of course, the "natural" use of water—so favored in the roman-tic era—had long been featured in the gardens of the Far East. In classical Chinese and Japanese gardens, water, regarded as a vital ingredient, appeared almost always in an entirely naturalistic way. But water in Asian gardens also had symbolic significance; for exam-ple, both the sight and the sound of water in Japanese gardens is part of the aesthetic importance of their traditional gardens.

Today water gardens have been inspired by these varied his-toric and cultural traditions and reinterpreted to accommodate con-temporary needs and tastes. As you visit gardens that feature water designs, you will perhaps identify some of these stylistic elements.

The Rock Garden

> It may appear at first that the collection of stones, etc., is designed to appear wild and irregular, little Art would be required in its construction; but this is so far from being the case, that perhaps rockwork is more difficult to design and execute than any other kind of garden scenery.
>
> —JANE LOUDON, ca. 1930

WE TAKE rock gardens for granted nowadays, enjoying the combination of hard, surprising stone and delicate, careful plantings. Many a rocky American hillside is planted these days with wildflowers and alpine specialties, and some such gardens are even created from the start.

But the rock garden does not have as long a history as most of the designs and styles of gardens we describe. In fact, the rock garden dates to 1777, when Sir Joseph Banks, a British naturalist (and pres-ident of the Royal Society some years later), visited Iceland. On a twelve-day hike to a volcanic mountain in Iceland, Banks collected the lava from the volcano's last eruption five years earlier. (He used it for ballast for his ship on the return to Britain.)

When he got home, he presented the hardened lava to the Chelsea Physic Garden, where it was combined with piles of stone from the old walls of the Tower of London, discarded bricks, and various other types of stone. Plants began to grow all over this huge and motley mound of rock.

Within fifty years, rock gardens were popular in Britain. Jane and John Loudon, noted writers on all subjects of gardening, described "rockwork" as fragments of rock "thrown together in an artistic manner, so as to produce a striking and pleasing effect, and to serve as a nest or repository" for a variety of plants. Rock gardens are more difficult to design than they look, they warned their readers. As the "cluttered" garden (much like the Victorian parlor) soon replaced the expansive, airy stretches of the previous era, the

rock garden with its many composite parts became more and more popular.

Among the early designs in private gardens for rockeries, as they were known, were an imitation Swiss mountain scene made of white marble to simulate snow and a naturalistic rocky hollow made from an abandoned quarry. Plants for these original gardens varied from traditional British ornamental shrubs and flowers to imported specimens, originating from rocky hillsides in other countries.

By midcentury many English rock gardens were devoted entirely to alpine plants in the Swiss style, even though the plants' native habitat on high, snowy mountains could not easily be transplanted to Britain. Advice proliferated on caring for such plants— described as "low, bushy, and evergreen" and "tiny and elfin"—and on how to design the rockeries. Before long the rock garden became synonymous with the alpine garden and a fashionable addition to many a country estate, where miniature mountains, gorges, valleys, waterfalls, and bridges appeared.

The alpine garden was the subject of intense interest to botanists and gardeners who traveled the world in search of rare plants that adapted well to their stony surroundings. The designs for such gardens were described by Reginald Farrer in *My Rock Garden*. He wrote derisively that there were three common ideas for rock gardens: the "Almond Pudding scheme," which has spiky pinnacles of limestone jutting up among the plants; the "Dog's Grave," with a pudding shape but its stones laid flat; and the "Devil's Lapful," which contains cartloads of bald, square-faced boulders dropped about anywhere, with plants dropped in between them. He preferred a naturalistic setting. (And so did many later garden designers, who went so far as to use imitation rocks to create "lifelike" landscapes.)

Today, the alpine idea is still popular, but it is no longer an imitative or confining design. There is great freedom of idea and layout in the American rock gardens we have visited. Many combine the

naturalistic features of a rocky terrain (with the huge boulders common to our part of the world) and a judicious use of stone walls and
stairways and other rocky additions. The plantings in these gardens
range widely from imported alpine delicacies to plants that lend
themselves to falling over stone walls. Raised beds, stone pools, and
tiny waterfalls are among the elements you might find.

The Asian Garden

> A lonely pond in age-old stillness sleeps,
> Apart, unstirred by sound or motion till
> Suddenly into it a little frog leaps . . .
>
> — BASHO (1644–94)

*G*ARDENS OF the Orient were the first to become living artistic
statements. Closely aligned with religious beliefs of Buddhism,
Taoism, and Shintoism, Chinese and Japanese gardens were places
of meditation and renewal. In an attempt to tame nature's wildness,
deliberately placed trees and plants were combined with materials
of long-lasting value, like wood, sand, and stone. Each element of
the garden was symbolic, designed for spiritual awareness as its
owners strolled through it.

Chinese "cup gardens"—ranging in size from picturesque lakes
surrounded by hills to small stone areas with a bonsai (artificially
pruned, miniature tree) in the center—were among the first sym-
bolically designed Asian gardens. The earliest cup garden is believed
to have been created by the great landscape painter and poet Wang
Wei (A.D. 699–759) during the T'ang dynasty. It was Wang Wei who
first articulated the close relationship of the Chinese garden to art,
poetry, and spirituality.

If you look at a traditional scroll painting of a Chinese landscape, in fact, it is hard to know which art is imitating which. For

the great Chinese gardens have the ambience of paintings, while the paintings seem inextricably bound up with the delicately designed traditional garden. Harmonious in design, the Chinese landscape is distinctive, with its careful balance of leaning trees and craggy rocks, arched bridges over reflective water, and gentle flowering plants.

The cup garden was surrounded (like the inside of a cup) by a wall, hedge, or other barrier in order to provide isolation from the chaos of the outside world. Within its boundaries, the cup garden drew the visitor's attention to accents—a particular plant or stone or body of water. The garden's purpose was introspection and privacy, using an artistic design and symbolism to bring close com-munication and union with nature and its forces.

The symbolic elements and design of ancient Chinese gardens strongly influenced the Japanese, who went on to create elaborate and exquisite gardens of their own. The Japanese stroll garden also

became a place for introspection: an orderly, aesthetic environment where balance, beauty, and harmony mirrored the proper harmony of the soul.

There is little that is accidental or uncalculated in a Japanese garden. Carefully placed, asymmetrical plantings—such as bamboo and katsura trees, ferns, delicate irises, or lilies—grow among symbolic settings. These important elements range from free-form ponds that reflect the sky, to statuary such as small deities or cranes (representing wisdom and long life), to raked sand (representing the ocean's tides), to carefully placed rocks and small stones (suggesting the earth's natural forms), to tiny islands in the pond (symbolizing clouds). Small buildings such as the familiar Japanese teahouse provide a haven of peace and beauty. To the Shintoists, spirits inhabit all natural phenomena, and the Japanese garden suggests no less than heaven on earth.

Southeast Asian gardens share many of the same designs and ideas, but in Thailand and Burma, for example, there is greater freedom from the precise symbolism of the Japanese. Though not as burdened by the meaning of each rock and bamboo shoot, these gardens are also spiritual

Major Asian Gardens in the Southeast

ALABAMA
Bellingrath Gardens

FLORIDA
Morikami Park

GEORGIA
Atlanta History Center
Riverwalk (Augusta)
Vines Botanical Gardens

SOUTH CAROLINA
Swan Lake Iris Gardens

TENNESSEE
Cheekwood
Memphis Botanic Garden

VIRGINIA
Lewis Ginter Botanical Garden
Maymont

WASHINGTON, D.C.
United States National Arboretum

sanctuaries adorned with sculptured deities, including small Buddhas set amid the greenery and flowers.

The Asian garden stunned and delighted Westerners who traveled to the East. In the seventeenth and eighteenth centuries, many aspects of Chinese artistry—including garden design and exotic plants—began to appear in European gardens and subsequently in America.

Today, in addition to many great Chinese and Japanese gardens carefully maintained in the United States, we also find Oriental plantings and landscape design intermixed with the more Western styles of many of our American gardens. Among the elements adopted in our own gardens are numerous exotic trees (ranging from Asian magnolias and rhododendrons to Japanese flowering cherries) and many flowers, including species of jasmine, poppies, azaleas, and lilies.

But even more obvious to our Western eyes are the elements of Asian design that have crept into our own formal and informal gardens: trickling water and delicate water-lily ponds, small arched bridges and waterfalls, "living still lifes" of stones and foliage so prized in Asian design, and garden areas created for meditation and harmony with nature.

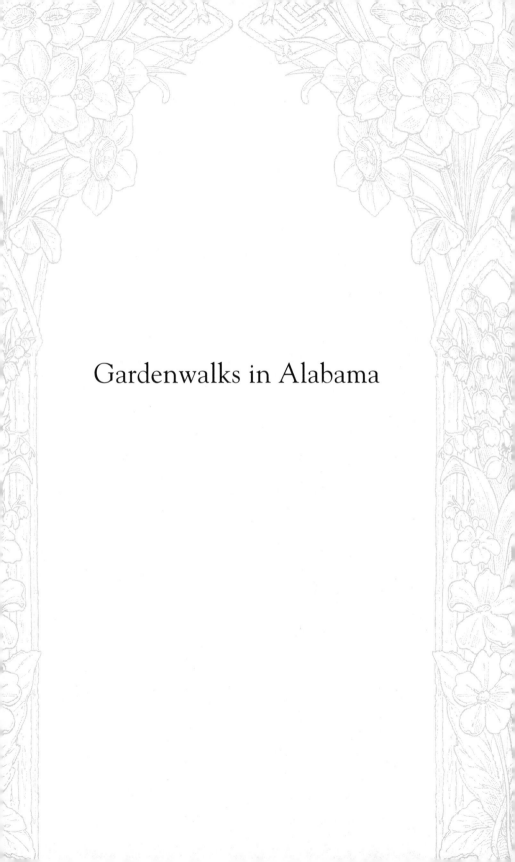

Gardenwalks in Alabama

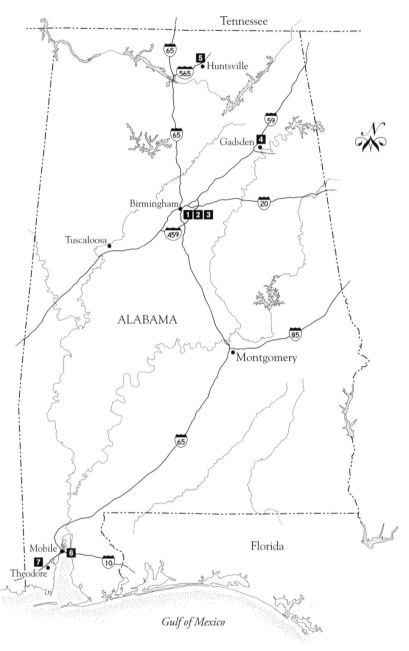

1. Arlington Antebellum Home and Gardens

331 Cotton Avenue SW, **Birmingham,** AL; (205) 780–5656;
www.informationbirlington.com/arlington/index.htm

*T*HIS GARDEN is best visited in springtime when the six acres are in colorful bloom. The eight-room antebellum mansion (also open to the public) is surrounded by green lawns, boxwood, and great oaks. Among the plantings are bright geraniums and coleuses, and from April to June you'll find many flowering magnolias, azaleas, dogwoods, and a lovely rose garden.

❀ **Admission:** Fee.

Garden open: Tuesday through Saturday, 10:00 A.M. to 4:00 P.M., Sunday 1:00 to 4:00 P.M.; closed city holidays.

Directions: Arlington is located approximately 1½ miles west of downtown Birmingham on First Avenue North, which becomes Cotton Avenue. From Interstate 65 south take the Sixth Avenue North exit; from I–65 north take the Third Avenue North exit. Then follow the signs.

2. Birmingham Botanical Gardens

2612 Lane Park Road, **Birmingham,** AL; (205) 414–3900;
www.bbgardens.org

A BOTANICAL GARDEN with sixty-seven acres, this site is divided into twelve special areas—some outdoors and some in conservatories. Anyone with a special interest in Asian gardens will enjoy the Japanese garden (considered to be one of the finest in the country), with a bonsai garden and a Zen garden. A traditional teahouse and lanterns in the Japanese garden were gifts from Japan.

Other major attractions are a rhododendron garden, a fern glade, and a rose garden (with some 2,000 bushes and 150 varieties). There are also a wildflower garden (created in what was once an old rock quarry), a magnolia garden, and gardens devoted to iris and crape myrtle, among others. Special features here include a sensory garden with a touch-and-see nature trail, a giant floral clock, naturalized acres particularly suitable for bird-watching, and an area devoted to new ideas for southern home gardeners.

Garden Shows and Festivals in Alabama

FEBRUARY
Camellia Show, Birmingham;
(205) 879–1227

APRIL
Iris Society Show, Birmingham;
(205) 879–1227

The greenhouses feature cacti and orchids among their many displays and seasonal exhibitions. A camellia house with 125 varieties is a favorite. With numerous displays, educational events, and propagation houses open to the public, this garden is truly inviting year-round to visitors with every kind of garden interest.

❁ **Admission:** Free.

Garden open: Daily dawn to dusk.

Directions: Located about 2 miles southeast of central Birmingham, the gardens are near the junction of U.S. Highways 280 and 31, near the zoo. Take Lane Park Road; the entrance to the gardens is the second driveway on the left.

3. The Charles W. Ireland Sculpture Garden

Birmingham Museum of Art, 2000 Eighth Avenue North,
Birmingham, AL; (205) 254-2565; www.artsbma.org

*D*ESIGNED BY a sculptor—an unusual occurrence—this garden is of interest both for its lovely landscape and its art.
Elyn Zimmerman, a New York environmental sculptor, planned the garden, dividing it into three separate areas. The largest pieces of sculpture are on the upper plaza, which is gracefully laid out with a pergola covered with wisteria vines. Its centerpiece is a great waterfall sculpture by Zimmerman; there are other contemporary works by Sol Lewitt, Mel Chin, and George Sugarman. The plaza is picturesque, with its rushing water over granite blocks, its curved garden wall, and its great cypress trees.

On another level is Red Mountain terrace, which also involves water. Here two rectangular pools designed by Valerie Jaudon are inlaid with colorful ceramic tiles in a mosaic pattern. Around the pools is a patio, itself surrounded by a delightful garden—particularly in springtime, when you'll find magnolias, dogwoods, and azaleas abloom midst the sculpture.

The third section of the garden is sunken and features temporary art installations. For those garden enthusiasts who enjoy seeing nature and art intermixed, this is an especially nice place to visit.

❀ **Admission:** Free.
Garden open: Tuesday through Saturday 10:00 A.M. to 5:00 P.M., Sunday noon to 5:00 P.M.
Directions: From Interstate 20 or Interstate 59, take the Twenty-second Street exit toward City Hall and Linn Park. The museum is in downtown Birmingham across Eighth Avenue from City Hall.

4. Noccalula Falls Botanical Gardens

1500 Noccalula Road, **Gadsden,** AL; (205) 543–7412

*T*HESE LOVELY sixty-five acres have a rare and beautiful site. They are along a rock gorge where the Black Creek River flows into a spectacular 90-foot waterfall. Though this is a major tourist site developed with a pioneer village, zoo, and new Habitat House with reptiles, the gardens themselves include acres and acres of natural woodlands and trails and, of particular note, 25,000 azaleas—something to see when in bloom all at once. There are giant evergreens, a picturesque covered bridge, flower beds, and a fine ten-acre botanical garden.

❀ **Admission:** Fee.
Garden open: Monday through Friday, 10:00 A.M. to 5:00 P.M., Saturday and Sunday 10:00 A.M. to 6:00 P.M.
Directions: From Gadsden, take U.S. Highway 278 north to Route 211. The park entrance is off Route 211.

5. Huntsville Botanical Garden

4747 Bob Wallace Avenue, **Huntsville,** AL; (256) 830–4447;
www.hsvbg.org

*T*HOUGH this is a small botanical garden, it has interesting specialties: Among them are a butterfly garden and butterfly house—a rare treat if you've never visited one. Most unusual is the lunar greenhouse. There are five acres of different types of gardens, including an aquatic garden, annuals, daylilies, ferns, herbs, and demonstration gardens. A recent addition is a miniature train surrounded by bonsai trees. There are also nature trails and many educational programs. This is a recommended place to take the children for a look at many different aspects of natural life.

❀ **Admission:** Fee.
Garden open: Monday through Saturday 8:00 A.M. to 6:30 P.M., Sunday 1:00 to 6:30 P.M.

Directions: Take Interstate 565 exit 15 onto Bob Wallace Avenue. The garden is east about a half mile on the right side of the road.

6. Mobile Botanical Gardens

5151 Museum Drive, **Mobile,** AL; (251) 342–0555;
www.mobilebotanicalgardens.org

*T*HIS FAIRLY NEW botanical garden is located within Municipal Park's one hundred lovely acres in the center of Mobile. Here you'll find a combination of gardens and woodland nature trails surrounded by native plants. Among the highlights are its collections of springtime blooms; visit in late March through May to see exotic azaleas, rhododendrons, and magnolias in full glory. Also featured are several specialty gardens including an herb garden, a fragrance and texture garden for the blind, and camellias, hollies, and ferns.

❀ **Admission:** Free.
Garden open: Daily dawn to dusk. Office open 8:00 A.M. to 5:00 P.M.
Directions: From I–65 take exit 5A (Springhill Avenue). Turn left onto Springhill Avenue and follow it until you see Langan Park ahead. Turn left onto Pfc. John New Street. Then turn left onto Museum Drive.

The Azalea Trail

Extending along 37 miles of Alabama roadside, Mobile's Azalea Trail winds its way through town and is best seen in March. Thousands of azaleas were originally planted in Mobile in the 1920s to create a tourist attraction. Hybrid varities were added beginning in the 1950s. The result is nothing short of remarkable. For a map visit Azalea Trail headquarters at 751 Government Street in Mobile.

7. Bellingrath Gardens

12401 Bellingrath Gardens Road, **Theodore,** AL; (251) 973–2217; www.bellingrath.org

ONE OF THE premier gardens in the Southeast, this is a don't-miss site for the garden tourist. Known as the Charm Spot of the Deep South, these sixty-five acres of formal estate gardens are spectacular, with plantings designed to bloom each season of the year. So whenever you visit, you'll find it worthwhile.

Mr. and Mrs. Walter Bellingrath began the gardens in 1928 with a collection of azaleas planted around their fishing camp. Visits to European gardens encouraged them to create a small formal garden at the site. Since then notable plantings have turned their vast estate into one of the showplaces of the South, with each month's display a spectacular event. (There is also a house filled with rare porcelains, silver, and antiques to visit.)

The ongoing progression of blooms includes a February and March extravaganza of hundreds of thousands of azaleas all flowering at once. Some of the shrubs are more than a century old. Similarly, an autumn display presents colorful chrysanthemums in vast array; there are 60,000 plants with millions of blossoms! (This is, in fact, the largest chrysanthemum garden in the world.) Other seasonal displays—each more stunning than the last—include camellias (March), lilies (April), roses (planted in a great circular garden abloom from spring through December), poinsettias, tulips, and many exotic plantings that enjoy the hot Alabama summertime, such as the colorful, tropically lush caladiums, dracaena, amaranthus, and dieffenbachia. Even August has its delights: African violets, salvias, orange ixora blossoms, and brilliant oleander.

Set among great live oak trees dripping with Spanish moss, the gardens include a great variety of venues, many suggested by garden styles around the world. Water is an important element. Among the attractions are an ecological Bayou Boardwalk (with views of all kinds of wildlife), conservatories of exotica, specialty gardens, a

Choosing an Outing in Alabama

Aquatic Gardens and
Gardens with Water Views
Bellingrath Gardens
The Charles W. Ireland Sculpture
Garden

Art in the Garden
The Charles W. Ireland Sculpture
Garden

Asian Gardens
Bellingrath Gardens

Birds and Other Animals
Noccalula Falls Botanical Gardens

Child-Pleasing Gardens
Huntsville Botanical Garden
Noccalula Falls Botanical Gardens

Conservatories and Botanic Gardens
Birmingham Botanical Gardens
Huntsville Botanical Garden
Mobile Botanical Gardens
Noccalula Falls Botanical Gardens

Formal Gardens
Bellingrath Gardens

Historic Houses and Plantations
Arlington Antebellum Home and
Gardens

Rock Gardens
Bellingrath Gardens
Birmingham Botanical Gardens

Rose Gardens
Bellingrath Gardens

sunken garden with a loggia, a butterfly garden, a seasonally planted grotto, extraordinary rock gardens (where many of the African violets grow), formal parterres, an Oriental-American garden, a canal, marshes, a river, and even a lake. A winding brick path takes the visitor through the expansive grounds.

With its brilliant bursts of color and magnificently large-scale, sweeping displays, this is the kind of garden that most of us can only dream about. (A Coca-Cola bottling fortune made it a reality.) Plan to spend a full day here, but remember: The gardens are extremely popular. Visit on off-peak days, if possible.

❀ **Admission:** Fee.
Garden open: Daily 8:00 A.M. to dusk.
Directions: Take U.S. Highway 90 to Theodore, then turn onto Bellingrath Gardens Road.

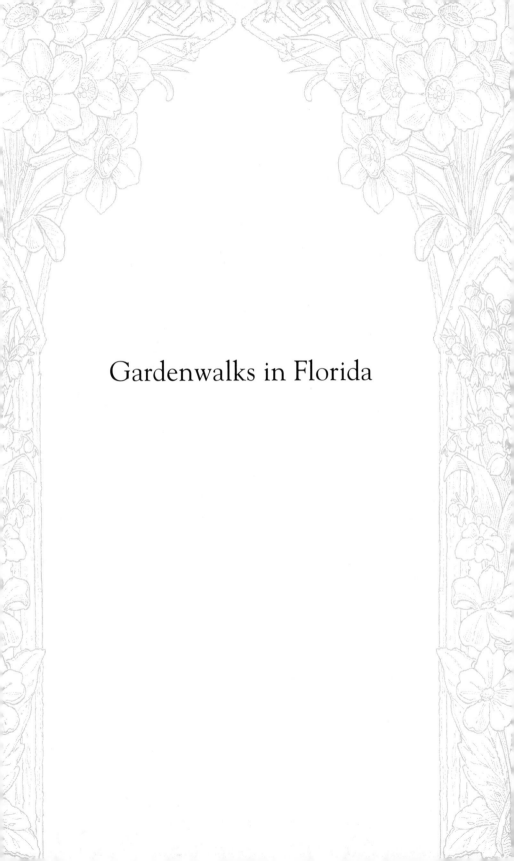

Gardenwalks in Florida

Alabama

Georgia

Atlantic
Ocean

Pensacola

Point Washington
22

28

Tallahassee

Jacksonville

10

Gulf of Mexico

Gainesville

6 Palatka **19**

Palm Coast **21**

Ormond Beach
Daytona Beach
Port Orange **23**

18

Orlando

Lake
Buena Vista **17**

11

29 **30**

Winter Haven

Melbourne **13**

33 **34**

Tampa

St. Petersburg **24**

Lake Wales **12**

Vero Beach **31**

Sarasota

25 **26** **27**

FLORIDA

West
Palm **32**
Beach **20** Palm
Beach

4 Delray
Beach

Fort Myers

5

Coconut Creek

1

16 Naples

Davie **3**

14 **15**

2 Miami
Coral Gables

Homestead

7 **8** **9**

1. Coconut Creek:
   Butterfly World
2. Coral Gables: Fairchild
   Tropical Garden
3. Davie: Flamingo Gardens
   and Arboretum
4. Delray Beach: Morikami Park
5. Fort Myers: Edison-Ford
   Winter Estates
6. Gainesville: Kanapaha
   Botanical Gardens
7. Homestead: Coral Castle
8. Homestead: Everglades
   National Park
9. Homestead: Fruit and
   Spice Park
10. Jacksonville: Cummer Museum
    of Art & Gardens
11. Lake Buena Vista:
    Walt Disney World Resort
    and Epcot
12. Lake Wales: Bok Tower
    Gardens
13. Melbourne: Florida Institute of
    Technology Botanical Garden
14. Miami: Simpson Park
    Hammock
15. Miami: Vizcaya Museum
    and Gardens
16. Naples: Caribbean Gardens
17. Orlando: Harry P. Leu Gardens
18. Ormond Beach: Rockefeller
    Gardens at the Casements
19. Palatka: Ravine State Gardens
20. Palm Beach: Cluett Memorial
    Garden
21. Palm Coast: Washington Oaks
    Gardens State Park
22. Point Washington: Eden
    Gardens State Park
23. Port Orange: Dunlawton Sugar
    Mill Botanical Gardens
24. Saint Petersburg: Sunken
    Gardens
25. Sarasota: Marie Selby
    Botanical Gardens
26. Sarasota: Ringling Museum
    of Art and Gardens
27. Sarasota: Sarasota Jungle
    Gardens
28. Tallahassee: Alfred B. Maclay
    State Gardens
29. Tampa: Busch Gardens
30. Tampa: Eureka Springs Park
31. Vero Beach: McKee
    Botanical Garden
32. West Palm Beach: Mounts
    Botanical Garden
33. Winter Haven: Florida Cypress
    Gardens
34. Winter Haven: Slocum
    Water Gardens

1. Butterfly World

Tradewinds Park, 3600 West Sample Road, **Coconut Creek,** FL; (954) 977–4400; www.butterflyworld.com

BUTTERFLY WORLD includes three acres of tropical gardens and the added attraction of thousands and thousands of colorful butterflies enjoying them. This intriguing spot includes different kinds of gardens: an English rose garden, a vine walk, a water garden, and a tropical rain forest. Also of note are an insectarium and nature walks. We recommend this gardenwalk for families with children, for here you will see not only attractive gardens but the interaction of insect life with the botanical—all in an attractive and fascinating environment.

Admission: Fee.
Garden open: Monday through Saturday 9:00 A.M. to 4:00 P.M., Sunday 1:00 to 5:00 P.M.
Directions: Butterfly World is part of Tradewinds Park, 10 miles to the north of Fort Lauderdale. Take the Florida Turnpike to Sample Road and head west a quarter of a mile.

2. Fairchild Tropical Garden

10901 Old Cutler Road, **Coral Gables,** FL; (305) 667–1651; www.fairchildgarden.org

THIS IS A major garden of tropical plants encompassing eighty-three acres. It is so large that you can take a tram around it, or you can walk through the noted palm and tropical flowering tree collection. There are lakes, shady areas, exotic plants, and collections of tropical wonders, such as rare orchids and bromeliads. An overlook of 18 feet—unusually high in this very flat section of Florida—enables you to get a view from above.

Considered to be the largest tropical garden of its kind in the continental United States, Fairchild is a must-see stop for garden enthusiasts who are interested in tropical species. For this is not only a display garden but a living laboratory, a botanical garden for both tourists and scientists. It was the brainchild in the 1930s of Robert Montgomery, a lawyer and accountant with a love of plants, and David Fairchild, a botanist. The garden was designed for them by William Lyman Phillips. His instructions noted that the place "should be a garden rather than a park," but there are nonetheless large open spaces as well as the magnificent trees and shrubs.

Plantings here are grouped according to botanical family and are offset with open space—lawns or lakes. The designer conceived of the arrangement as a series of "openings"—from one section to the next, from large tranquil spaces to densely planted sections. Areas of the garden offer a great variety of shapes, textures, and colors. There is a palm glade (700 species of palms grow at Fairchild); a rock garden; a rain forest; a rare-plant house; a fern collection; and many tropical flowering plants including bougainvillea, hibiscus, frangipani, ylang-ylang, and that plant with the wonderful name and daily-changing colored blossoms: the yesterday, today, and tomorrow shrub.

❀ **Admission:** Fee.

Garden open: Daily 9:30 A.M. to 4:30 P.M.

Directions: From Miami Beach, take Interstate 95 south to U.S. Highway 1 (South Dixie Highway). Go south on US 1 to Southwest Forty-second Avenue (LeJeune Road). Turn left onto Southwest Forty-second Avenue and drive south to the roundabout. Enter the roundabout and take the second right onto Old Cutler Road. Drive 2 miles on Old Cutler Road. The Fairchild entrance will be on your left.

3. Flamingo Gardens and Arboretum

3750 Flamingo Road, **Davie,** FL; (954) 473-2955;
www.flamingogardens.org

*T*HIS IS as much a nature museum as a garden, with all kinds
of natural life—from flamingos in their native habitat to rain
forest, citrus grove, waterfowl, and tropical flora and fauna of many
different types. You can ride through the gardens and arboretum on
a tram for more than a mile, viewing wildlife and growing things,
including the world's largest collection of tropical butterflies called
heliconias. In addition to seeing some twenty-one champion trees,
you'll get a real taste of what a rain forest is really like. There is also
an aviary and a museum devoted to the history of the Everglades.

❈ **Admission:** Fee.

Garden open: Daily 9:30 A.M. to 5:30 P.M. from October through May;
closed Monday June through September.

Directions: The gardens are 1 mile west of Fort Lauderdale–Hollywood
International Airport. From the airport take Interstate 595 west to
exit 1B (Flamingo Road); at the traffic light turn left onto Flamingo
Road and go south for 2 ½ miles. The garden entrance is on the left.

4. Morikami Park

4000 Morikami Park Road, **Delray Beach,** FL; (561) 495-0233;
www.morikami.org

*F*OR A CHANGE of pace from Florida's lush tropical gardens,
you will enjoy this quiet Japanese museum and garden. Here
you can learn about aspects of Japanese culture through permanent
and changing exhibitions, and you can wander through the serene
1-mile guided nature trail and view a magnificent bonsai collection.

Morikami Gardens was founded by George Sukeji Morikami,
who first came from Japan to Florida with a group of farmers in 1906.
Though most of the colony disbanded, Morikami was able—at the
age of eighty-nine, and after a long career in farming and real

estate—to satisfy a long desire to create a gift to the state of Florida. In 1976 he donated 200 acres to Palm Beach County and had an authentic Japanese garden and museum constructed. Since the climates of Florida and Tokyo are so different, the planners adapted tropical plants from all over the world to the Japanese design.

But the clean-raked sands, carefully placed rocks, pools of koi fish, and gently running water are all thoroughly traditional to Japanese gardens, and above all the peaceful stillness of the environment is typical of the great Eastern gardens. Bamboo walls enclose the bonsai collection. If you are not already aware of the Japanese garden ethos—with its unions of opposites, asymmetrical plantings, symbolic statuary, and reflective water—this garden will expand your knowledge and your enjoyment tremendously.

❀ **Admission:** Fee.
Garden open: Tuesday through Sunday 10:00 A.M. to 5:00 P.M.; closed holidays.
Directions: Take I–95 to the Linton Boulevard exit, to Morikami Park Road.

5. Edison-Ford Winter Estates

2350 McGregor Boulevard, **Fort Myers, FL;** (239) 334–7419; www.edison-ford-estate.com

*T*HOMAS EDISON and Henry Ford made their winter homes next door to one another in Fort Myers. Each had a taste for gardens; today you can tour both estates together. You'll find Edison's riverfront estate (including his house and laboratory, now a museum) as well as a fourteen-acre botanical garden. In Fort Myers Edison conducted botanical experiments and devised inventions for which he is so famous.

You can walk among the garden's impressive array of trees, many planted by the inventor himself, and see what is claimed to be the largest banyan tree in the country (though it was only

2 inches high when given to Edison). Other rare trees include a sloth tree from the West Indies, sapodillas, a sausage tree, a 100-foot hibiscus, and many more. Much of the vegetation was destroyed by the 2004 hurricanes, but the banyan tree and most of the other trees are still standing, and the gardens are being brought back to life.

A visit here includes a fascinating combination of history and botany and invention; you can even see an exhibit relating to the inventor's attempts to produce synthetic rubber from goldenrod.

✿ **Admission:** Fee. Reservations required.

Garden open: Monday through Saturday 9:00 A.M. to 5:30 P.M., Sunday noon to 5:30 P.M.

Directions: From Interstate 75 take exit 22 (Colonial Boulevard). From Colonial Boulevard turn right onto McGregor Boulevard (Route 867). The entrance to the estates is approximately 2 miles on the right.

6. Kanapaha Botanical Gardens

4700 Southwest Fifty-eighth Drive, **Gainesville**, FL;
(352) 372–4981; www.kanapaha.org

*K*ANAPAHA BOTANICAL GARDENS, which cover sixty-two acres, is both a collection of eight specialty gardens and a great wildlife sanctuary with original Indian trails and walks taken by the early American naturalist William Bartram. Although the gardens experienced some hurricane damage in 2004, much of that has been repaired and the gardens' rare trees and unusual carnivorous plants, bamboos, lotuses, and other exotic species still thrive, as do all kinds of Florida wildlife, from birds to alligators.

Gardens Shows and Festivals in Florida

FEBRUARY
Camellia Month, Orlando;
(407) 246–2620

APRIL
Sarasota Orchid Festival,
Marie Selby Botanical Gardens;
(813) 366–5731

OCTOBER
Sunrise Hibiscus Society Show,
West Palm Beach;
(407) 783–2576

DECEMBER
Camellia Christmas,
Tallahassee; (904) 487–4115

And what specialty gardens these are! Here you'll find gardens devoted to everything from bamboo to herbs, wildflowers, and spectacular water lilies. Don't miss the garden of hummingbirds, where flowers and plants attract dozens of these tiny creatures. Or the butterfly garden—one of the best around—where masses of exquisite butterflies flutter about.

You'll also enjoy a vinery with exotic vines from around the world growing on ornamental lattices, and a sunken garden (in a natural sinkhole), where ferns and palms and various unusual plants abound. There are also a carnivorous garden, a water garden, a rock garden, a bog garden, and the state's largest public bamboo garden. If you delight in lilies, come in August or September when the rarest bloom, but from February through the spring Kanapaha Gardens are awash in color as well.

❀ Admission: Fee.

Garden open: Monday, Tuesday, Wednesday, and Friday 9:00 A.M. to 5:00 P.M., Saturday and Sunday 9:00 A.M. to dusk.

Directions: Take I–75 to exit 384 (Southwest Archer Road/Route 24). The garden entrance is on Southwest Archer Road.

7. Coral Castle

28655 South Dixie Highway, **Homestead,** FL; (305) 248–6345; www.coralcastle.com

*T*HIS FASCINATING sculpture/architecture site, situated within a walled compound, is no ordinary garden. It conjures up visions of an ancient druid realm. Immense gates (one weighing nine tons!) reminiscent of Stonehenge open into a world created in the 1920s entirely by Edward Leedskalnin, a Latvian émigré. Built as a reclusive home for himself and a longed-for bride, it includes a two-story tower and curious outdoor garden rooms, all chiseled from coral rock. The rooms contain handmade stone furniture—beds, tables, love seats, a couch, and bathtub—as well as bold sculptures shaped like obelisks, moons, and stars.

The fiercely independent and eccentric owner conceived of this ten-acre site as his castle. Wishing to be self-sufficient, he planted vegetables and fruit trees, flowering vines, shrubs, and flowers. These gardens, interspersed among the sculptures, feature species native to South Florida as well as subtropical exotics.

Surprisingly, Leedskalnin welcomed occasional visitors to his private world. A bell is still located next to the front gate, with a sign instructing you to ring twice—no more, no less—as it did during his lifetime.

❀ **Admission:** Fee.
Garden open: Daily 9:00 A.M. to 6:00 P.M.
Directions: From the Florida Turnpike south take exit 5 (288th Street). Turn right off the exit and go 2 miles; turn right onto 157th street. Coral Castle will be on the right.

8. Everglades National Park

U.S. Highway 1, **Homestead,** FL; (239) 695-3101;
www.everglades.national-park.com

*Y*OU CAN view this vast ecological spread by foot, boat, tram, or car, and you can rent both canoes and bikes. This is a natural botanical garden, with typical Everglades bogs and plants and wildlife. A flamingo area is also home to pelicans and egrets, and 345 different species of birds have been spotted in the park. Under the canopy of the hardwood forest there are a hundred types of butterflies—some of them rare. For those of us most interested in Everglades plant life, a pontoon service takes visitors into the heart of the swamp where wildflowers and tropical plants grow in profusion.

❀ **Admission:** Fee.
Garden open: Daily. Interpretive center open 8:00 A.M. to 5:00 P.M.
Directions: Take the Florida Turnpike/Route 821 south to the Florida City exit. Turn right at the first traffic light onto Palm Drive and follow the signs to the park.

9. Fruit and Spice Park

24801 Southwest 187th Avenue, **Homestead,** FL; (305) 247-5727

*I*NSTEAD OF flowers you'll discover an extraordinary collection of exotic fruits, spices, nuts, and herbs growing here—500 varieties from every corner of the world. A new exhibit is the herb and spice garden, and a greenhouse is being built to accommodate a collection of ultratropical plants. This unique park, which covers twenty acres, was founded in 1944. An intriguing concept—you'll not only find it fascinating to look at, but you'll enjoy the wonderful exotic fragrances that fill the air. Visit this heady spot and bring a picnic (and purchase exotic fruits and nuts on the premises). Bring the children on this outing; they will be fascinated by seeing and tasting here.

✿ **Admission:** Fee.

Garden open: Daily 10:00 A.M. to 5:00 P.M.

Directions: The park is located on 187th Avenue (Redlands Road), between Coconut Palm Drive (Southwest 248th Street) and Campbell Drive (Southwest 312th Street), just west of US 1/Dixie Highway.

10. Cummer Museum of Art & Gardens

829 Riverside Avenue, **Jacksonville,** FL; (904) 356–6857; www.cummer.org

*T*HIS 2½-ACRE garden surrounding a fine art museum was begun a century ago at its charming site along the St. Johns River. These are formal gardens replicating the Villa Gamberaia garden in Italy. The Italianate- and English-style design features bulbs and flowering shrubs and evergreens; the best time for a visit to see the flowers and shrubs in bloom is spring. The Cummer Museum art collection features works from ancient Greece to modern times. But the gardens are a period piece, a fine example of the formal gardens of the past.

✿ **Admission:** Free.

Garden open: Tuesday through Friday 10:00 A.M. to 4:00 P.M., Saturday noon to 5:00 P.M., Sunday 2:00 to 5:00 P.M.

Directions: The gardens are located on the north bank of the St. Johns River. From I–95 north take exit 350A (Riverside Avenue). Follow the signs to Riverside Avenue and look for the museum on the left.

11. Walt Disney World Resort and Epcot

Interstate 4 and Route 535, **Lake Buena Vista,** FL; (407) 824–4321; www.waltdisneyworld.com

*W*HILE YOU may not have come to these popular sites primarily to see gardens, you will be delighted to discover the scope of horticultural pleasures here. The 30,500-acre site has enough flowers, trees, and other plants to interest anyone with a

Choosing an Outing in Florida

Aquatic Gardens and
Gardens with Water Views
Alfred B. Maclay State Gardens
Everglades National Park
Marie Selby Botanical Gardens
Rockefeller Gardens
   at the Casements
Slocum Water Gardens
Vizcaya Museum and Gardens

Arboretums
Flamingo Gardens and Arboretum
Florida Institute of Technology
   Botanical Garden

Art in the Garden
Cummer Museum of Art & Gardens
Coral Castle
Vizcaya Museum and Gardens

Asian Gardens
Morikami Park

Birds and Other Animals
Busch Gardens
Butterfly World
Caribbean Gardens
Everglades National Park
Flamingo Gardens and Arboretum
Sunken Gardens

Child-Pleasing Gardens
Busch Gardens
Butterfly World
Fruit and Spice Park

Marie Selby Botanical Gardens
Ringling Museum of Art and Gardens
Sarasota Jungle Gardens
Sunken Gardens

Conservatories and Botanic Gardens
Eureka Springs Park
Kanapaha Botanical Gardens
Marie Selby Botanical Gardens
McKee Botanical Garden
Mounts Botanical Garden

Famous Landscape Designer Gardens
Bok Tower Gardens
   (Frederick Law Olmsted)

Formal Gardens
Alfred B. Maclay State Gardens
Ringling Museum of Art and Gardens
Vizcaya Museum and Gardens

Garden Rooms
Coral Castle

Italianate Gardens
Cummer Museum of Art & Gardens
Vizcaya Museum and Gardens

Notable Americans' Gardens
Edison-Ford Winter Estates
   (Henry Ford and Thomas Edison)
Rockefeller Gardens at the Casements
   (John D. Rockefeller)

Romantic Gardens
Harry P. Leu Gardens
Vizcaya Museum and Gardens

taste for horticultural beauty. Indeed, the size and number of flower gardens is dazzling: More than three million bedding plants are displayed in 300,000 square feet of flower gardens each year. And there are topiary and theme gardens, trees from fifty countries as well as the United States, and a nature preserve. The landscape is strategically planted to add character, color, mood, and backdrop to one of the world's busiest stages. (An overall picture of the size and scope of the horticultural efforts here is suggested by the fact that it requires no fewer than 630 people to see to the landscape.)

In addition to the carefully landscaped grounds throughout (like the palm-lined boulevard at the Disney–MGM Studios), certain areas are specially devoted to garden pleasures. As you organize your time here, plan to see the major garden areas.

Most formal and elegant are the Le Nôtre Gardens in the France Showcase at Epcot, where baroque-style French gardens have been re-created in all their splendor—including a *parterre de broderie* (a garden laid out in embroidery patterns). Also at Epcot is a six-acre agricultural showcase, which includes a boat ride through greenhouses and experimental growing areas. The largest bedding area at Epcot covers 20,000 square feet and is planted with seasonal blooms year-round; this vast flower bed contains up to 20,000 plants. Another spot to see at Epcot is the topiary garden of specially pruned trees in geometric shapes at Journey into Imagination. The gardens at Epcot are showcased for six weeks each spring at the International Flower and Garden Festival.

A must-see for garden lovers is the rose garden at Cinderella Castle in the Magic Kingdom. Here there are forty varieties of roses—some 13,000 plants. The rose garden is abloom year-round. And while at Disney's Animal Kingdom, a visitor interested in jungle plants will find the landscape filled with exotic species.

The horticultural ambience ranges from the very civilized to the wild—from the carefully maintained 200 whimsical topiary shapes (including Disney characters) and thousands of hanging flower baskets, to the 11,000-acre Walt Disney Wilderness Preserve, which is devoted to the restoration anad preservation of an adjacent wilderness. The preserve protects native species of flora and fauna at the headwaters of the Kissimmee River.

❀ **Admission:** Fee.

Garden open: Daily; hours vary seasonally.

Directions: Walt Disney World is 22 miles southwest of Orlando on Interstate 4 and Route 535 in Lake Buena Vista.

12. Bok Tower Gardens

11151 Tower Boulevard, **Lake Wales,** FL; (863) 676–1408; www.boksanctuary.org

*D*ESIGNED BY the great landscape designer Frederick Law Olmsted, these gardens are special. Edward Bok, for whom they are named, was a publisher and author from Holland who created these gardens for public enjoyment in 1929. In his effort to beautify the landscape, he had a dramatic marble and coquina stone bell tower built and the gardens planted around it. (You can hear one of the world's greatest carillons—fifty-seven bells—played daily at every half hour, with a recital at 3:00 P.M.)

The gardens are located at one of the highest points in the state of Florida. When Olmsted undertook the design, the owner asked him to create a garden that would "touch the soul with beauty and quiet." The resulting landscape is filled with flowering trees and winding paths. The 128 acres are planted with camellias (blooming November through March), magnolias, and azaleas (December through April), as well as a fine collection of palms. There is also a nature observatory overlooking a pond. This is a gentle and lovely place, and there are many special events. Bok is known to have said, "Wherever your lives may be cast, make the world a bit better or more beautiful because you have lived in it." He took his own advice to heart.

❋ **Admission:** Fee.
Garden open: Daily 8:00 A.M. to 6:00 P.M.; last admission at 5:00 P.M.
Directions: Bok Tower is located 3 miles north of Lake Wales. Take County Road 17A (Burns Avenue) to Tower Boulevard.

13. Florida Institute of Technology Botanical Garden

150 West University Boulevard, **Melbourne,** FL;
(321) 674-8000; www.fit.edu

*I*F YOU ARE intrigued by palm trees, this is the place to visit. More than 2,000 palm trees of some one hundred species grow in this thirty-acre garden, which is adjacent to the landscaped Florida Tech campus. You'll find a series of different habitats in this natural preserve, ranging from a lush grouping of hickories and oaks and other hardwoods to sandy uplands with palmettos and pines.

The botanical garden is a good place for a walk; you can traverse it on a milelong trail with wooden bridges and paved paths.

❁ **Admission:** Free.
Garden open: Daily sunrise to sunset.
Directions: From downtown Melbourne take Country Club Road 1 mile south of New Haven Avenue, or U.S. Highway 192, to West University Boulevard.

14. Simpson Park Hammock

55 Southwest Seventeenth Road, **Miami**, FL; (305) 856–6801

*S*URPRISINGLY SITUATED right in the heart of downtown Miami, these eight-and-one-half acres give us an idea of what the natural life of southern Florida once looked like—a subtropical jungle. Here you'll see the native trees and plants of the area, along with resident wildlife that represent the area as it was about one hundred years ago. Today, the area is cared for—and provides a home for—many horticultural groups, including the local garden clubs who keep it going.

❁ **Admission:** Free.
Garden open: Daily 10:00 A.M. to 5:00 P.M.
Directions: From US 1 (Brickell Avenue) in Miami, turn onto Southwest Fifteenth Road. Turn left onto Southwest Miami Avenue, then right onto Southwest Seventeenth Road to enter the park.

15. Vizcaya Museum and Gardens

3251 South Miami Avenue, **Miami**, FL; (305) 250–9133;
www.vizcayamuseum.org

*T*HIS PALATIAL waterside house and its gardens bring a touch of the Renaissance to South Florida. There is a seventy-room Italian Renaissance palazzo with a great collection of objets d'art and furnishings from the first to the eighteenth centuries. And of special interest to us, you'll find a wonderful twelve-acre subtropical garden based on Renaissance design.

Shaped like a giant fan spread out on a hillside, the garden is spectacular (and noted throughout the country as perhaps the finest Italianate garden in America), with its elegant architectural design, fountains, parterres, pavilions, lagoons with islands, water displays, shell-lined grottoes, and sculpture—as well as its plantings. This is a garden that takes the European idea of a formal garden to heart; it offers not just pretty flowers and trees, but a true sense of design and an elegant intermingling of art and nature. In the classical Renaissance style, the garden becomes an extension of the villa itself.

Villa Vizcaya, on the shore of Biscayne Bay, was designed to be the winter home of James Deering, of the International Harvester fortune, who settled in Miami for his health. Before building he traveled to Italy to survey the most beautiful gardens and palazzos. With the aid of Paul Chalfin, a painter and curator, he began collecting and planning for his own magnificent Italianate home and garden. Begun in 1914, the estate was built by a thousand artisans, many brought from Italy; the gardens took more than nine years to develop under the guidance of a noted landscape architect, Diego Suarez.

Like its Italian counterparts, it is primarily an evergreen garden, a haven of cool shade, reflective water, fountains, and antique art. Color here is used as an accent rather than the rule. Where Italian plants would not thrive in the humid climate, all kinds of ingenious alternatives were developed. Thus, though the garden may seem to re-create a Mediterranean ambience, it is actually filled with native plants—displayed in thoroughly Italianate style. The fan-shaped formal gardens are the heart of Vizcaya's design, yet there are gardens and art all around the property. Among the many treats here are the topiary shrubs and trees, the complex patterns of pathways and balustrades, the Maze Garden, the Theater Garden (which is a miniature version of a terraced ancient outdoor theater), the Secret Garden (complete with hidden grottoes), and the Fountain Garden, where there is an authentic seventeenth-century Italian fountain. Don't miss the domed garden house, called the Casino, the Peacock Bridge, and the marvelous collection of antique stone statuary throughout. On the shoreline is a U-shaped seawall, where an artistic Venetian-style stone barge landing accommodated the owner's gondola.

Some say that the best view of this unforgettable garden is from the second-floor windows or the terrace of the villa. But be sure to walk through its labyrinth of paths and pavilions anyway. You will not find another garden like it in this country.

🌼 **Admission:** Fee.

Garden open: Daily 9:30 A.M. to 4:30 P.M.

Directions: Viscaya is located in the north Coconut Grove area, overlooking Biscayne Bay. From the north take I–95 south to exit 1A. Turn right onto South Miami Avenue. Turn left at the third light into Vizcaya.

16. Caribbean Gardens

1590 Goodlette Road, **Naples**, FL; (239) 262–5409; www.napleszoo.com

*T*HIS TROPICAL SETTING is home to both animals and plants. Parrots and other rare birds fly through the gardens' fifty-two acres of jungle and plants. There are stunning greenhouse collections of bromeliads and orchids as well as great palms and cypress. You can walk through the gardens or take a tram ride through the dense cypress groves and the acres of palm trees. This is a good outing for children since, in addition to the many birds and jungle growth, there is a zoo and animal shows.

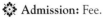 **Admission:** Fee.

Garden open: Tuesday through Sunday, 9:30 A.M. to 5:30 P.M.

Directions: Take I-75 to exit 107 and turn onto Pine Ridge Road, going west. Continue just under 4 miles and turn left (south) onto Goodlette-Frank Road. The zoo and gardens are on the left just over 3 miles ahead.

17. Harry P. Leu Gardens

1920 North Forest Avenue, **Orlando,** FL; (407) 246-3622;
www.leugardens.org

*C*AMELLIAS ARE a specialty in this large, lush fifty-six-acre garden in the heart of the historic district of Orlando and on the shore of Lake Rowena. Botanical collections feature all kinds of tropical plants and palms, and a rose collection covers a full acre. In fact, there are more than 2,000 varieties of plants here. Created in 1936, the garden has had a long time to mature, and it is a delightful place to wander along boardwalks, footbridge, and pathways, amid many gazebos and fountains. If you need a respite from the nearby Disney hoopla, visit these lovely acres.

Harry P. Leu's extraordinary collection of camellias has a serendipitous history. He was searching for a profitable crop to grow on his oak-shaded lands. During travels in India and Tibet, he and his wife were fascinated by a shade-loving camellia whose leaves were a rare ingredient in the finest British teas. He decided to import the plant for his own acres, and it did indeed prosper. The camellia turned out to be the wrong species for tea— though it had a magnificent Asian blossom much like a rose. Leu gave up the idea of tea and instead began these beautiful camellia gardens, ordering dozens of additional species of the Asian plants. Leu gave the gardens to the city of Orlando in 1961; it has been a major attraction ever since.

In addition to the great collection of 2,000 camellias—Florida's largest—you'll find a number of floral displays, including a giant clock made of flowers and a lily circle, and many areas devoted to specific plantings: an azalea area, a ravine garden (which features bird of paradise, bananas, flowering vines, and ferns), and a conservatory with orchids and other tropical plants. Other specialties include ginger and impatiens and flowers native to the area.

To see the camellias at their best, visit from October through March. You can also visit a restored historic house from the late 1800s.

❀ **Admission:** Fee.

Garden open: Daily 9:00 A.M. to 5:00 P.M.

Directions: From I-4 take exit 85 (Princeton Street) and follow the signs to the gardens.

18. Rockefeller Gardens at the Casements

25 Riverside Drive, **Ormond Beach,** FL; (386) 676-3216

*H*ERE YOU'LL find an authentic restoration of a two-acre garden on the Halifax riverfront that belonged to John D. Rockefeller Sr. in the early 1900s. There are citrus trees, a grand promenade, and a generally attractive air to these gardens, with streams and small bridges and a variety of seasonal flower displays during the year. The Rockefeller mansion, called the Casements, is across the river and open for tours. (Not far away, you'll find the Ormond War Memorial Art Galleries and Gardens. On a four-acre site, this semitropical park features stands of native bamboo, flowering trees and shrubs, and many water plants.)

Admission: Free.

Garden open: Weekdays 9:00 A.M. to 5:00 P.M., Saturday 9:00 A.M. to noon.

Directions: From I–95 take exit 268. Go east on Route 40; at the Intracoastal Waterway, cross the bridge. Turn right on Riverside Drive to the garden entrance on the left.

19. Ravine State Gardens

1600 Twigg Street, **Palatka,** FL; (386) 329–3721; www.floridastateparks.org/ravinegardens

*Y*OU CAN either drive or walk through these 153.6 acres of subtropical gardens and a 1.8-mile drive. Beautifully set in a natural ravine with a surrounding landscape of blooming shrubs and flowers, these gardens are partly formal, partly natural. Natural species are favored. Azaleas are the featured attraction from January to April, with more than 100,000 of them (fifty varieties) abloom then.

Formed by water flowing through the sandy west shore of the St. Johns River, the ravine became covered with indigenous shrubs, pines, magnolias, dogwoods, and many other species of trees. In the 1930s the park was established, and plantings of azaleas and camellias were added to complement the flowering dogwoods and other springtime shrubs. There are also a water-lily reflection pond and terrific hikes. Tours are offered during azalea season.

Admission: Free.

Garden open: Daily 8:00 A.M. to sunset.

Directions: Take Route 20 south from Palatka to Twigg Street.

20. Cluett Memorial Garden

Church of Bethesda-by-the-Sea, South County Road and
Barton Avenue, **Palm Beach,** FL; (561) 655-4554

*I*T IS ALWAYS a special treat to find a hidden garden! To reach this surprisingly large, formal tropical garden, you enter through the east arcade of a 1925 Gothic church. Privately maintained by the Cluett family, this extensive garden features many exotic plantings and changing flower displays; it is ornamented with pergolas, pools, and fountains. For a quiet and lovely oasis in the heart of Palm Beach, make a stop here.

❀ **Admission:** Fee.
Garden open: Daily 9:00 A.M. to 5:00 P.M.
Directions: From US 1 in West Palm Beach, take Route A1A east, then turn south on South County Road. The gardens are on the left at Barton Avenue.

21. Washington Oaks Gardens State Park

6400 North Oceanshore Boulevard, **Palm Coast,** FL;
(386) 446-6780; www.washingtonoaksstatepark.com

*W*ITH THE Atlantic Ocean and the Mantangas River just beside you, you can walk on a boardwalk and enjoy both the water vistas and the fine formal gardens in these state gardens in the north of Florida. An unusual combination of the formal and the natural, this site is particularly interesting. These 390 acres include all kinds of natural plants, rock formations, and a native hardwood hammock forest, as well as an abundant selection of azaleas, roses, camellias, and exotic species. This is a lovely spot and one that will capture the attention of both garden lovers and wanderers who prefer exploring the rocks and forest.

❀ **Admission:** Fee.
Garden open: Daily 8:00 A.M. to sunset.

Directions: The park is located in northern Florida near Route A1A, 2 miles south of Marineland.

22. Eden Gardens State Park

181 Eden Gardens Road, **Point Washington**, FL; (850) 231–4214; www.floridastateparks.org/edengardens

*N*OW PART OF the Florida park system, Eden Gardens is the former home of William Henry Wesley, a lumber baron who lived here a century ago. There is a restored Greek revival mansion (which you can tour for a taste of affluent turn-of-the-twentieth-century life); an eleven-acre garden featuring azaleas and camellias; a fine "mirror" garden of roses; and great oak trees dotting the lawns. Visit in March for the best of the spectacular azalea display or from October through May for camellias galore; you'll enjoy the moss-draped live oaks year-round.

❁ **Admission:** Fee.

Garden open: Daily 8:00 A.M. to sunset.

Directions: The gardens are located off U.S. Highway 98 in the Florida Panhandle, 1 mile west of Point Washington (and 30 miles west of Panama City) on County Road 395.

23. Dunlawton Sugar Mill Botanical Gardens

950 Old Sugar Mill Road, **Port Orange**, FL; (386) 767–1735; www.dunlawtonsugarmillgardens.org

*T*HIS FAIRLY NEW ten-acre botanical garden boasts a variety of fine collections as well as a natural area for hiking (including the Ivy Lane and the Florida Hammock Trail, a bog trail, and the Audubon Trail). Built on the ruins of a mid-eighteenth-century English sugar mill that was destroyed in the Seminole Indian wars, it is a romantic combination of ruins and gardens. There are collections of camellias and magnolias, a water garden, and orchids in the trees. Daylilies and azaleas are also featured. A xeriscape garden is devoted to plants that grow in very dry climates, and a greenhouse offers garden-grown plants for a small donation. Look for the four stone dinosaurs guarding the pathways.

❀ **Admission:** Free.
Garden open: Daily 8:00 A.M. to 6:00 P.M.
Directions: From Daytona take US 1 south to Herbert Street in Port Orange. The gardens are 1 mile west off Herbert Street on Old Sugar Mill Road.

24. Sunken Gardens

1825 Fourth Street North, **Saint Petersburg,** FL; (727) 551-3100

*A*NY EXOTIC plant aficionado won't want to miss the many tropical plants found in this eight-acre garden, which includes 50,000 varieties of subtropical plants set in each year and a rare collection of orchids—more than 1,000 examples. The variety here is enormous, from colorful vines to rare African violets to bromeliads and ferns. There is an aviary with tropical birds—peacocks and parrots—and a jungle section devoted to other animals. (Unfortunately, there are also a variety of touristy attractions—including alligator wrestling—and a vast number of visitors. Try to visit in off-peak times.)

❀ **Admission:** Fee.
Garden open: Monday through Saturday 10:00 A.M. to 4:30 P.M., Sunday noon to 4:30 P.M.
Directions: Take Interstate 275 to exit 24. Turn left off the exit onto Fourth Street North, then turn right to the garden entrance.

25. Marie Selby Botanical Gardens

811 South Palm Avenue, **Sarasota**, FL; (941) 366-5731;
www.selby.org

*A*NY ORCHID enthusiast should make
this a must-see site. Orchids and
bromeliads are the specialty: 6,000 of
them. Their delicate colors and fragrance
make this garden a rare experience.
(They range from the most endangered of
species to the more familiar.) But there is
much more to see here. In the eleven-acre
botanical gardens there are some twenty different theme gardens and seven greenhouses.
The collection has more than 20,000
plants—an extraordinary number for any
garden.

Many of the plants were collected in
the wild, and there are exotic plants as
well as more common varieties. In fact, many
of the botanical species here were collected in faraway places such
as Brazil, Borneo, Ecuador, Indonesia, and Costa Rica.

Among the theme gardens are a butterfly garden (a perennial
favorite), a bamboo pavilion, a waterfall garden, palm and banyan
groves, a succulent garden, water lilies, and a spectacular hibiscus
garden. Also featured in the lush environment are oddities like carnivorous pitcher plants, malabar spinach from Sri Lanka, vegetable
sponge from Africa, and the world's largest collection of African
violets. There are tropical edibles like papayas, cassavas, figs, and
pineapples. With its location along Sarasota Bay, the botanical gardens offer a Baywalk Sanctuary with an elevated boardwalk that
wanders through a mangrove swamp. In the Tropical Display House

there are myriad lush plantings, many of which dangle above you from a 10-foot-tall volcanic rock wall.

Another unusual feature is the collection of epiphytes (plants that feed on air and moisture) that grow on twelve ancient oaks. A visit here will truly give you a sense of the tropical jungle—not just of the artificial amusement park variety, but of the real botanical type—an experience not to be missed.

❀ **Admission:** Fee.

Garden open: Daily 10:00 A.M. to 5:00 P.M.

Directions: From I–75 take exit 210 (Fruitville Road, formerly exit 39) and go west about 7 miles all the way to the end. Turn left onto U.S. Highway 41, go through three sets of traffic lights, and take the first right on Palm Avenue just after the large curve. The entrance to the gardens is at the end of the block on the right.

26. Ringling Museum of Art and Gardens

U.S. Highway 41, **Sarasota,** FL; (941) 355–5101; www.ringling.org

*H*ERE YOU'LL see the noted Ringling Museum of Art, a mansion (patterned after two hotels in Venice) and a delightful Circus Museum, the restored 1798 Italian Asolo Theater (offering many performances), as well as thirty-eight acres of plantings. For the garden enthusiast, a visit here will include the sumptuous 350-foot museum court garden—an elegant combination of plants and statuary and fountains—plus a formal rose garden, a parterre garden, and a secret garden. The gardens are part of a large and impressive complex representing aspects of all of the arts.

❀ **Admission:** Fee.

Garden open: Daily 10:00 A.M. to 5:30 P.M.

Directions: The site is located on US 41, 3 miles north of Sarasota.

27. Sarasota Jungle Gardens

3701 Bayshore Road, **Sarasota,** FL; (941) 355–5305;
www.sarasotajunglegardens.com

*S*ARASOTA'S OLDEST tourist attraction, the Jungle Gardens
are formally arranged with lush garden trails. These winding
brick paths take you through an
untamed landscape; in contrast, once
you get to the gardens, you'll be
able to enjoy thousands of
plants—and birds both wild and
tame, among them pink flamingos
and cockatoos. Major horticultural attractions include gardenias,
banana groves, bougainvilleas, hibiscus, fern gardens, and traditional palms.
There is plenty to amuse the family here:
Shows of tropical birds—trained by prisoners in a California jail—
are a popular attraction, and there is a collection of 3,000 shells and
a display of many jungle reptiles.

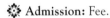

❀ **Admission:** Fee.

Garden open: Daily 9:00 A.M. to 5:00 P.M.

Directions: Take US 41. Two miles south of Sarasota/Bradenton
Airport, look for Myrtle (Thirty-seventh) Street and Bayshore Road,
2 blocks west of the highway. Turn onto Bayshore Road.

28. Alfred B. Maclay State Gardens

3540 Thomasville Road, **Tallahassee,** FL; (813) 987–5082,
(888) 800–5447; www.floridastateparks.org/maclaygardens

*T*HIS BEAUTIFUL 300-acre site is a former private estate and
now a state park. There are formal gardens, flowering trees
(including dogwood, magnolia, and cherry), and demonstration

gardens. The Maclays began creating their extensive garden in 1923, and over the years it matured into a lovely spot—particularly in winter and early spring when the Maclays were in residence.

Twenty-eight acres of the extensive estate are landscaped, some of them around a large picturesque lake. Though Alfred Maclay favored azaleas and particularly camellias, he planted many exotic species too. There are familiar blooms like pansies, daylilies, and irises. This is thought to be one of the South's most extensive collection of azaleas and camellias (to see these in bloom, visit in March). Notice the architectural feel to many of these gardens; there are archways, walkways, circular flower beds, and such attractions as a camellia walk, a walled garden (which surrounds a courtyard with a small pool), and the Lake Vista, which has a reflecting pool bordered by white azaleas and palms and cypress trees.

❀ **Admission:** Fee.

Garden open: Daily 8:00 A.M. to sunset.

Directions: Located about 6 miles north of Tallahassee, the gardens' entrance is on U.S. Highway 319, just past the intersection with Interstate 10.

29. Busch Gardens

3000 Busch Boulevard, **Tampa,** FL; (813) 977–6606; www.buschgardens.com

*I*F YOU LIKE bustling environments with things to do, see, and buy, then don't miss these famous gardens. Included in the 300-acre park are flowers, tropical trees, and shrubs, as well as a good-size zoo, bird and dolphin shows, sky ride, monorail, restaurant, and brewery tour. Eight different theme sections evoke the spirit of turn-of-the-twentieth-century Africa, here called the Dark Continent. Among the thematic exhibits are sections devoted to Nairobi and baby animals, Morocco and a North African ambience, the

Rare Trees

Torreya State Park in western Florida offers something few other parks can claim: *Torreya taxifolia,* or stinking cedar, a rare and endangered species of torreya tree found only in certain areas of the Florida panhandle and adjacent Georgia. The 1,063-acre park, located along Highway 12 between Bristol and Greensboro, has been called the Garden of Eden because it also includes many trees that are described in the Bible. For information call (850) 643-2674.

Serengeti Plain and its native wildlife, and the Bird Gardens and Aviary with more than 2,000 specimens. There are seasonal and tropical plantings throughout this entertainment complex.

❀ **Admission:** Fee.
Garden open: Daily 9:00 A.M. to 6:00 P.M.
Directions: From Tampa go 8 miles north on I-275. Go east on Busch Boulevard to Busch Gardens' entrance.

30. Eureka Springs Park

6400 Eureka Springs Road, **Tampa,** FL; (813) 744-5536

*T*HIRTY-ONE ACRES here are devoted to a botanical garden of rare and unusual plants, all of them native to Florida. In addition to conservatories featuring orchids and other tropical plants, the park offers extensive outdoor gardens with walkways ornamented by trellises, interpretive trails, and a variety of appealing walks. Less well known than its neighbor, Busch Gardens, this park is a serious botanical garden for those with a taste for horticultural and aesthetic pleasures.

Admission: Free.
Garden open: Daily 8:00 A.M. to 6:00 P.M.
Directions: From I–75 going south, exit at Dr. M. L. King Boulevard. Turn right. Go to U.S. Highway 301. Turn right at the second light (Sligh/Breckenridge); at the stop sign turn right. After 1 ½ miles turn left to entrance.

31. McKee Botanical Garden

350 U.S. Highway 1, **Vero Beach,** FL; (772) 794–0601; www.mckeegarden.org

*O*NE OF THE oldest botanical gardens in the state—and an early tourist attraction—McKee Botanical Garden was developed in 1932. It quickly became known for its beautiful orchids and water-lily collections and for its hybridizing of exotic plants. Now a major project of the Indian River Land Trust, the garden has been named to the National Register of Historic Places. It is undergoing exten-sive renovation due to hurricane damage, but the restoration is well on its way to completion and the garden is open to the public. If water lilies and exotic plants are your interest, this is an attraction you won't want to miss.

🌼 **Admission:** Fee.
Garden open: Tuesday through Saturday 10:00 A.M. to 5:00 P.M., Sunday noon to 5:00 P.M.
Directions: From I–95 south take Indrio Road east to US 1. Continue north on US 1 to Vero Beach. McKee Botanical Garden is on US 1 at the southern gateway of Vero Beach.

32. Mounts Botanical Garden

531 North Military Trail, **West Palm Beach,** FL; (561)
233–1749; www.mounts.org

A VARIETY OF gardens here include citrus and
tropical fruit trees, a fern house, a
lily pond, a touch garden, and gardens
devoted to hibiscus, roses, and herbs.
Despite major hurricane damage in
2004, the gardens are now restored
and open to the public. This thirteen-
acre botanical garden has an unusual
menu of programs and educational
events dealing with such subjects as
salt-tolerant plants and native species;
its horticultural programs are one of its
major objectives. But even if you just come to
see the pretty growing things, you will find plenty
to interest you.

✻ **Admission:** Free.
Garden open: Monday through Saturday 8:30 A.M. to 4:30 P.M.,
Sunday 1:00 to 4:00 P.M.
Directions: From I–95 take the Southern Boulevard exit west to Mil-
itary Trail, then go north on Military Trail half a mile. The gardens are
on your left, across from Palm Beach International Airport.

33. Florida Cypress Gardens

6000 Cypress Garden Boulevard, **Winter Haven,** FL;
(863) 324–2111; www.cypressgardens.com/gardens.asp

T HIS IS A very large (200-acre) extravaganza, and one any
garden enthusiast will want to visit. It is planted with spectacular tropical and native plants and is certainly a well-known

tourist attraction. Founded in 1936 in what was once a swamp by a retired advertising executive named Richard Pope, Cypress Gardens was designed specifically with beauty and attractiveness (and certainly some commercial interest) in mind. *Life* magazine once referred to it as a photographer's paradise, and indeed it has been used as a site for movies and photo shoots and visited by thousands and thousands of tourists. (Some say that Cypress Gardens is where Florida tourism began.) Though Pope was laughed at for choosing this site—he was known as "Swami of the Swamp" and "Maestro of the Muck"—his enterprise has become one of the most-visited sites in the state. There are all of the usual tourist attractions and more, including a zoo, water-skiing and ice-skating exhibitions, and all kinds of events—both garden and nongarden related. Nonetheless, just as all of the past visitors have found the gardens magnificent, so will you!

With one of the world's largest collections of tropical and subtropical plants in the world, Cypress Gardens offers vast areas of flowering beauty, and you needn't walk to see it all. You can survey the garden through canal-boat tours, railroad tours, kiddie rides, and guided tours. Most notable is the Island in the Sky—a sixteen-story, 150-foot ride that soars above the park. There is a man-made Mediter-

Florida Highway Wildflowers

Several interstates offer wonderful wildflower displays at different times of year. You'll find crimson clover on Interstate 10 from Pensacola to Tallahassee (March to April), phlox on Interstate 75 from Tampa to the Georgia state line (April to May), blanketflower on Route A1A from Saint Augustine to Route 201 in Flagler (June to August), and coreopsis and goldenrod on U.S. Highway 98 from Panama City to Perry (August to December).

ranean waterfall (in this flat landscape!) and numerous fountains, walkways, formal gardens, and changing displays.

Theme gardens include a rose garden (with 500 types of roses), collections of orchids, gardenias, a forest garden, a butterfly garden (in a great Victorian glasshouse), vegetable and fruit gardens, a biblical garden (with some twenty-five species mentioned in the Bible), an Oriental garden, a French garden, educational exhibits, and no fewer than 8,000 different varieties of plants from ninety different countries. Giant cypress trees, many with Spanish moss dripping from them, loom over delicate plants and pathways. Every plant is labeled both in Latin and English.

There are numerous special garden events here too, each as flamboyant and extravagant as the next. For example, springtime brings extensive topiary displays (the Easter Bunny and a giant inchworm, among others) and a Victorian garden party event, in which creeping fig vine is used to create dozens and dozens of topiary figures. Forty thousand poinsettias decorate the grounds around Christmastime, and in fall the chrysanthemum blooms are said to number 2.5 million!

A visit here can be easily combined with the nearby Slocum Water Gardens in Winter Haven.

✿ **Admission:** Fee.
Garden open: Daily 9:30 A.M. to 5:30 P.M.
Directions: Cypress Gardens are in central Florida, 4 miles southeast of Winter Haven. Take Route 540 and follow signs.

34. Slocum Water Gardens

1101 Cypress Gardens Road, **Winter Haven,** FL; (863) 293-7151; www.slocumwatergardens.com

*T*HIS DELIGHTFUL 7½-acre water garden includes ponds, fountains, goldfish, and aquatic plants. But the real specialty here is water lilies—one hundred varieties of them. These acres of water gardens are truly a fascinating sight; if you've never visited an extensive water garden, you will be delighted by the sight, especially as you walk the paths above the water. You can also purchase and bring home some of the water lilies from this garden. This is one of the rare retail establishments included in the book; it is well worth visiting, whether you choose to buy plants or just wander about.

❀ **Admission:** Free.

Garden open: Monday through Friday 8:00 A.M. to 4:00 P.M., Saturday 8:00 A.M. to noon.

Directions: Take Route 540 east from Winter Haven to Cypress Gardens Boulevard.

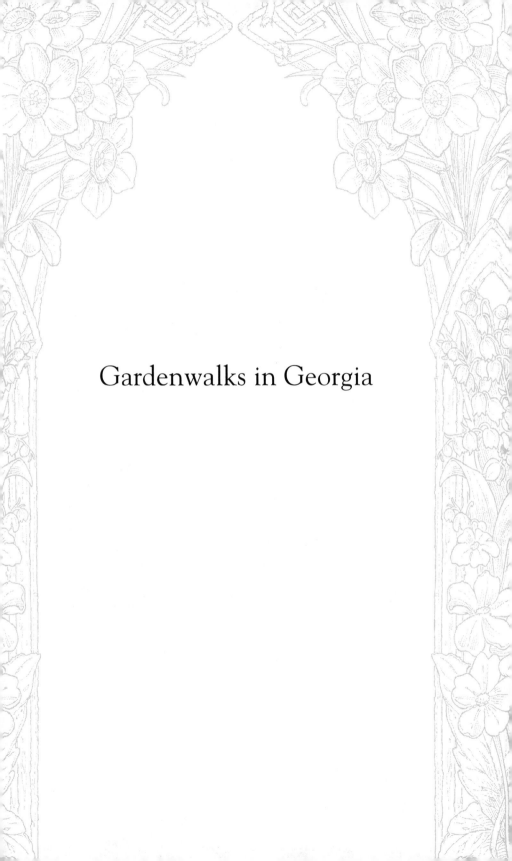

Gardenwalks in Georgia

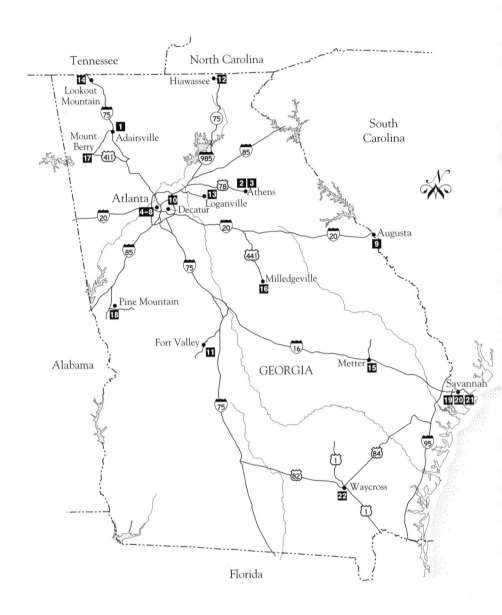

1. Adairsville: Barnsley Gardens
2. Athens: Founders Memorial Garden
3. Athens: State Botanical Garden of Georgia
4. Atlanta: Atlanta Botanical Garden
5. Atlanta: Atlanta History Center
6. Atlanta: Cator Woolford Gardens at the Frazer Center
7. Atlanta: The Gardens of H. M. Patterson & Sons
8. Atlanta: Robert L. Staton Rose Garden
9. Augusta: Riverwalk
10. Decatur: Georgia Perimeter College Botanical Garden
11. Fort Valley: Massee Lane Gardens
12. Hiawassee: Fred Hamilton Rhododendron Garden
13. Loganville: Vines Botanical Gardens
14. Lookout Mountain: Rock City Gardens
15. Metter: Guido Gardens
16. Milledgeville: Lockerly Arboretum
17. Mount Berry: Oak Hill at the Martha Berry Museum
18. Pine Mountain: Callaway Gardens
19. Savannah: Chatham County Garden Center and Botanical Gardens
20. Savannah: Forsyth Park
21. Savannah: Owens-Thomas House and Gardens
22. Waycross: Okefenokee Swamp Park

1. Barnsley Gardens

597 Barnsley Gardens Road,
Adairsville, GA;
(770) 773–7480, (877) 773–2447;
www.barnsleyresort.com

HESE beguiling gardens in the rolling northwest Georgia mountains combine the romantic ruins of an Italianate villa with many acres of landscaped grounds and flower gardens within a brand-new luxury resort. Once the much larger country estate of Godfrey Barnsley, an Englishman who came to Georgia in the nineteenth century to seek his fortune in cotton, the property has had a long and rich history, one also tinged with tragedy. (It was the scene of a family murder in the 1930s.) In 1841 Barnsley built this rather extravagant estate—which he called Woodlands—for his wife, Julia, and their growing family. An avid amateur botanist and gardener, it seems he based his landscape designs on the published manuals of Andrew Jackson Downing, the most renowned landscape architect of the time. With its many exotic plants from around the world, as well as hundreds of native rhododendrons and azaleas, Woodlands was a real showplace. So much so that during the Civil War, General McPherson and his troops were careful not to damage it.

Unfortunately, during the late nineteenth century, the property suffered from lack of care; on top of everything else, a vicious tornado left the manor house without a roof in 1906. The sad deterioration of Woodlands was reversed in the 1980s, when Prince Hubertus Fugger of Germany bought the estate. It has since undergone extensive restoration. The romantic ruins of the main house have been reclaimed from a jungle of wisteria vines and preserved, as have other historic structures on the property, and the once-fabled gardens have been brought back to life.

The haunted-looking brick mansion is now the picturesque setting for an art gallery and museum documenting the history of the site. You will want to walk around its arched passageways and explore it, as well as the surrounding gardens, fields, and woods.

Among the garden's many pleasures are a boxwood parterre with Renaissance-style fountain, a vast collection of roses (some 150 species), broad lawns with herbaceous borders, rock and bog gardens, a group of ponds surrounded by ornamental grasses and other plantings, a wildflower meadow, and conifer and silver bells hills. You are free to explore on your own or take a guided tour conducted by a horticulturist or historian, depending on your interests.

❀ **Admission:** Fee.
Garden open: Daily 9:00 A.M. to 6:00 P.M.
Directions: Take Interstate 75 north through downtown Atlanta to exit 306 (Adairsville). Turn left and go about a mile and a half, go through two intersections, and then take the second left and follow signs. After about 5 miles on Hall Station Road, turn right onto Barnsley Gardens Road. The gardens will be on the left after 2½ miles.

2. Founders Memorial Garden

325 South Lumpkin Street, **Athens,** GA; (706) 542–4776; www.uga.edu/gardenclub

*C*REATED AS A living tribute to the twelve Georgia ladies who in 1891 formed the first garden club in the nation (there are now almost 10,000 such organizations), this is a gracious 2½-acre garden on the leafy grounds of the University of Georgia campus. It was conceived in the early 1940s by Hubert Owens, head of the university's Department of Landscape Architecture, not only to honor the founders but also to provide an outdoor laboratory of regional ornamental plants for both students and visitors.

Existing historic buildings—a picturesque 1857 historic Greek revival house, a small kitchen building, and a smokehouse—became the backdrops for the elegant garden. Featured are gracefully flowing garden rooms, including a formal boxwood parterre, a perennial garden, a courtyard of paving stones arranged in circles, terraces overlooking the landscape, a camellia walk and arbor, and a more free-form, shaded garden with azaleas, rhododendrons, ground covers, and stone paths.

One of the favorite areas within the beautifully maintained site is the colonial boxwood garden. Surrounded by a white picket fence, it combines dwarf evergreen hedges trimmed in circular motifs, brick walkways, and beds of native peach, Cherokee rose, and cotton boll. Beside it, a small terrace flows into the perennial, or serpentine, garden, so called because of its undulating brick wall surrounding a broad lawn and collection of annuals and perennials. Nearby is the outstanding camellia collection (dedicated to Owens) and arboretum of mature trees. Throughout the garden you will find some of the best examples of Georgia and Piedmont species in the South, including double-flowering dogwood, magnolia, leatherleaf viburnum, and flowering quince.

A fitting memorial to those dedicated garden lovers of the nineteenth century, the garden is a serene oasis that invites contemplation and careful study or a leisurely stroll in a historic setting.

❀ **Admission:** Free.

Garden open: Daily dawn to dusk.

Directions: The gardens are located on the University of Georgia campus at the intersection of South Lumpkin Street and Bocock Drive. Follow signs to the campus from U.S. Highway 78.

3. State Botanical Garden of Georgia

The Garden Club of Georgia, 2450 South Milledge Avenue,
Athens, GA; (706) 542-1244; www.uga.edu/botgarden

*A*PTLY describing itself as "a living laboratory," this 313-acre botanical garden of the University of Georgia is dedicated to the study and enjoyment of plants and nature. With its specialty gardens, miles of winding woodland trails (color coded for easy identification), and pristine, modern conservatory, it provides the ideal setting for a nice long gardenwalk.

Its theme gardens (with more in the planning stage) include many seen in other botanic sites: a shade garden, dahlia garden, ground cover collection, trial garden, native flora garden, rose garden, annual/perennial garden, and new heritage garden, among others. But more unusual—and especially inviting—is the international garden. (You can enjoy a nice view of it from the airy tea room in the visitor center.) Here, alongside a stream and over an arched, flower-filled stone "flower bridge," a sequence of horticultural collections flow gracefully into one another, portraying the important historic connections between people and plants and the evolution of botanical gardens. These beautiful and enlightening exhibits feature plants from the Middle East and the Mediterranean, Spanish America, the American South, and the Orient; herb collections used for dye, fragrance, ceremonial, and culinary purposes; examples of threatened and endangered species and thoughts on conservation; and displays honoring historic personages—such as John Bartram—whose tireless efforts in plant gathering have significantly furthered the study of botany.

The gardens on these vast grounds (all well marked and clearly identified) connect via gently sloping paths, many shaded with laurel, magnolia, dogwood, viburnum, azalea, rhododendron, and other native species. The conservatory contains fine collections of orchids; tropical food, beverage, and spice crops; and exotic palms.

For an unexpected pleasure after seeing the gardens, stop at the Day Chapel, a 1994 soaring structure made of cypress and glass, peacefully set in thick woods on the other side of the gardens.

❀ **Admission:** Free.

Garden open: Daily 8:00 A.M. to dusk.

Directions: From U.S. Highway 129/441 south of the city center, go to the bypass, head east, and turn right on South Milledge Avenue to the garden entrance.

4. Atlanta Botanical Garden

1345 Piedmont Avenue, **Atlanta**, GA; (404) 876-5859;
www.atlantabotanicalgarden.org

A LAVENDER wisteria vine covering a wood trellis graces the entrance of this delightful thirty-acre urban oasis, located at the northern end of Atlanta's Piedmont Park. Within lies a world of spectacular flowering trees and blossoms, from pink and white dogwoods, to cherries, azaleas, and crab apples. Springtime features masses of wildflowers, tulips, hyacinths, pansies, and irises. An All-America Rose Selections Garden (the setting for many weddings) adds elegance and charm. You will also find a rock garden, an herb and knot garden, a vegetable garden, and a woodland trail with native shrubs.

Garden Club of Georgia

Throughout the South countless garden organizations have helped restore historic gardens. The Garden Club of Georgia is one such group of dedicated volunteers. Local chapters of the club have contributed to the renovation of LeConte Woodmanston Rice Plantation and Botanical Garden off U.S. Highway 17 near Riceboro. In 1810 Louis LeConte founded a fine botanical garden here, and now sixty-four acres of the original 3,300-acre plantation are being restored. To visit LeConte Woodmanston, call (912) 884-6500. To learn more about the Garden Club of Georgia, visit www.uga.edu/gardenclub.

But the centerpiece of the Atlanta Botanical Garden is without doubt its dazzling conservatory. Opened in 1989, the Dorothy Chapman Fuqua Conservatory encloses 16,000 square feet of tropical and desert climatic zones. More than 6,000 plants flourish in this house of glass, many of which are rare or endangered. In the desert environment is a rich collection of succulents. Under the massive tropical rotunda (which is 50 feet tall and visible throughout the garden), a dramatic 14-foot cascade tumbles over volcanic lava, surrounded by exotic orchids, ferns, and high Madagascar palm trees. Brightly colored parrots fly around freely to the sounds of poison dart frogs that come from the rain forest in South America and are nearly extinct. You could well imagine yourself in a real jungle!

The garden also has collections of carnivorous plants. Just outside the conservatory is a bog featuring some of these curiosities, including Venus flytraps. Children will enjoy this site and will be fascinated by these displays.

The Atlanta Botanical Garden is a very pleasant place to visit, whether you are here to get ideas for your own garden or simply to enjoy its natural beauties.

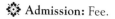 **Admission:** Fee.

Garden open: Tuesday through Sunday 9:00 A.M. to 6:00 P.M.

Directions: From I–75 through Atlanta, exit at North Avenue (east); pick up Piedmont Avenue going north and Piedmont Park will be on your right. The botanical garden is at the north end of the park.

5. Atlanta History Center

130 West Paces Ferry Road NW, **Atlanta**, GA; (404) 814–4000; www.atlhist.org

HE ATLANTA HISTORY CENTER, situated on what was once a private estate with surrounding woods, chronicles the natural and historic evolution of the region through a collection of indoor and outdoor exhibits. There is much to see on these spacious grounds in addition to a museum and library, from the reconstructed nineteenth-century Georgia farm buildings to the many delightful gardens and winding woodland trails. You should allow time to savour it all.

The centerpiece of the site is the Swan House and its lovely enclosed boxwood garden. This classic-style mansion, designed by Philip Shutze in the late 1920s for the prominent Inman family, contains furnishings and artifacts reflecting the glamour of that era.

The formal Italianate garden features a boxwood parterre meticulously restored to its original splendor, a gracious central fountain basin, elegant columns, urns, potted hydrangeas, grassy borders, gravel paths, and carefully arranged plantings. Perennial beds, re-created after extensive research on which plants might have originally been there, are now filled with peony, iris, phlox, hosta, and candytuft. It's difficult to imagine that this quiet and peaceful garden is in the middle of a lively city.

Among the other garden offerings at the center are an Asian-American garden, complete with stylish gazebo and Japanese maples, exotic azaleas, and hydrangeas; an enticing, shaded garden on the site of an abandoned quarry, enhanced by a stream, water-fall, and granite outcrops; a rhododendron garden with flowering native shrubs and trees; a group of charming nineteenth-century-style flower, herb, and vegetable gardens outside the rustic farm buildings; and the newest of all, the Gardens for Peace.

The latter, an intimate, circular forest garden within the Swan Woods Trail, offers ferns, rhododendrons, evergreens, wildflowers, and small stone benches for rest and contemplation. Featured at one end is a bronze sculpture called *The Peace Tree*, depicting five life-size figures clasping hands around a tree. This garden is the first of a network of international gardens (others are presently located in Tbilisi, Georgia, and in Madrid) whose purpose is to promote world peace and respect for the environment.

You can also enjoy a stroll through the half-mile Swan Woods Trail. Referred to as an outdoor laboratory, the trail wanders past azaleas, tulip poplars, magnolias, and other woodland species of the Georgia Piedmont and is dotted with little signs describing in detail the ecosystem of the region.

❀ **Admission:** Fee.
Garden open: Monday through Saturday 10:00 A.M. to 5:30 P.M., Sunday noon to 5:30 P.M.; closed holidays.
Directions: From I–75 through Atlanta, go to the northern part of city. Take exit 255 and turn left to pick up West Paces Ferry Road. Go approximately 2⁷⁄₁₀ miles. The Atlanta History Center will be on your right.

6. Cator Woolford Gardens at the Frazer Center

1815 Ponce de Leon Avenue NE, **Atlanta**, GA;
(404) 377–3836, ext. 13; www.cwgarden.com

*N*ESTLED in historic Druid Hills, a leafy Atlanta enclave designed more than a century ago by the prolific Frederick Law Olmsted, this secluded garden is a serene oasis of flowers, columns, grassy areas, and woods. Once part of the thirty-three-acre estate of entrepreneur Cator Woolford, it was originally a private garden and was restored and redesigned in the 1920s by a prominent Philadelphia landscape architect. When the property was sold to the Children's Rehabilitation Center in the 1940s, it became a therapeutic garden to enhance the nature experiences of people with disabilities. Now it's a favorite site for outdoor weddings and other social events—not surprisingly, in view of its romantic setting.

The centerpiece of the six-acre garden is a broad lawn surrounded by colorful plantings, including pansies, irises, peonies, phlox, azaleas, old-fashioned roses, and decorative grasses, as well as a graceful columnade. Winding paths lead to a rock garden, wildflower glen, and bog garden along a little stream flanked with bamboo. The pretty woodland walkways, within a deep virgin forest, are dotted with dogwoods, azaleas, and other native shrubs. Many of the garden structures—stone benches, archways, and columns—add a touch of old-world charm.

✥ **Admission:** Free.

Garden open: Daily dawn to dusk

Directions: From Interstate 75/85, take exit 248C onto Freedom Parkway/Route 10 until it dead-ends at Ponce de Leon Avenue. Turn right onto Ponce de Leon and travel 1⁶⁄₁₀ miles, then turn right onto Clifton Road. Travel approximately 30 yards, then turn left onto South Ponce de Leon Avenue. The garden is reached via the last driveway on the right.

7. The Gardens of H. M. Patterson & Sons

Spring Hill, 1020 Spring Street NW, and Oglethorpe Hill, 4550 Peachtree Road NE, **Atlanta**, GA; (404) 876–1022

A WALK in a garden surrounding a funeral home might not strike most people as an especially inviting proposition, but a visit to either of these two similar sites might revise this view.

The gardens at Spring Hill, situated on a busy midtown street corner, are the earlier of the two sites. Conceived in the late 1920s by architect Philip Shutze to complement his elegant design for the house, the gardens at Spring Hill are divided into two sections, one formal, the other less so. On the north end of the building is the intimate, partially enclosed formal area, with symmetrical rows of boxwoods, geometric flower beds, and grassy cutouts. A graceful female statue and a small fountain with a basin of aquatic plants add classical touches. The south garden features a gently sloping hillside of colorful flowers and shrubs amid rocks and stone pathways.

Spring Hill and Oglethorpe Hill have been managed by the same Patterson family since the beginning, and the gardens, with minor exceptions, have shown the same continuity in design and plantings over the decades.

❀ **Admission:** Free.
Garden open: Call before visiting.
Directions: Spring Hill is on the corner of Spring and Tenth Streets, adjacent to I–75/85. Oglethorpe Hill is on Peachtree Road, a block past Oglethorpe University, half a block from the intersection with Ashford Dunwoody Road.

8. Robert L. Staton Rose Garden

Fernbank Museum of Natural History, 156 Heaton Park Drive NE, Atlanta, GA; (404) 929–6300; www.fernbank.edu/museum

*T*HIS ONE-ACRE delight of fragrance and color is a must for any rose fancier. Here you can find just about every type of rose you have ever heard of, from miniatures to hybrids to climbing roses. There are altogether about 1,300 plants representing some 250 varieties, all coming from three sources: All-America Rose Selection test plants, American Rose Society Award of Excellence Miniature test plants, and donated named roses. Some are in tidy rows of rectangular beds outlined in brick, while others climb gracefully onto wooden trellises. Most flowers are labeled, except for those that are undergoing a period of evaluation to determine their suitability for the local climate.

The rose garden bears the name of its founder, a precocious rosarian who joined the American Rose Society while still in his teens. Later, while working for the Fernbank Science Center, he came up with the idea for the garden.

Because of Atlanta's long growing season, the rose garden is in bloom from early May well into fall, until the first frost.

❄ **Admission:** Free.

Garden open: Daily sunrise to sunset.

Directions: The garden is on the grounds of the Fernbank Museum of Natural History. From downtown Atlanta, go north on Peachtree Street to Ponce de Leon Avenue and turn right. Go 3³⁄₁₀ miles to Clifton Road and turn left. Go ¹⁄₁₀ of a mile to the museum entrance and turn right.

9. Riverwalk

Sixth Street to Tenth Street, **Augusta,** GA; (706) 823–6600

*S*INCE 1987 Augusta has been blessed with a most picturesque gardenwalk along its Savannah riverfront. During the 1980s, when city leaders around the country began to understand the commercial and aesthetic value in revitalizing their downtowns, Augusta conceived of the idea of creating walkways to take advantage of the spectacular river scenery.

The riverwalk is along two promenades, about 5 city blocks in length. One, built on top of a levee dating from the early 1900s, commands striking views of both city and river; the other, just above the riverbank, affords a closer look to the water.

A Formal Blue Garden

An enchanting garden within the sixty-four-acre Pendleton King Park in the middle of Augusta is known as the Southern Blue Garden. And for good reason: Here you'll see only blue blossoms, such as the most unusual lilac chaste tree. Included in the park is a touch-and-smell herb garden, which will be of particular interest to the visually impaired. You'll find the garden on Kissingbowen Road in Augusta.

The beautifully landscaped promenades are endowed with dogwoods, azaleas, river birch trees, and other varieties native to the region. A Japanese garden—something of a surprise in this kind of setting—is included on the grounds, as are the more likely picnic tables, park benches, playground, and dock. You will find the combination of river views and garden pleasures irresistible.

❀ **Admission:** Free.
Garden open: Daily dawn to dusk.
Directions: Riverwalk runs from Sixth Street to Tenth Street alongside the Savannah River.

10. Georgia Perimeter College Botanical Garden

3251 Panthersville Road, **Decatur,** GA; (404) 244–5001; www.gpc.edu

*I*N THE suburban town of Decatur, just east of Atlanta, you'll find this little botanical garden tucked away behind the modern buildings of a local college and a high school. At first glance you might think of it as a modest garden—that is, until you realize how ambitious it actually is.

Begun in 1990 by the students of the college (then named Dekalb College), its mission has been to preserve and propagate native plant species. Through the dedication and hard work of individuals and local organizations, the site (also known as the Wildflower Center of Georgia) is presently the state's largest all-native garden. And it is still expanding. Eventually, some 2,000 species will be represented.

The grounds feature rare, hard-to-grow, sometimes endangered species situated on four acres within a floodplain. In the front of the botanic garden are raised beds of sun-loving flowers, shrubs, and small trees bearing such names as hairy sumac, white beardtongue, blazing star, streamside wild indigo, Barbara's button, and blanket-flower. Behind, in a woodland with a creek, are the shade plants. You can walk along a nature trail and view fern, iris, black cohosh, azalea, needle palm, orchid, Jack in the pulpit, and Carolina phlox, to cite only a few.

Everything is carefully labeled throughout the garden. Indeed, if it weren't for the fact that this is, after all, an educational facility, you might wish to see fewer of the somewhat distracting little white markers. But you can learn a great deal here and enjoy the garden at the same time.

❀ **Admission:** Free.

Garden open: Daily dawn to dusk.

Directions: From Interstate 285 take Panthersville Road (just to the west of the Candler Road intersection). The garden is located behind the parking area, adjacent to the Occupational Education building.

11. Massee Lane Gardens

100 Massee Lane, **Fort Valley,** GA; (478) 967–2358; www.camellias-acs.org

*T*HE CENTERPIECE of this ten-acre garden in the heart of Georgia is the camellia. The site, surrounded by a landscape of peach and pecan trees, boasts one of the largest camellia collections anywhere in the world (more than a thousand varieties) and is, in fact, the headquarters of the American Camellia Society.

In 1936, when a severe storm devastated what was then land dedicated to growing peach trees for commercial use, the owner, Dave Strother, began cultivating camellias. His passion for this glorious, colorful blossom became such that he eventually founded the American Camellia Society. In 1965 he donated his farm acreage and collection to the society.

The camellia, an ancient flower first appreciated by the Chinese some 4,000 years ago, is one of those rarities that bloom during the winter months. When most other flowers lie dormant, it shines in brilliant pinks, reds, and whites. The time to visit these gardens is between November and April, with a peak during February and early March.

Massee Lane offers other garden pleasures besides the camellia, however. There are smaller gardens featuring roses, perennials, daylilies, and even an enclosed Japanese garden. Also on the grounds are a camellia greenhouse as well as a new greenhouse for other plants, a children's garden, an extensive library (with rich collections on camellias), a museum, and a gallery displaying porcelain birds.

❀ **Admission:** Fee.
Garden open: Monday through Saturday 9:00 A.M. to 5:00 P.M., Sunday 1:00 to 5:00 P.M., from December through March; Monday through Friday 9:00 A.M. to 4:00 P.M. from April through November.
Directions: From I–75 take exit 149 to Route 49 south to Fort Valley. The garden entrance is on Route 49, about 5 miles south of Fort Valley.

12. Fred Hamilton Rhododendron Garden

1311 Music Hall Drive, **Hiawassee**, GA; (706) 896–4191; www.georgia-mountain-fair.com/hamgar

*A*s ITS name indicates, this garden celebrates the glorious rhododendron—and in an enthusiastic way. On these seventeen acres in northern Georgia, quite close to the North Carolina border, some 2,000 rhododendron plants representing 400 varieties are on display. From spring to early fall, rhododendron lovers from all over congregate at this site, the state's largest such specialty garden, some for its annual rhododendron festival.

The creation of Fred and Hazel Hamilton, the garden was at first a private spot about 3 miles from its present site. When the Hamiltons donated the garden to the Georgia Mountain State Fair in 1982, its many plants were moved to its current location near Lake Chatuge. Since that time, more and more plants have been added, with more to come.

In addition to the featured rhododendrons, you'll find azaleas, dogwoods, tulip magnolias, and quite a number of wildflower varieties. The blooming peak is from the last week of April to early June, so plan accordingly.

❁ **Admission:** Free.

Garden open: Daily dawn to dusk.

Directions: The garden is located on the grounds of the Georgia Mountain Fairgrounds. From Atlanta take Interstate 985 to Gainesville to U.S. Highway 129 north to Cleveland. In Cleveland, pick up Route 75, which takes you through Helen. At the stop sign at the end of Route 75, turn left on Route 76 west; the fairgrounds are 1 mile past the town of Hiawassee.

13. Vines Botanical Gardens

3500 Oak Grove Road, **Loganville**, GA; (770) 466-7532; www.vinesbotanicalgardens.com

*V*INES BOTANICAL GARDENS, one of the newer gardens in the region, is also one of its most idyllic. On twenty-five immaculate acres outside a small town just east of Atlanta, it features a landscape of colorful plantings set around a picturesque lake complete with bridge, fountains, swans, and geese. Beyond are a group of charming gardens, some graced with antique statuary and yet more fountains, others set along streams and ponds.

For its short history the site has undergone several incarnations, from being the private estate of Charles and Myrna Adams in the mid-1980s, to becoming a public garden in the 1990s, to later being taken over by the Vines Botanical Gardens Foundation (named after Mrs. Adams's father, Odie Vines), to being yet again privatized, finally to becoming a county park.

Among the garden pleasures are the Asian garden, a peaceful tableau of irises, azaleas, rhododendrons, and Japanese maples along a pond and stream; the White Garden, with a white gazebo framing all-white blossoms; the Rose Colonnade Garden, featuring four statues representing the seasons, classic columns with climbing wisterias, and a profusion of antique roses; Pappy's Garden, a colorful collection of old-fashioned flowers on a gentle slope; and the Brook Garden, including a rock-lined stream and terraced garden of shrubs and perennials.

Connecting the gardens are intertwining paths and boardwalks, stone steps, little bridges, and wooden pavillions. The elegant manor house, set high on the hill with spectacular views of the lake and gardens, is now home to various amenities, including a popular restaurant.

❀ **Admission:** Free.

Garden open: Daily 10:00 A.M. to dusk.

Directions: The gardens are located just off US 78 on Route 20 in Loganville (between Athens and Atlanta). From Atlanta via US 78, turn left on Brand Road in Loganville and left again on Oak Grove Road to the entrance.

14. Rock City Gardens

1400 Patten Road, **Lookout Mountain,** GA; (706) 820–2531;
www.seerockcity.com

*R*ock City Gardens is a craggy landscape of paths and steps and narrow bridges winding among huge rocks and ravines high on a mountain. You walk on self-guided trails, alongside hundreds of species of wildflowers, shrubs, and other plants native to this mountain region. Those with a sense of adventure and enough agility to negotiate challenging places (with such names as Fat Man's Squeeze, Needle's Eye, and Balanced Rock) are rewarded with a glorious view encompassing seven states.

Actually, Rock City Gardens is part of Lookout Mountain, a favorite tourist destination just outside of Chattanooga, Tennessee, extending into Georgia and even Alabama (our walk is technically in Georgia, with access from Tennessee). Rock City became an attraction during the lean Depression years, when the entrepreneurial Garnet and Frieda Carter decided to charge admission to their most unusual ten-acre property on top of Lookout Mountain. To publicize their Rock City Gardens, they hired people to paint "See Rock City" on hundreds of barn roofs along major highways from the Gulf Coast to the Great Lakes.

After this unconventional gardenwalk, you might stop at the nearby Lookout Mountain Natural Bridge, a natural rock arch, where groups of Spiritualists used to conduct séances and other ceremonies. This quiet, uncommercial spot is a pleasant place for a picnic.

❁ **Admission:** Fee.

Garden open: Daily 8:30 A.M. to dusk; closed Christmas.

Directions: From Atlanta take I–75 north all the way to Chattanooga, Tennessee. When I–75 meets with Interstate 24, take I–24 west toward downtown Chattanooga. Get off at exit 178 south, the Lookout Mountain/Market Street exit. Go straight to the traffic light on Broad Street and take a left. Follow the signs to Rock City.

Choosing an Outing in Georgia

American History Gardens
Founders Memorial Garden

*Aquatic Gardens and
Gardens with Water Views*
Guido Gardens
Okefenokee Swamp Park
Riverwalk
Vines Botanical Gardens

Arboretums
Lockerly Arboretum

Art in the Garden
Barnsley Gardens

Asian Gardens
Atlanta History Center
Riverwalk
Vines Botanical Gardens

Child-Pleasing Gardens
Atlanta Botanical Garden
Atlanta History Center
Barnsley Gardens
Callaway Gardens
Oak Hill at the Martha Berry
   Museum
Okefenokee Swamp Park

Conservatories and Botanic Gardens
Callaway Gardens
Chatham County Garden Center
   and Botanical Gardens
Vines Botanical Gardens

Formal Gardens
Atlanta History Center
Oak Hill at the Martha Berry
   Museum

Garden Rooms
Founders Memorial Garden

Historic Houses and Plantations
Owens-Thomas House and Gardens

Informal and English-Style Gardens
Oak Hill at the Martha Berry
   Museum

Italianate Gardens
Atlanta History Center
Barnsley Gardens

Medicinal and Herb Gardens
State Botanical Garden of Georgia

Rock Gardens
Atlanta History Center
Barnsley Gardens
Rock City Gardens

Romantic Gardens
Barnsley Gardens
Cator Woolford Gardens
   at the Frazer Center

Rose Gardens
Robert L. Staton Rose Garden

Specialty Gardens
Callaway Gardens (azaleas)

Fred Hamilton Rhododendron Garden

Massee Lane Gardens (camellias)

Unusual Themes

Atlanta Botanical Garden (carnivorous plants)

Guido Gardens (garden for Evangelical broadcasts)

Oak Hill at the Martha Berry Museum (goldfish)

Urban Settings

Forsyth Park

Riverwalk

15. Guido Gardens

600 North Lewis Street (Route 121), **Metter,** GA; (912) 685–2222; www.the-sower.org

THIS PRETTY, three-acre oasis of fountains, brooks, waterfalls, and bright blossoms is more than your standard pleasure garden. Indeed, it is the setting for television and radio broadcasts that are heard by some thirty million people worldwide. For many years, Dr. and Mrs. Guido have preached their evangelical Christian message from this site, which was donated to them thirty years ago by the local mayor so that they could pursue their ministry.

The well-kept garden features native Georgia plants—dogwoods, pines, and many, many azaleas. Other highlights include a water garden complete with rocks, exotic koi fish and lily pads, a picturesque gazebo, and a chapel in a peaceful pine grove. There are benches for quiet meditation and soft background music for additional inspiration. A recent innovation is a tomb (much like Jesus's tomb in Nazareth), surrounded by plants from the period—palm trees and cacti. Visitors are invited to take a guided tour of the adjacent Sower Studio, production home of the broadcasts.

Admission: Free.

Garden open: Daily dawn to dusk.

Directions: Metter is located between Macon and Savannah off of Interstate 16. Take I–16 to exit 104 and drive 2 miles north into Metter.

16. Lockerly Arboretum

1534 Irwinton Road, **Milledgeville**, GA; (478) 452–2112;
www.lockerlyarboretum.org

*L*OCKERLY ARBORETUM is a living laboratory dedicated to
the conservation, beautification, and study of plants. Here,
on forty-seven acres right in the middle of the state, you can examine
more than 6,000 species, from native azaleas, hostas, rhododendrons,
camellias, and grasses to exotic tropical or desert plants.

The best way to see this untouristy site is by foot, along well-
marked and maintained trails. Bring a copy of the detailed map,
available at the office. (You can also drive to most displays.) Among
the arboretum's many offerings are a sand tracking bed (with animal
footprints); a vineyard; an aquatic garden; a berry bramble; specialty
beds with herbs, irises, lilies, and perennials; a climax forest (still
developing); a butterfly garden; and two greenhouses and a museum.

The arboretum was the creation of Edward J. Grassman, a New
Jersey nature and ornithology enthusiast, whose mission was to educate students of all ages, encouraging them to share their botanic
knowledge with others.

✤ **Admission:** Free.
Garden open: Monday through Friday 8:30 A.M. to 4:30 P.M., Saturday
1:00 to 5:00 P.M.
Directions: From Atlanta take I–20 east to exit 114 (Madison). Turn
right onto U.S. Highway 441 south. Follow US 441 south to Milledgeville (about 45 miles).

17. Oak Hill at the Martha Berry Museum

189 Mount Berry Station, **Mount Berry,** GA; (706) 291–1883;
www.berry.edu/oakhill

*T*HE 170-ACRE gardens at Oak Hill, among Georgia's oldest
and most venerable, will appeal to both nature and history
devotees. Situated near Rome, in an agricultural region rich with

limestone, the gardens surround a gracious antebellum plantation house, one of the few in Georgia that survived the Civil War unscathed. There is a great deal to see at this site: the gardens themselves, the manor, a museum, and a vast and impressive college campus right next door.

The grounds near the house are exquisitely landscaped with formal gardens. Beyond are rolling parklands with meadows, ponds, and nature trails. The oldest remaining garden at Oak Hill, the Formal Garden, was begun by Frances Berry in the early years of the Civil War. Her daughter, Martha, added the enchanting Sunken Garden many years later. But Martha's interests were primarily educational rather than botanical; indeed, the tiny log-cabin school she built on her inherited land to educate local children was the nucleus of Berry College, now a 30,000-acre campus adjacent to Oak Hill's mansion and gardens. You might also be interested in seeing the Original Cabin, dating from 1873 (known as the "birthplace of Berry College"), not to mention Berry College itself, best seen by driving through its extensive campus.

Before visiting the gardens you might like to take a quick tour of the museum and mansion, which will give you an interesting overview of Martha Berry, her family, and the evolution of the

Garden Shows and Festivals in Georgia

MARCH
Macon Cherry Blossom Festival, Macon; (912) 751–7429

Tour of Homes and Gardens, Savannah; (912) 234–8054

MAY
Rose Show and Extravaganza, Atlanta; (404) 876–5858

JUNE
Daylily Show, Augusta; (706) 736–5893

AUGUST
Midsummer Night's Dream Tour of Ponds, Atlanta; (404) 975–0277

property. The Martha Berry Museum also exhibits paintings from the family collection by Thomas Sully and others.

The gardens were opened to the public in 1972. Among their many delights is Frances Berry's Formal Boxwood Garden, with its gracious flagstone walkways outlined in boxwood and its flower beds, fountain pool, and adjoining rose garden. Paths lead to the nearby Goldfish Garden (a favorite of Martha's), complete with pond, traditional knot garden, and outer beds of annuals and perennials. The picturesque Sunken Garden, also called the Terrace Garden, features a charming stone fountain surrounded by flowering cherry trees given to Martha by the emperor of Japan in the early 1930s; beneath them are thousands of daylilies that are in full bloom in early April and then again in July. Other garden highlights include the Sundial Garden (annuals and perennials), three greenhouses containing more than 25,000 plants, hillside nature trails with daffodils and other native plants, the wildflower meadow, and the All-America Selection Display Garden (one of only five in the state).

❀ **Admission:** Fee.

Garden open: Tuesday through Saturday 10:00 A.M. to 5:00 P.M., Sunday 1:00 to 5:00 P.M.; closed on major holidays.

Directions: Oak Hill is about an hour and twenty minutes from Atlanta. Take I–75 north to exit 290 (Rome/Canton, Route 20) and turn left onto Route 20. Travel approximately 2 miles to the end of the road, turn left at the light, then take an immediate right onto U.S. Highway 41 north. Drive 2 8/10 miles and bear right onto U.S. Highway 411 (Rome exit). Travel 17 3/10 miles and turn right at light onto the East Rome Bypass (also called Georgia Loop 1). After passing the fifth traffic light, look for the museum entrance on the left.

18. Callaway Gardens

Route 18, **Pine Mountain**, GA; (800) 282-8181;
www.callawaygardens.com

$\mathcal{C}$ALLAWAY GARDENS, one of the premier family resorts and gardens in the country, is a vast, 2,500-acre site in the rolling Appalachian foothills. Here, on ancient territory known as Pine Mountain (some geologists claim it is the oldest land in America), people of all ages can find relaxation, inspiration, and an appreciation of the natural world. Among Callaway's many offerings are 13 miles of scenic drives, bicycle trails, woodland walking trails rich with wildflowers, acres of garden conservatories and flower beds, and a large fruit and vegetable garden. (There are even golf courses, a 175-acre lake stocked for fishing, a large man-made beach, and tennis courts.) Callaway also boasts one of the most magnificent azalea collections anywhere—thousands upon thousands of azaleas representing some 750 varieties.

The creators of this extraordinary place were Cason and Virginia Callaway, who in the 1930s acquired a large tract of land that had been worn down by generations of cotton cropping. Originally meant as their private family retreat, the property evolved into a much more ambitious project, as they bought more and more land, restored forests, formed lakes, built trails through the woods, and created "gardens prettier than anything since the Garden of Eden." Opened to the public in 1952, the site was dedicated to enhancing people's appreciation of nature through its many horticultural and education displays and activities.

There are many garden pleasures to be found at Callaway. The John A. Sibley Horticultural Center (opened in 1984), among the most advanced greenhouse-garden complexes anywhere, includes five acres of indoor and outdoor displays. Its conservatory features exotic collections as well as major floral themes that are continually changed according to season. Its outdoor gardens not only

Blossoms in an Old Cemetery

Bonaventure Cemetery in Savannah offers a chance to see heirloom plants and more. This picturesque old site was once a plantation. Today it is filled with camellias, azaleas, wisteria, and jasmine beneath canopies of live oaks and Spanish moss. Visit the cemetery at 350 Bonaventure Road.

include lawns graced with old-fashioned flower beds and mixed borders but also—much to the delight of children—flowers shaped into fanciful creatures, such as peacocks or even dinosaurs.

Children will also love the recently renovated Cecil B. Day Butterfly Center, with its rich collections of tropical plants and butterflies contained within a spectacular 7,000-square-foot octagonal glass space. Just outside the conservatory are small butterfly gardens, showing visitors which plants to cultivate in order to attract these handsome insects.

The seven-and-a-half-acre Fruit, Vegetable, and Berry Garden (now providing much of the several restaurants' delicious produce) was planned as a demonstration garden. Callaway and his wife felt that people should be given the opportunity to observe the growing of fruits and vegetables.

Visitors can enjoy walking, biking, or birding along the Azalea Trail and Azalea Bowl, Laurel Spring Trail, Rhododendron Trail, Holly Trail, Wildflower Trail, and Mountain Creek Trail. Note that you can rent bicycles to tour the gardens, which are also accessible by car and tram.

❀ **Admission:** Fee.

Garden open: Daily 9:00 A.M. to 6:00 P.M from May through September; check hours during other months.

Directions: Pine Mountain is sixty minutes southwest of Atlanta. Take Interstate 85 south to Interstate 185 south (exit 21). From I–185, exit onto U.S. Highway 27 (exit 42). Follow US 27 south to Pine Mountain, where you'll turn right onto Route 354 west. Proceed to Route 18 and the entrance will be on the left.

19. Chatham County Garden Center and Botanical Gardens

1388 Eisenhower Drive, **Savannah**, GA; (912) 355–3883

*I*T COMES AS a surprise to learn that these charming gardens are on land once used as a prison farm. In 1991 the property was given to a nonprofit organization to be developed into gardens and an educational center. A historic 1840s wooden farmhouse about to be demolished was transported to these premises to serve as the garden center headquarters.

Since its official opening in 1997, the ten-acre site has served to educate the public in conservation, horticulture, landscape design, even garden therapy. Courses and lectures are routinely given in botany and related fields, tours of these and other botanical gardens are conducted, and the already fine collection of native trees (some quite mature), shrubs, and flowers is being enlarged.

An army of dedicated volunteers maintains impeccably the Azalea and Camellia Garden, the Native Plant Garden, the Kitchen Garden, the Herb Parterre, the Four Seasons Garden, the Rose Garden, the Shade Garden, and the Children's Garden, among others. The property includes a picturesque pond, an inviting forest with nature trails, meadows filled with wildflowers, and even an ongoing archaeological dig where students can be seen busy at work.

Bear in mind that although you are free to walk around the gardens on your own at any time, you can only visit the restored farmhouse during the week, when the center is open.

✿ **Admission:** Free.

Garden open: Daily from dawn to dusk. Center open Monday through Friday 10:00 A.M. to 2:00 P.M.

Directions: From downtown Savannah take Harry S. Truman Parkway south off of President Street. Exit on Eisenhower Drive, which runs east–west through the center of the city of Savannah. The garden center is just west of the Bacon Park golf course.

20. Forsyth Park

Park Street and Whitaker Street, **Savannah,** GA; (912) 651–6610

*S*AVANNAH is not only celebrated for its charming historic houses but also for its delightful squares, that string of intimate, jewel-like commons, some of which have graced the city for well over 200 years. These rectangular, impeccably maintained oases—twenty-four in all—contain the inevitable oaks (yes, dripping with Spanish moss), azaleas and other blossoms, and fountains and monuments.

Forsyth Park, sometimes referred to as the Last Square because of its location, is also the city's largest park. Encompassing twenty-one acres, it includes parkland with gardens and a magnificent central fountain. This restored 1858 cast-iron fountain, a replica of one in Cuzco, Peru, is a favorite Savannah landmark.

The gardens are a colorful collection of azaleas, magnolias, and palmettos punctuating the atmospheric oak trees. Completing the beautifully tended gardens is a fragrance garden for the blind, with its many differently textured plants.

✿ **Admission:** Free.

Garden open: Daily dawn to dusk.

Directions: From Route 25, turn right onto Martin Luther King Jr. Boulevard. After 1 ⁷⁄₁₀ miles, turn left onto West Park Street. The garden is at the intersection of Park and Whitaker Streets.

21. The Owens-Thomas House and Gardens

124 Abercorn Street, **Savannah**, GA; (912) 233-9743

*T*HIS ELEGANT house with its enclosed garden stands out among Savannah's historic sites. Considered to be one of the best examples of English Regency architecture in the country, the stylish house was designed by a young English architect named William Jay (one of the first professionally trained architects practicing in the United States) and built between 1816 and 1819. After its original owner, Richard Richardson, suffered financial losses, it became an elegant boardinghouse (where the Marquis de Lafayette stayed and delivered a speech in 1825), then it was purchased by the Owens family. In 1951 the house was bequeathed by Margaret Thomas, the Owens's granddaughter, to the Telfair Academy of Arts and Sciences for use as a museum.

The intimate (one-eighth-acre), walled garden is an English-style parterre, with a small central fountain, stone walkways, and flower beds bordered with short, clipped boxwood. Here you will see varieties of azaleas, nandinas, junipers, old-fashioned roses, and mock oranges, among other plants suited to the temperate Savannah climate. Although not added until the 1950s, the garden has the feeling of one dating from the early 1800s. Installed in what used to be the stable yard of the house, it is surrounded with walls now mostly covered with vines.

The house (which can be visited only by guided tour) has an outstanding collection of decorative arts, including fine furniture, paintings, porcelains, and locally made textiles. You can walk around the garden on your own, savoring its peaceful and charming aura.

❀ **Admission:** Fee.

Garden open: Tuesday through Saturday 10:00 A.M. to 5:00 P.M. Sunday and Monday 2:00 to 5:00 P.M.; closed January and major holidays.

Directions: From I–16 into Savannah, take exit 165 (Route 204) south to Abercorn Street.

22. Okefenokee Swamp Park

U.S. Highway 1 South, **Waycross,** GA; (912) 283–0583;
www.okeswamp.com

A REMARKABLE adventure awaits you, one that will take
you deep into what has been called America's greatest
natural botanical garden. The Okefenokee Swamp Park, a National
Wildlife Refuge located within nearly a half-million acres of wetlands in southeastern Georgia, is richly endowed with unusual plants
and animals.

This vast, jungly wilderness of forests, islands, and water-lily-
filled waterways surrounded by great stands of overhanging live oaks
and towering cypress can be visited on foot via walking trails and
boardwalks, by small railway, or—for those who wish to explore the
deeper reaches of the swamp—by boat. (Boat tours of all kinds are
available.)

The park offers interpretive exhibits, wildlife shows, and lectures, and it offers a lagoon amphitheater, living swamp observatory,
nature center, animal habitats, and 90-foot observation tower. Anyone who has a spirit of adventure and is intrigued by rare flora or
fauna—and who does not mind a few tourist trappings that inevitably surround such a site—will find this a memorable experience.

❀ **Admission:** Fee.

Garden open: Daily 9:00 A.M. to 5:30 P.M.; closed Thanksgiving and
Christmas.

Directions: Okefenokee is located 8 miles south of Waycross, off of
U.S. Highway 1 south on Highway 177.

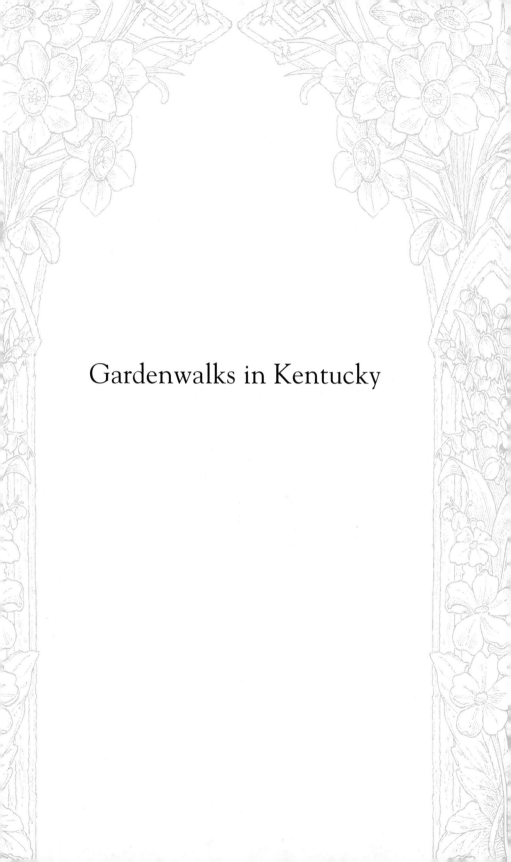

Gardenwalks in Kentucky

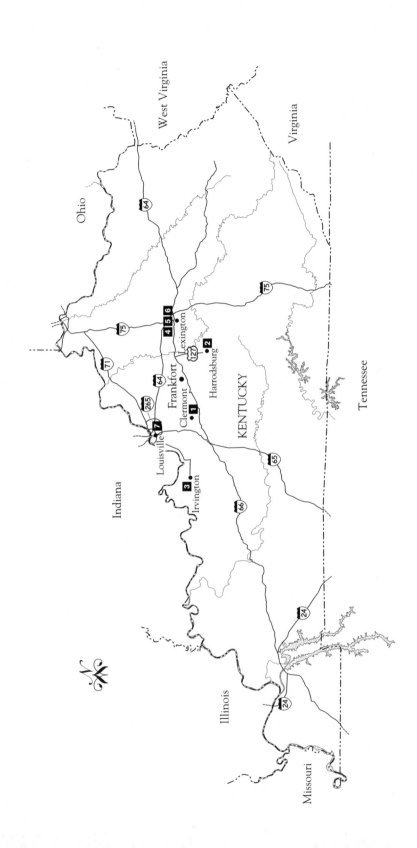

1. Clermont: Bernheim Arboretum and Research Forest
2. Harrodsburg: Shaker Village of Pleasant Hill
3. Irvington: Broadmoor Gardens and Conservatory
4. Lexington: Ashland
5. Lexington: Lexington Cemetery
6. Lexington: University of Kentucky Arboretum
7. Louisville: Louisville Nature Center and Beargrass Creek State Nature Preserve

1. Bernheim Arboretum and Research Forest

Route 245, **Clermont**, KY; (502) 955–8512;
www.bernheim.org

*I*T's HARD to imagine that overfarmed
land once occupied this site. In the late
1920s Isaac Bernheim, a young, conservation-
minded German immigrant living in Louisville,
gave this 10,000-acre tract to the state for the creation
of a nature sanctuary. Over the years it has evolved into a forest complemented by wide-open meadows and a beautifully maintained
arboretum. Recent developments at this forward-looking arboretum
include a new visitor center (the "greenest" building in the region)
and three new trails featuring Kentucky trees and Kentucky ecosys-
tems.

Much of the deep and extensive wilderness is kept as a research
forest for state universities and colleges, and it is an ideal refuge for
a rich variety of birds and other animal species. The public part of
Bernheim includes some 35 miles of hiking trails amidst woodland
and the parklike arboretum.

This is an unusually well-tended arboretum: Its 250 acres contain nearly 2,000 carefully labeled plants. A scenic road takes you
past stretches of meadows, ornamental gardens, and ponds—where
you will likely see hundreds of waterfowl. Self-guided trails loop
through wooded areas and fields, amid flowering trees and shrubs
(azaleas, rhododendrons, dogwoods, crab apples), lush grasses, and
wildflowers. Among the arboretum's special offerings are its highly

regarded holly collection (one of the best in the country), as well as its ginkgoes, oaks, and horsechestnuts.

A nature center provides exhibits of flora and wildlife as well as workshops and classes, and you can watch horticulturalists at work in the new greenhouses through an open viewing room.

❀ **Admission:** Free weekdays; fee on weekends.

Garden open: Monday through Saturday 9:00 A.M. to 5:00 P.M., Sunday noon to 4:00 P.M.

Directions: Clermont is about 30 miles south of Louisville. Take Interstate 65 to Route 245. The gardens are about 5 miles east on Route 245.

2. Shaker Village of Pleasant Hill

3501 Lexington Road, **Harrodsburg,** KY; (859) 734–5411;
www.shakervillageky.org

*S*ET AMID 2,700 acres of bluegrass farmland lies this restored Shaker village of some thirty original buildings. Although not technically a garden, this popular historic site does include small medicinal and herb gardens in keeping with the Shaker tradition, plus a new heirloom garden using historic seeds. One visits Shaker Village for the total experience, gardens included.

The Shakers, a nineteenth-century American utopian sect, believed in living a quiet and peaceful life apart from the rest of a world they viewed as disorderly and decadent; their communities were isolated and self-sufficient. In addition to making the graceful, simple furniture and other functional crafts they are so well known for, they cultivated vegetable and herb gardens for their own use. These tended to be small and intimate—and always tidy and pleasing to the eye.

You can take a self-guided tour through the buildings as well as the gardens (best seen during the summer months) and the recently added 40 miles of trails for hiking. You will see working studios featuring weaving, furniture making, and candlemaking, among other crafts. The village was built along an unusually picturesque stretch of the Kentucky River, which the Shakers used for commerce with the outside world. As part of your tour you can enjoy a delightful hourlong river excursion on the sternwheeler *Dixie Belle*, available several times daily.

❀ **Admission:** Fee.
Garden open: April through October: daily 10:00 A.M. to 5:00 P.M. November through March: daily 10:00 A.M. to 4:30 P.M. Closed Thanksgiving and Christmas.
Directions: From Interstate 66 take exit 59 (the Blue Grass Parkway). Go south on U.S. Highway 127. Exit at Harrodsburg and follow signs.

3. Broadmoor Gardens and Conservatory

U.S. Highway 60 East, **Irvington,** KY; (270) 547–4200

*T*HIS VAST (400-acre) site offers many a garden pleasure— from extensive water gardens with pools, fountains, and waterfalls, a tropical plant conservatory, and miles of wildflower gardens. There are rose gardens, iris-lily gardens, and garden statuary too, adding a European flavor to this Kentucky landscape.

It was largely in Europe that the creators of Broadmoor found their inspiration. While visiting Holland's Kukenhoff Gardens and other famous European gardens during the mid-1980s, Mary Ann Tobin and Brucie Beard decided to build their own public garden on a 2,400-acre farm just 50 miles southwest of Louisville. In keeping with the farmlike ambience (and perhaps with children in mind), they added quite a variety of

Garden Shows and Festivals in Kentucky

JUNE
Garden Tour, Louisville;
(502) 452–9920

JULY
Bluegrass Hemerocallis Society, Lexington; (606) 299–8269

animals—swans, peacocks, guinea hens, and pigmy goats—as well as delightful animal topiaries.

But Broadmoor is not just for children. Any and all visitors—from sometime gardeners to professional horticulturists to families on a picnic outing—are bound to enjoy this lovely spot.

✿ **Admission:** Fee.

Garden open: Friday through Sunday noon to 6:00 P.M.

Directions: Broadmoor is located 50 miles southwest of Louisville. Take U.S. Highway 60 south from U.S. Highway 31W (from Louisville) to Bewley–Guston Road.

4. Ashland

120 Sycamore Road, **Lexington,** KY; (859) 266-8581; www.henryclay.org

ASHLAND, one of Lexington's most appealing destinations, combines a gracious historic house with formal gardens. Once the estate of the illustrious statesman Henry Clay, the "Great Compromiser," and his wife, Lucretia, it is now a museum containing nineteenth-century family memorabilia surrounded by twenty acres of gardens and woodland. And what lovely grounds these are!

The Clays, both great garden lovers, wanted a grand landscape to complement their elegant mansion (designed in part by Pierre L'Enfant, the brilliant architect/designer of Washington, D.C.). In their heyday, in the early to mid-1800s, these gardens were vast, encompassing some 600 acres that included orchards along with parterres and other planted areas.

The present garden is much smaller, but it retains the spirit and style of the original. Lovingly tended by the Garden Club of Lexington, it features geometric flower beds, brick walls covered with ivy, carefully clipped boxwood hedges, and many, many old-fashioned blossoms. Depending on when you visit, you'll find roses, daylilies, geraniums, dahlias—and a wonderful collection of peonies.

If you stroll beyond the formal area, you'll discover some unusual trees, including a ginkgo (Clay brought this species to Kentucky), and nineteenth-century outbuildings such as two round icehouses, smokehouses, and carriage houses.

You can explore Ashland on your own, although guided tours are available.

✿ **Admission:** Fee.

Garden open: April through October: daily dawn to dusk. November, December, February, and March: Tuesday through Sunday dawn to dusk. Closed January and holidays.

Directions: Ashland is in central Lexington just off of U.S. Business Route 421 on Sycamore Road.

5. Lexington Cemetery

833 West Main Street, **Lexington,** KY; (859) 255–5522; www.lexcem.org

*A*LTHOUGH beautiful cemeteries tend to be carefully planted and well cared for, they are not necessarily places for a gardenwalk. Lexington Cemetery is one of the exceptions, offering a spectacular arboretum and two formal garden areas along with many historic monuments.

The cemetery dates from 1849, a time when the idea of the public park was taking hold across the country. In that spirit, it was conceived not only as a burial site but also as a peaceful spot for families to spend leisurely moments.

Amid these 170 bucolic acres are 200 varieties of trees (including an ancient linden tree, weeping cherries, ginkgoes, southern magnolias, panicle hydrangeas, and many evergreens). The three-acre garden area has a delightful sunken garden and colorful displays of bulbs, roses, irises, and lilies, among other flowers. Adding to the quiet and dignified aura are the unusual memorials (Henry Clay was among those buried here), some adorned with striking statuary.

Choosing an Outing in Kentucky

American History	*Art in the Garden*
Shaker Village of Pleasant Hill	Lexington Cemetery
Aquatic Gardens and	*Birds and Other Animals*
Gardens with Water Views	Broadmoor Gardens and Conservatory
Broadmoor Gardens and	
Conservatory	*Child-Pleasing Gardens*
	Broadmoor Gardens and Conservatory
Arboretums	
Bernheim Arboretum and	*Formal Gardens*
Research Forest	Ashland
University of Kentucky	*Notable Americans' Gardens*
Arboretum	Ashland (Henry Clay)

A stroll in this lovely spot is sure to please those who love gardens and nature as well as history.

❀ **Admission:** Free.

Garden open: Daily 8:00 A.M. to 5:00 P.M.

Directions: The cemetery is located in central Lexington on US Business 421 (not the bypass), also called West Main Street.

6. University of Kentucky Arboretum

Alumni Drive, **Lexington,** KY; (859) 257–9339; www.uky.edu/Arboretum

*T*HOUGH relatively young (1991), this lovely arboretum is remarkably well established. The fact that it is evolving makes it an interesting place to visit to see the process of creating a landscape.

Since 1996 more than 3,000 flowering shrubs and trees have been planted, and more are being added. As you walk about in this peaceful setting (somewhat removed from the bustling campus), you can enjoy a variety of demonstration gardens (including "idea gardens" to inspire amateur as well as professional gardeners), an herb and knot garden, and even fountains. Recent additions include 1,500 rose plants, an All-America Selections test garden, a home-demonstration garden, a children's garden, and a wheelchair-accessible garden.

A 2-mile trail called a Walk across Kentucky is being developed; it will feature native plants from the state's seven geophysical areas. Beyond it is a bluegrass woodland, where you are welcome to continue your nature exploration.

The arboretum has an ambitious program of special events throughout the year: lecture series and seasonal displays, art exhibits, band concerts, stargazing events, apple tastings, a Shakespearean festival, and winter nature walks.

❀ **Admission:** Free.

Garden open: Daily dawn to dusk.

Directions: The arboretum is located on the University of Kentucky campus near Commonwealth Stadium. From Interstate 64 and Interstate 75 north through downtown Lexington, take exit 115 (Newtown Pike/Route 992) and go south. Drive 4 miles on Newtown Pike. Turn left onto West Main Street, and turn right at the third intersection (Upper Street). Drive through the campus and turn left onto Alumni Drive.

7. Louisville Nature Center and Beargrass Creek State Nature Preserve

3745 Illinois Avenue, **Louisville**, KY; (502) 458-1328; www.louisvillenaturecenter.org

*L*OCATED in the heart of the city, the nature center and adjacent preserve offer a forest habitat rich with many varieties of animal and plant life.

While the center is the educational facility for promoting the study of nature (it features programs for children and adults, lectures, hands-on demonstrations, and many inviting excursions), the preserve is the actual laboratory for this work. Here, within some forty-one acres of second-growth forest, you can see more than 180 species of trees and flowering shrubs as well as hundreds of birds. (Bird-watching is a favorite activity here.) Springtime brings masses of delicate wildflowers, with guided walks for those so inclined.

✿ **Admission:** Free.

Garden open: Tuesday through Saturday 9:00 A.M. to 5:00 P.M.

Directions: From Interstate 264 exit onto Poplar Level Road North. Turn right onto Trevilian Way, then take the first left onto Illinois Avenue for 1 block.

Gardenwalks in Louisiana

As our readers surely know, some of Louisiana's gardens were damaged by 2005's hurricanes. However, every effort is being made to bring the gardens back to their original beauty. Please be sure to phone or check the Internet before visiting the gardens in this state.

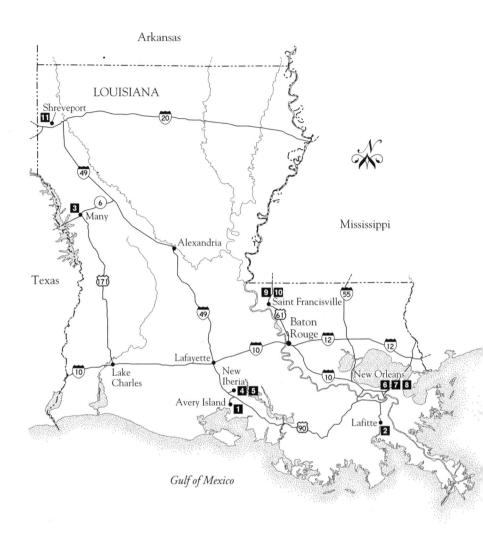

1. Avery Island: Jungle Gardens
2. Lafitte: Victoria Inn
3. Many: Hodges Gardens
4. New Iberia: Rip Van Winkle Gardens
5. New Iberia: Shadows-on-the-Teche
6. New Orleans: Longue Vue Gardens
7. New Orleans: New Orleans Botanical Garden
8. New Orleans: Old Ursuline Convent
9. Saint Francisville: Afton Villa
10. Saint Francisville: Rosedown Plantation and Gardens
11. Shreveport: The Gardens of the American Rose Center

1. Jungle Gardens

Highway 329, **Avery Island**, LA; (337) 369–6243;
www.tabasco.com/tobasco_history/visit_avery_island.cfm

*T*RUE TO its name, Jungle Gardens is a
lush habitat for exotic plants and animals in a naturalistic environment. Within
its 200-or-so acres are groves of palm
and bamboo and live oak, swamp-
lands and lagoons with alligators
cruising about lazily, and thou-
sands of snowy egrets and herons. But the site
is more than a haven for the exotic. It offers an eclectic collection of tropical, subtropical, and temperate species from
around the world.

On this salt dome hill, just after the Civil War, the McIlhenny
family cultivated rows of hot red peppers for making Tabasco sauce,
their sensational new invention. (You can still see thousands of these
colorful plants and visit the nearby Tabasco factory.) It was not
until some years later that Edward McIlhenny, family heir and amateur naturalist, introduced to his garden hundreds of unusual plants
and animals from his worldwide travels. He apparently liked the idea
of mixing rare with native plants, and Jungle Gardens, an imaginative combination of these, was launched.

Today's gardens include lotus and papyrus from the Nile, iris
from Siberia, bamboo from China, as well as thousands of camellias
(one of the best collections in Louisiana), azaleas, magnolias, and
other local favorites. Among the garden's special viewing treats are
the thousands of egrets that have thrived here thanks to Edward

McIlhenny's efforts to save this once-endangered species. Visitors enjoy watching the graceful white birds as they fly over marshlands in search of food.

The gardens are served by 7 miles of winding drives and walking paths that lead to various points of interest, with some surprises along the way. Among these is the not-to-be-missed Chinese pagoda (housing an authentic eleventh-century Buddha) perched high atop a stone cairn. Enjoy a fine view of it from the bayou while surrounded by ducks, geese, and swans.

✿ **Admission:** Fee.

Garden open: Daily 9:00 A.M. to 5:00 P.M.; closed holidays.

Directions: Avery Island is 120 miles southwest of New Orleans. Take Interstate 10 from New Orleans to U.S. Highway 90 south. Exit at Route 14; pick up Route 329 to Jungle Gardens.

2. Victoria Inn

4707 Jean Lafitte Boulevard, **Lafitte,** LA; (800) 689–4797; www.victoriainn.com

*I*F YOU ARE a fan of the iris (the state flower of Louisiana), you won't want to miss a visit to this charming Victorian-style bed-and-breakfast. Picturesquely set on the bayou near Jean Lafitte National Historical Park, some 22 miles south of New Orleans, Victoria Inn is surrounded by unusually pretty gardens shaded by canopies of giant live oaks. You will be enchanted with the variety of native and hybrid irises on display here—masses of them!— including the so-called Victoria Inn iris, named after the inn. Although the garden is inviting at all times, it is especially beautiful in spring during iris season.

There is much to explore in these approximately three acres as you stroll along flower-lined walkways, with pretty water vistas to admire at every turn. Among the delights are a Shakespearean herb garden (which features examples cited by the Bard), an intimate antique rose garden, and a small wooden bridge arching over the bayou, from where you might spot turtles, alligators, or even blue herons. Garden benches and swings are located in scenic spots for resting, reading, or contemplation.

You are always welcome to walk through the garden at your leisure, whether or not you are a guest at the inn, and you might well be tempted to prolong your visit to include dinner at the inn's gastronomic restaurant, which features many local specialties.

If you wish to explore this wondrous region a bit further, we recommend the nearby Jean Lafitte National Historical Park, where there are at least 11 miles of raised boardwalk that takes you through scenic natural swampland.

✺ **Admission:** Free.

Garden open: Call for information about hours.

Directions: Take I–10 toward New Orleans and follow signs for U.S. Business Route 90 West/West Bank; cross the Mississippi River Bridge to West Bank. After about 6 miles take exit 4B and follow signs for Jean Lafitte; go left onto Route 45/Barataria Boulevard, then left onto Route 3134. Cross the bridge and again take Route 45 (now called Jean Lafitte Boulevard) for another 7 miles, through the town of Jean Lafitte. Cross the bridge over Goose Bayou and follow signs for Victoria Inn.

3. Hodges Gardens

U.S. Highway 171, **Many,** LA; (318) 586–3523;
www.hodgesgardens.com

*H*ODGES GARDENS, situated within an abandoned stone quarry in the low, rolling pine hills of western Louisiana, was the creation of A. J. and Nona Trigg Hodges, two forward-thinking conservationists. In the 1940s, when few others were concerned about the consequences of deforestation, they purchased a 4,700-acre tract of land on a ridge to create an experimental arboretum.

Choosing an Outing in Louisiana

American History
Shadows-on-the-Teche
Old Ursuline Convent

Aquatic Gardens and
Gardens with Water Views
Longue Vue Gardens

Art in the Garden
Rosedown Plantation and Gardens

Birds and Other Animals
Jungle Gardens

Child-Pleasing Gardens
Jungle Gardens

Conservatories and Botanic Gardens
New Orleans Botanical Garden

Formal Gardens
Afton Villa

Garden Rooms
Afton Villa
Longue Vue Gardens

Historic Houses and Plantations
Rosedown Plantation and Garden
Shadows-on-the-Teche

Informal and
English-style Gardens
Afton Villa
Hodges Gardens

Notable Americans' Gardens
Rip Van Winkle Gardens
(Joseph Jefferson)

Rock Gardens
Hodges Gardens

Romantic Gardens
Afton Villa
Longue Vue Gardens

Rose Gardens
The Gardens of the American
   Rose Center
New Orleans Botanical Garden
Rosedown Plantation and
   Gardens

Tropical, Subtropical,
and Swamp Gardens
Jungle Gardens

Within it was a stone quarry rich with wildflowers, unusually shaped rocks, and seedling pines, which was found to be an ideal spot for a woodland garden. They created a 225-acre lake, streams, walks, footbridges, and an animal haven (with mostly elk and deer).

The garden (referred to as "a garden in the forest") includes seventy acres carefully landscaped to accentuate the dramatic rock formations and different levels of the terrain. The many flower beds (almost one hundred) are in bloom for most of the year. In spring you can enjoy a lovely rose garden on a slope above the lake, as well as plantings of tulips, bulbs, pansies, anemones, and flowering trees and shrubs. In summer hydrangeas and water lilies reign; in autumn, chrysanthemums; and in winter, camellias. A conservatory and greenhouses contain palms, orchids, and bromeliads, among other exotic plants.

There are miles of drives past scenic points (don't miss the extraordinary view from Observation Point over the pine tops and lake into East Texas) and hiking trails through the woods. An unexpected and interesting feature is an unusual remnant from the past: a 40-foot petrified tree trunk, thought to be an ancestor of the avocado and probably thousands of years old.

❀ **Admission:** Fee.
Garden open: Daily dawn to dusk; closed Christmas and New Year's.
Directions: Located 75 miles south of Shreveport, Hodges Garden is 15 miles south of Many. Take Interstate 49 south to the intersection with Route 6, turn right and go to Many. Pick up U.S. Highway 171 at Many; the garden entrance is south of town.

4. Rip Van Winkle Gardens

5505 Rip Van Winkle Road, **New Iberia**, LA; (337) 359–8525; www.ripvanwinklegardens.com

*S*ET DEEP IN Cajun country on a twenty-five-acre salt dome surrounded by the flat marshlands typical of the region, these romantic English gardens are on a site claiming an intriguing past. Here a pirate named Jean Lafitte once sought refuge and, according to local lore, buried his treasure. Then, in the nineteenth century, the "island" became the winter retreat of Joseph Jefferson, the highly regarded American actor, famous for portraying Rip Van Winkle. He built a charming house, now the garden's museum, in a style reflecting Moorish architectural details he had noted while visiting his friend Washington Irving in Spain. Apparently President Grover Cleveland used to visit here, taking his naps in the cool shade of the live oak trees near the house. But it was not until the Bayless family bought the property in 1917 that the gardens came to be.

Rip Van Winkle Gardens was originally named Live Oak Gardens because of the magnificent gnarled and weathered specimens found here, some dating back 300 years. (Two are named for the pirate Lafitte, whose mysterious pots of old coins were supposedly once found nearby.) The gardens surround the house and, combining English naturalism with a lush, moss-draped exotic ambience, are a delight to explore.

Paths (some through thick, tropical growth) lead to a secluded iris garden surrounded by bamboo; an Alhambra garden with terraces and pools; a camellia garden; a rock garden; a small Japanese tea garden, with lovely water views over a lagoon and lake, and many magnolias. Traditional plants—roses, camellias, and azaleas—blend in gracefully with oleanders, gardenias, and hibiscus, and there are broad lawns with vistas and a tropical glen. Don't miss the fine collections of bamboos and gingers. You will find something to enjoy year-round, whether in the inviting outdoor gardens or in the greenhouses whose collections of orchids, camellias, and tropical plants are well worth a visit.

❁ **Admission:** Fee.

Garden open: Daily 9:00 A.M. to 5:00 P.M.

Directions: From Lafayette take I–49 south/US 90 east toward New Iberia. Turn right onto Route 675 toward Jefferson Island. Follow Route 675 to the Jefferson Island sign and turn right into the gardens.

5. Shadows-on-the-Teche

317 East Main Street, **New Iberia,** LA; (337) 369–6446;
www.shadowsontheteche.org

*T*HE SHADOWS," now a National Trust Historic Site, includes a gracious 1830s plantation house surrounded by a lush, secluded garden. The two-and-a-half-acre property, once part of a much larger (158-acre) sugarcane plantation, is enclosed within clusters of bamboo and thick, green foliage. Within are inviting shaded pathways beneath massive live oaks draped with Spanish moss.

The present garden was created in the 1920s by William Weeks Hall, great-grandson of the original family owners. A keen enthusiast of landscape design (he was, in fact, a painter), he restored the badly overgrown landscape, transforming it from a functional property with just a few decorative gardens to an exclusively aesthetic pleasure.

In front of the house—considered one of the best examples of plantation house architecture in the country—are the magnificent live oaks, as well as collections of camellias and aspidistras. A small formal garden on the side of the house features elephant ears and yet more camellias, with a backdrop of southern magnolias. The garden behind the house is built around a Victorian-style summerhouse along the bayou. Among the plant groupings are shell gingers, sweet olives, crape myrtles, rice paper plants, and azaleas. A well-documented and informative guided tour conducts you through the house and gardens, but you can also walk around the grounds on your own.

❀ **Admission:** Fee.

Garden open: Daily 9:00 A.M. to 4:30 P.M.

Directions: Take US 90 south from I–10. Exit at Route 14 and head east to New Iberia and to East Main Street in town.

Louisiana Project Wildflower

If you're a wildflower fancier, you'll be glad to know that the Louisiana Department of Transportation is encouraging the growth of many species of wildflowers along various highways. One of the communities involved in this ongoing project is Lafayette (others are Monroe, Alexandria and, most recently, New Orleans). Look for native stands of verbena, coreopsis, and other species on highways in the region, or contact Louisiana Project Wildflower for a map by writing to 637 Ginard Park Drive, Lafayette, LA 70503. Or call (337) 268-5544.

6. Longue Vue Gardens

7 Bamboo Road, **New Orleans**, LA; (504) 488-5488;
www.longuevue.com

*H*ERE ON the outskirts of this romantic, historic city is a garden of water delights. Designed with Moorish features reminiscent of the Alhambra and Generalife Gardens in Granada, Longue Vue includes, among its pleasures, a formal court with reflecting pool and jets, canals, and many, many fountains—twenty-three, in fact!

In the early 1940s Edith and Edgar Stern decided to complement their Greek revival mansion with an elegant formal garden. The deliciously cooling waterworks that make the garden so special and inviting—especially during the sultry Louisiana summers—were added later, in the mid-1960s.

The gardens are mostly divided into rooms. A welcoming allée of oaks leads to the grand house and terrace overlooking the gardens. The central focus of the grounds is the Spanish Court. Surrounded by the shade of a loggia, it is graced with a rectangular mirrorlike pool in which delicate fountains make a gracefully arched pattern.

On both sides of the court are enclosed boxwood gardens with colorful potted plants and fountains, some replicas of those in the Alhambra.

Longue Vue also includes gardens that are not in the Spanish mode, such as a wildflower garden (with native varieties), a yellow flower garden, and a Pan garden. The Discovery Garden is dedicated to children who want to learn about gardens in a hands-on fashion: Here they can dig and discover natural pleasures on their own.

❀ **Admission:** Fee.

Garden open: Call or visit the Web site for hours and restoration updates.

Directions: From I–10 through the Bayou St. John–Lakefront area of the city, turn right onto Monticello Street (south). Just after the Metairie Cemetery, you'll find Longue Vue on Bamboo Road. Detailed directions are on the garden's Web site.

7. New Orleans Botanical Garden

City Park, 1 Palm Drive, **New Orleans,** LA; (504) 483–9386; www.neworleanscitypark.com/nobg.php

*T*HIS LOVELY botanical garden, the only one of its kind in Louisiana, features a vast collection of trees, shrubs, and flowers that thrive in this semitropical environment. Set within a public park that was once the site of a large plantation, it was created as a WPA project during the Depression and contains some 2,000 varieties.

Majestic live oaks—the kind you picture when thinking of southern landscapes—are among the garden's many offerings. Other features include secluded rooms enclosed with white *Camellia sasanqua,* a water-lily pond, fountains, statuary, and a formal parterre of roses in geometric patterns. There is a butterfly walk too, as well as an aromatic garden of ginger and herbs. A lovely azalea garden complemented by magnolias and camellias stands on the eastern end of the garden. A well-equipped conservatory contains orchids, ferns, bromeliads, and other tropical plants that can be enjoyed year-round.

❄ **Admission:** Fee.
Garden open: Call or visit the Web site for hours and restoration updates.
Directions: From I–10 west take the Metairie Road/City Park exit and turn left onto City Park Avenue. From I–10 east take Interstate 610 to the Canal Boulevard exit, and turn left onto City Park Avenue.

8. Old Ursuline Convent

1100 Chartres Street, **New Orleans**, LA; (504) 529–3040

*T*HE OLD URSULINE CONVENT is the oldest remaining build-ing in the Mississippi Valley and now a historic landmark. Located within the French Quarter, it is among the city's most important and most picturesque historic relics.

Its long and fascinating history reflects the turbulent events (fires, hurricanes, battles, massacres) that engaged New Orleans from its beginnings. Here the dedicated and indefatigable nuns took in orphaned children, tended the sick and poor, and taught and counseled the young. When the nuns were moved to a new convent in 1824, the site became the home of the bishop.

It was not until 1941 that the existing garden was laid out. The garden was based on plans from the old Royal Botanical Gardens that once existed across the street. Comprising six geometrically shaped parterres with carefully clipped borders in the formal eighteenth-century style, it was the work of the local garden club. The city agreed to maintain it, provided that the garden be open to the public.

A guided tour will take you through the garden, the Old Ursu-line Convent, and the adjacent St. Mary's Church, also of historic significance.

Admission: Fee.

Garden open: Call for hours and restoration updates.

Directions: Located in the French Quarter, this site is at the intersection of Chartres Street and Ursulines Street, several blocks northeast of Jackson Square.

9. Afton Villa

U.S. Highway 61, **Saint Francisville**, LA; (225) 635–6773

*A*FTON VILLA is that quintessentially romantic southern garden, complete with a welcoming allée of live oaks laced with Spanish moss, languid statues amid lush plantings, and the haunting atmosphere of an evocative past—including a forlorn family cemetery. On this spot more than a century ago, a forty-room Gothic revival mansion was built with extensive formal gardens that terraced down into a ravine. Over the years the house and garden underwent cycles of neglect and restoration, until finally in the 1970s the garden at least was brought back to life.

Using the unearthed brick and stucco remains of the mansion as its framework, the new owners created a ten-acre formal garden surrounded by natural parkland. (The ruins of the old plantation house now contain a courtyard garden.) The formal area includes five terraces enclosed with traditional boxwood hedges, connected with stone steps and brick walkways. The first of these rooms is a colorful parterre of tulips, daylilies, and camellias, while others combine Italian marble statues with the plants.

Beyond the sweetly fragrant gardens and green lawns lie the woodland. Here live oaks, wisteria, tulip trees, and cedars are interspersed with literally thousands of azaleas. An interesting historic footnote holds that these colorful azaleas are the actual descendants of a lone survivor of past gardens, known as the Pride of Afton.

✿ **Admission:** Fee.
Garden open: Daily 9:00 A.M. to 4:30 P.M. from March through June and from October through November.
Directions: Take U.S. Highway 61 north from Baton Rouge. The garden entrance is on US 61 north of Saint Francisville.

10. Rosedown Plantation and Gardens

12501 Route 10, **Saint Francisville,** LA; (225) 635–3332;
www.crt.state.la.us/crt/parks/rosedown/rosedown.htm

*R*OSEDOWN PLANTATION State Historic Site, a twenty-eight-acre antebellum site, reflects Old South culture in both in its elegant mansion and surrounding grounds. The elaborate gardens, a combination of seventeenth-century-style French gardens and more naturalistic English gardens, still contain some of the original plantings, making them among the nation's most important historic plant collections. Representing well over 150 years of continuous operation, they are also among the nation's oldest gardens.

Situated along a picturesque road once dotted with other prosperous plantations, the gardens were the creation of Martha and Daniel Turnbull. Like others of the southern gentry, they had traveled throughout Europe partly in search of beautiful art objects and antiquities. Many of the statues they collected on these trips are still found on the grounds. Martha's horticultural abilities were considerable for her time. She meticulously planned then for many years maintained—eventually all by herself—her gardens. Fortunately, she kept a detailed garden journal, one that proved useful when the eight-year re-creation of the gardens began in 1956.

Among Rosedown's special offerings are its magnificent rose gardens. These contain antique specimens rarely found in modern rose gardens, including burr roses (called chinquapin roses in the South) and China roses. Also not to be missed are the camellia, azalea, and cryptomeria collections (the Turnbulls were among the earliest to import these cultivars, and some of the azalea plants are more than a hundred years old); the fern gardens; and the herb and medicinal gardens. And, not surprisingly, here too is that gracious icon of many southern plantations: a magnificent avenue of live oaks, some 200 years old, welcoming visitors to the house and gardens.

❀ **Admission:** Fee.
Garden open: March through October: daily 9:00 A.M. to 5:00 P.M. November through February: daily 10:00 A.M. to 4:00 P.M. Closed Thanksgiving, Christmas, and New Year's Day.
Directions: Located 35 miles north of Baton Rouge, Rosedown is on Route 10 at Saint Francisville. Take US 61 north from Baton Rouge to Route 10.

11. The Gardens of the American Rose Center

8877 Jefferson-Paige Road, **Shreveport,** LA; (318) 938–5402; www.ars.org

*I*F YOU ARE a particular fan of roses, you won't want to miss these gardens. Comprising forty-two acres surrounded by woodland, they are after all the showcase for the American Rose Society. As such, they offer at least 20,000 rosebushes displayed in sixty individual gardens representing 450 varieties.

The site, a tribute to America's favorite flower, includes every name in the rosarian lexicon you could possibly come up with, from the All-America Rose Selections to miniature roses and the latest in hybrids. But this is more than just an outdoor museum: Amateur gardeners wanting practical ideas for their own backyards can visit its more intimate theme gardens, oriented to family needs.

❀ **Admission:** Fee.

Garden open: Monday through Friday 9:00 A.M. to 5:00 P.M., Saturday 9:00 A.M. to 6:00 P.M., Sunday 1:00 to 6:00 P.M., from April through October.

Directions: Take Interstate 20 west from Shreveport for 14 miles. Take exit 5 and follow the signs to the Rose Center on Jefferson-Paige Road.

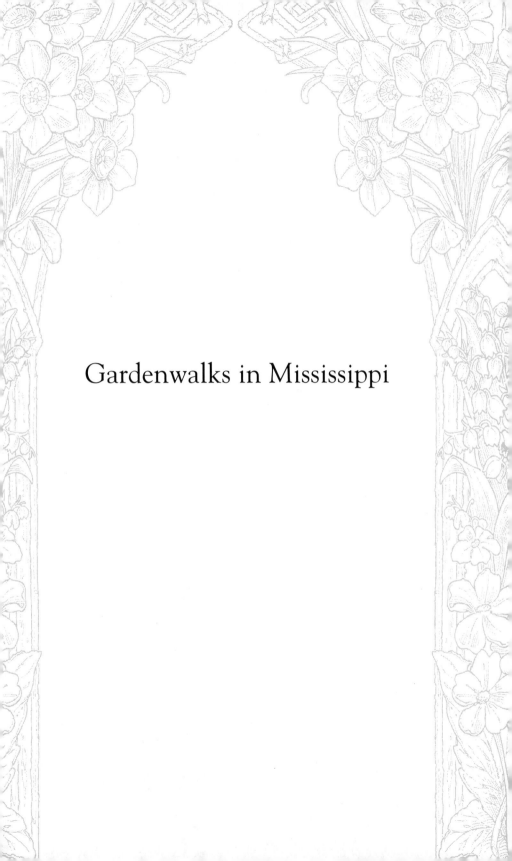

Gardenwalks in Mississippi

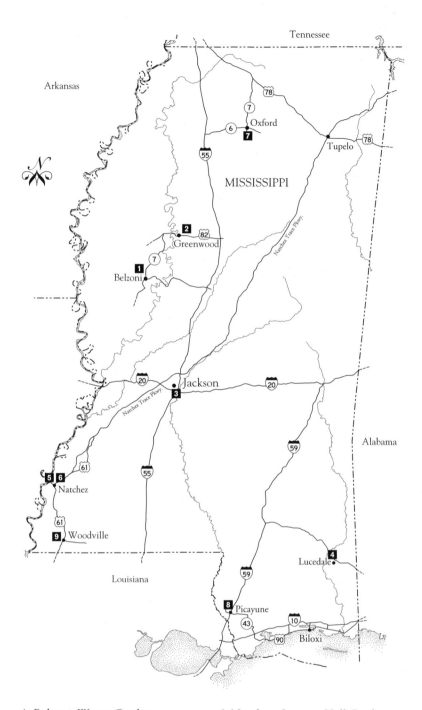

1. Wister Gardens

500 Henry Road, **Belzoni,** MS; (662) 247–3025

*T*HIS IS an elegantly landscaped, lush fourteen-acre estate surrounding a colonial house. There are broad lawns and a small decorative lake populated by black swans, African geese, and flamingos. Wister Gardens has a nice Deep South ambience, with gazebos and serpentine paths through the trees. Some 8,000 azaleas bloom in springtime, as do numerous bulbs (including 4,000 tulips) and a variety of lovely fruit trees. There are more than 120 varieties of trees and shrubs here. Also of note are the chrysanthemums of autumn and the camellia displays in winter.

✿ **Admission:** Free.

Garden open: Daily 9:00 A.M. to 5:00 P.M.

Directions: Belzoni is a small town in the Mississippi Delta. Wister Gardens is just north of Belzoni on Route 7.

2. Florewood River Plantation State Park

U.S. Highway 82, **Greenwood,** MS; (662) 455–3821

*T*HIS RECONSTRUCTION of an 1850s Mississippi plantation is situated on one hundred acres near the Yazoo River in the heart of cotton country. You'll find a fully revived picture of the nineteenth-century Mississippi Delta cotton industry, including the reconstructed mansion; the museum with the Whitney gin; the smokehouse and blacksmith's, potter's, and candle maker's shops; and demonstrations by guides in antebellum costume. (In the fall you can help pick cotton.)

Of particular interest of course are the gardens, set in the park-like grounds surrounding the mansion. They are pleasingly planted with Japanese boxwood, crape myrtle, live oak, peach, pear, dwarf plum, and southern wax myrtle. There are also other kinds of gardens: vegetables and vast fields of cotton, corn, sorghum, and peas.

❀ **Admission:** Fee.
Garden open: Tuesday through Saturday 9:00 A.M. to 5:00 P.M., Sunday 1:00 to 5:00 P.M.; closed major holidays.
Directions: Take Interstate 55 to U.S. Highway 82. Florewood is 2 miles west of Greenwood.

3. Mynelle Gardens

4736 Clinton Boulevard, **Jackson**, MS; (601) 960–1894

*T*HIS IS a seven-acre informal garden with a delightful air all its own. Developed in 1920 by a noted local gardener named

Choosing an Outing in Mississippi

American History
Monmouth Plantation

Arboretums
The Crosby Arboretum

Historic Houses and Plantations
Florewood River Plantation
   State Park
Monmouth Plantation
Rosemont Plantation

Informal and English-style Gardens
Mynelle Gardens
Wister Gardens

*Medicinal and
Herb Gardens*
Mynelle Gardens

Notable Americans' Gardens
Rosemont Plantation
   (Jefferson Davis)
Rowan Oak
   (William Faulkner)

Unusual Themes
Palestine Gardens

Mrs. Mynelle Westbrook Haywood (and since 1973 owned by the city of Jackson), Mynelle Gardens has a collection of Mississippi favorites planted in a series of lush and picturesque settings. Among them are an English bog garden, a medical and herb garden, a rustic garden, an old-fashioned garden, and its pièce de résistance: a Japanese garden. Plants range from amaryllises, daylilies, gardenias, pinks, and camellias; to roses and Asiatic magnolias; to a number of rare and ancient specimens—some dating from the seventeenth century. (This is the kind of pretty setting that suggests weddings!) There are several nice walks as well as wheelchair-accessible trails.

❀ **Admission:** Fee.
> **Garden open:** March through October: daily 9:00 A.M. to 5:00 P.M.; November through February: daily 8:00 A.M. to 4:15 P.M.
> **Directions:** From Interstate 220/U.S. Highway 49 through Jackson, exit at Clinton Boulevard. Turn west onto Clinton; the garden entrance is on the right.

4. Palestine Gardens

Palestine Gardens Road, **Lucedale,** MS; (601) 947–8422;
www.palestinegardens.org

*T*HIS IS one of those great oddities we come across as we travel the country: a twenty-acre garden that is a scale model of the Holy Land. Here you'll find the plants mentioned in the Bible, as well as miniature replicas of such ancient cities as Jerusalem, Bethlehem, Capernaum, and Jericho. This nondenominational site is open to all. It's one of those gardens in which an abstract idea has been fully realized.

❀ **Admission:** Fee.
> **Garden open:** Tuesday through Friday 9:00 A.M. to 4:00 P.M., Saturday 9:00 A.M. to 5:00 P.M., Sunday 1:00 to 4:00 P.M., from March through November.
> **Directions:** Lucedale is near the Alabama border. Going south from

Hattiesburg on U.S. Highway 98, turn left onto North Bexley Road about 3½ miles, and turn right onto Palestine Gardens Road, a dirt road.

5. Monmouth Plantation

36 Melrose Avenue, **Natchez,** MS; (601) 442–5852;
www.monmouthplantation.com

*M*ONMOUTH, a fine house built about 1818, was the home of prominent Natchez citizen and Mexican War hero Gen. John Anthony Quitman and his wife, Eliza Turner Quitman. The general was known to be the richest man in Natchez in his day, and his antebellum house and gardens were suitably magnificent. Great oaks dripping with Spanish moss surrounded the house. He imported forty trees and vines from France and grew peaches, pears, nectarines, olives, figs, and many flowers in separate formal beds. Even one of his gardeners was imported—from England.

Monmouth had a long and colorful history, including terrible destruction during the Civil War, the burning of some of the great oaks for firewood, and a fall into decay and ruin. In 1977 the place was bought and restored by a couple from California, and today the reconstructed, replanted Monmouth is a National Historic Landmark and is open to the public. Thoroughly and lovingly restored, Monmouth's gardens are a delight. Neat brick walks crisscross the grounds, while a gazebo and small pond add interest to the collection of flowers, especially the camellias.

Natchez is noted for its antebellum houses and gardens. This garden, like Stanton Hall, below, can be visited all year. Other Natchez mansions and gardens—including Hope Farms, Rosalie, D'Evereux, and Cherokee—are open on special days in spring and fall; call Natchez Pilgrimage at (800) 442–2011 for information on all of the city's historic houses and gardens.

✦ **Admission:** Fee.

Garden open: Daily; closed Christmas. Tours are offered every forty-five minutes from 9:30 A.M.

Directions: Monmouth Plantation is within Natchez city limits. Entering town from U.S. Highway 61 (from Baton Rouge), take a left at the fifth traffic light onto Melrose-Montebello Parkway. Go through the flashing light, continue to the next traffic light, and take a left onto John Quitman Parkway. Monmouth Plantation is on the left.

6. Stanton Hall Gardens

401 High Street, **Natchez**, MS; (601) 442–6282

*D*ATING FROM 1851, this is a fine antebellum mansion with grounds that feature live oaks, azaleas, camellias, daylilies, caladiums, and other pleasures. The opulent, elaborate, Greek revival house is well worth a visit, with its great columns, imported marble mantels, chandeliers, and glamorous staircase. And it is appropriately located in an inviting Deep South garden setting. Visit in spring or summer for the best viewing of flowering shrubbery under the live oaks.

✦ **Admission:** Fee.

Garden open: Daily 9:00 A.M. to 5:00 P.M.

Directions: From U.S. Highway 61/84 north of the city, exit at St. Catherine Street. Turn right onto Union Street and turn left onto 401.

Garden Shows and Festivals in Mississippi

MARCH
Mynelle Gardens Spring Plant Festival, Jackson; (601) 960–1894

SEPTEMBER TO NOVEMBER
Fall Garden Tours, Hattiesburg; (601) 799–3211

7. Rowan Oak

Old Taylor Road, **Oxford,** MS;
(662) 234–3284; www.olemiss.edu

*I*F YOU are visiting Mississippi, you will not want to miss William Faulkner's 1840s home and its garden at the University of Mississippi. It is now a National Historic Landmark. No recent figure is so identified with the state and its landscape as Faulkner, and here you will see not only the great writer's fine antebellum house, with its columned portico and library and writing room (with his Underwood typewriter still in place), but the lovely garden he created too. The hedge-bordered rose garden is the high point of the tree-shaded outdoor setting, which includes a stable and smokehouse.

❀ **Admission:** Free.

Garden open: Tuesday through Saturday 10:00 A.M. to noon and 2:00 to 4:00 P.M., Sunday 2:00 to 4:00 P.M.; closed university holidays.

Directions: From Jackson take I–55 north for 150 miles. Take the Batesville/Oxford exit off I–55. Proceed east on Route 6 toward Oxford for 26 miles. Once in Oxford, take the second exit, Coliseum Drive, onto the campus of "Ole Miss."

8. The Crosby Arboretum

370 Ridge Road, **Picayune,** MS; (601) 799–2311; www.msstate.edu

*T*HE CROSBY ARBORETUM has the admirable aim of specializing in plants native to its Pearl River habitat. Among its plantings are many delightful wildflowers, and in May it sponsors a wildflower weekend when thousands of native species are in bloom. There are more than 300 species of indigenous shrubs and trees planted here.

❀ **Admission:** Fee.

Garden open: Wednesday through Sunday 9:00 A.M. to 5:00 P.M.

Directions: The arboretum is close to the Louisiana border. From New Orleans take I–10 east to Route 43 north toward Picayune. The arboretum is off of Route 43.

9. Rosemont Plantation

Route 24 East (Main Street), **Woodville, MS**; (601) 888–6809; www.rosemontplantation.com

*T*HE BOYHOOD home of Jefferson Davis, Rosemont is a circa-1810 modest "planter's cottage" set amid 300 acres of plantation lands and a charming garden. Five generations of the Davis family lived at Rosemont. The cool gardens are shaded by evergreen magnolias and great live oaks draped with Spanish moss. In spring and summer you'll see the tiny magenta roses that climb up the white latticework of the house; these are just part of the elaborate rose gardens originally planted in the early 1800s by Jane Davis, the Confederate president's mother.

❀ **Admission:** Fee.

Garden open: Tuesday through Saturday 10:00 A.M. to 4:00 P.M. from March through December 15.

Directions: Located in the southwest corner of the state, Woodville is reached via US 61 from Natchez. Rosemont is 1 mile east of town center on Route 24 (Main Street).

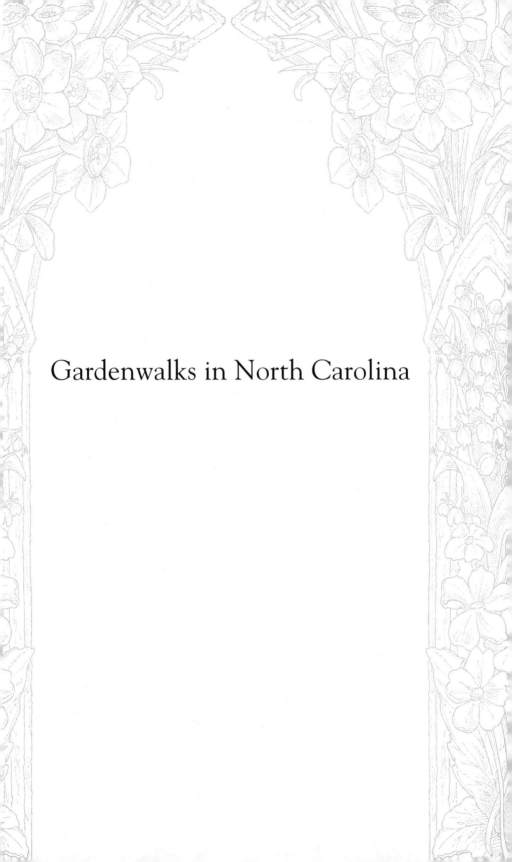

Gardenwalks in North Carolina

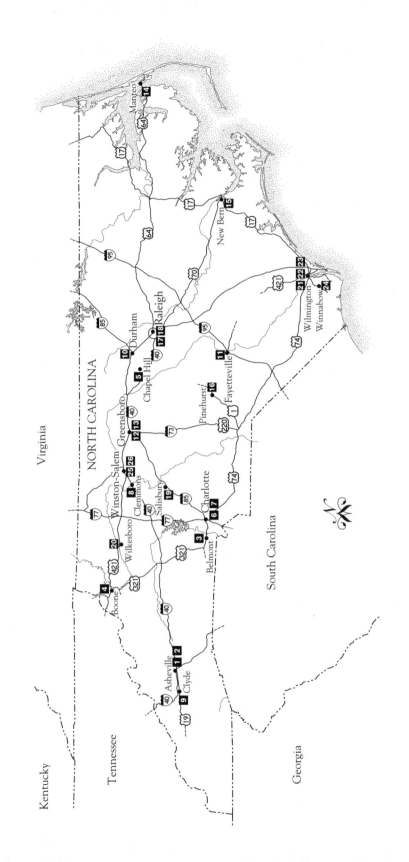

1. Asheville: Biltmore Estate
2. Asheville: Botanical Gardens at Asheville
3. Belmont: Daniel Stowe Botanical Garden
4. Boone: Daniel Boone Native Gardens
5. Chapel Hill: North Carolina Botanical Garden
6. Charlotte: University of North Carolina at Charlotte Botanical Gardens
7. Charlotte: Wing Haven Gardens and Bird Sanctuary
8. Clemmons: Tanglewood Arboretum and Rose Garden
9. Clyde: Campus Arboretum of Haywood Community College
10. Durham: Sarah P. Duke Gardens
11. Fayetteville: Cape Fear Botanical Garden
12. Greensboro: Greensboro Arboretum
13. Greensboro: Greensboro Bicentennial Garden and Bog Garden
14. Manteo: Elizabethan Gardens
15. New Bern: Tryon Palace Gardens
16. Pinehurst: Sandhills Horticultural Gardens
17. Raleigh: J. C. Raulston Arboretum
18. Raleigh: Raleigh Municipal Rose Garden
19. Salisbury: Elizabeth Holmes Hurley Park
20. Wilkesboro: Wilkes Community College Gardens
21. Wilmington: Airlie Gardens
22. Wilmington: Greenfield Gardens
23. Wilmington: New Hanover County Extension Service Arboretum
24. Winnabow: Orton Plantation Gardens
25. Winston-Salem: Old Salem
26. Winston-Salem: Reynolda Gardens of Wake Forest University

1. Biltmore Estate

One North Park Square,
Asheville, NC; (800) 543–2961;
www.biltmore.com

*T*HE BILTMORE ESTATE is not just a garden, though the gardens are well worth
a visit on their own. The 250-room mansion
remains the largest private residence in the
United States. Built for the grandson of Cor-
nelius Vanderbilt; it is now a historic landmark, a turn-of-the-
twentieth-century Renaissance-style château in the heart of the
Blue Ridge Mountains. You should certainly visit it when you come
to see the gardens, since the very steep admission fee covers both
house and grounds, the latter including a winery.

The grounds, designed by America's master landscape architect, Frederick Law Olmsted, cover 8,000 acres of beautiful rolling
terrain. With this kind of pedigree, the Biltmore is clearly a garden
lover's paradise. Huge, glamorous, partly formal and partly woodsy,
the estate gardens truly have something for every taste. A few high
points include the 50,000 spring bulbs in a walled garden (considered one of the finest English-style gardens in the nation), with
tulips and daffodils planted in geometric color patterns. The same
area is planted with myriad chrysanthemums in fall. A notable rose
garden displays one hundred varieties blooming from mid-spring
through late fall. In the wooded areas there are azaleas and forsyth-
ias and dogwoods aplenty adorning the lovely landscape in the Glen
and along the walkways. A formal Italian garden has three pools

with aquatic plants (including Egyptian lotus and water lilies), statuary, and benches.

A brief sketch of your garden tour might include beginning at the side of the mansion in the arbored terrace draped with three seasons of flowering vines and overlooking the formal Italian garden. A lush shrub garden, featuring huge banks of snowball viburnum and azaleas, borders the path to the great walled tulip garden and the magnificent rose garden. You will find the conservatory farther down the path, shielded from view by a tall holly hedge. Inside you'll find a palm garden, hydrangeas, orchids, and other delights. Next is the azalea garden (we visited in spring!), starring the Piedmont azalea native to the Blue Ridge area. A small creek with stepping-stones and Japanese bridge leads to the woodsy landscape beyond.

All of the gardens are accessible and inviting to wanderers. We judge a visit here to be a full day's adventure.

❀ **Admission:** Fee.

Garden open: Daily 9:00 A.M. to 5:00 P.M.; call for special hours and events.

Directions: From Interstate 40 take exit 50. Go north less than a mile to Biltmore.

2. Botanical Gardens at Asheville

University of North Carolina, 151 W. T. Weaver Boulevard, Asheville, NC; (828) 252–5190; www.ashevillebotanicalgardens.org

*H*ERE, in this Southern Appalachian region, plants native to the area are preserved and showcased on ten beautiful acres. A prize-winning garden for the blind and spectacular wildflower trails are among the many fine elements of these botanical gardens. Designed by noted landscape architect Doan Ogden (who also created the gardens at Haywood Community College in Clyde and the Daniel Boone Native Gardens in Boone), the garden's overall ambience is one of informality, with rhododendrons, dogwoods,

Craggy Gardens Rhododendrons

Brilliant flame azaleas and wild Catawba rhododendrons grow profusely in the 600-acre mountainous Craggy Gardens site along the Blue Ridge Parkway north of Asheville. These rhodies bloom later than their lower-elevation cousins, so visit in June and July to see the blossoms at their peak. Craggy Gardens offers several trails. The one at milepost 364.1 offers panoramic views, and another links the visitor center and bookshop at milepost 364.6 to a large picnic area. The observant visitor may spot wildflowers such as violets, blackberry, mayapple, and Turk's-cap lily.

and other spring blooms in profusion. Specialties include a sunshine garden, an azalea garden, and a sycamore area. (You can also see earthworks from the Battle of Asheville.) There are many trails through meadows and woods. For best viewing visit between early April and mid-June, but at any time you'll find interesting things going on; there is a botany center and year-round activities, such as the three-day Annual Wildflower Pilgrimage.

❀ **Admission:** Free.

Garden open: Daily dawn to dusk.

Directions: From Interstate 240, which goes through Asheville, take Merrimon Avenue (U.S. Highway 25) north for 1 ²⁄₁₀ miles. Turn left onto W. T. Weaver Boulevard and continue for ½ mile. The garden entrance is on the right.

3. Daniel Stowe Botanical Garden

6500 South New Hope Road, **Belmont**, NC; (704) 825–4490; www.stowegarden.org

*T*HIS IS A fairly new garden, but the aim of its creator (a retired executive named Daniel Stowe) to create a vibrant conservancy and large public garden is already evident. Eventually some 400 acres will be included. Phase one—the ten acres already landscaped and cultivated—offers fine display gardens, conservatories, many water features, and lots of birds. Specialties include daylilies, native plants and shrubs, a kitchen garden, and all kinds of seasonal plantings. There are a children's garden, a gazebo, a knot garden, several border gardens arranged by color, and a butterfly garden, among other completed areas. A white garden has just been created.

It is always interesting to see a great garden in its early stages, and this one is already well on its way. Best time to visit is springtime.

❀ **Admission:** Free.

Garden open: Monday through Saturday 9:00 A.M. to 5:00 P.M., Sunday noon to 5:00 P.M.; closed Christmas.

Directions: Take Interstate 77 toward Charlotte. Belmont is to the west of Interstate 85 after its intersection with I–77. From I–85 north take the New Hope Road exit and turn right onto New Hope Road. After 11 miles, the garden entrance is on your right.

4. Daniel Boone Native Gardens

U.S. Highway 421/321, **Boone, NC;**
(828) 264–6390

*T*HESE TEN ACRES are a good place for a self-guided tour; a brochure is available at the entrance, and you can wander through the North Carolina plants, identifying native species as you go. The designer was Doan Ogden, the creator of distinctive gardens at Asheville and Clyde as well. Named for Daniel Boone, the frontiersman and explorer (whose hand-hewn log cabin is here), the gardens are informal and very pretty, with pools, meadows, a sunken garden, a bog garden, a fern garden, a rock garden, and a meditation garden. Specialties include native flora like azalea, honeysuckle, clematis, dogwood, Black Mountain heart cherry, wildflowers, and a variety of other blooms that make this section of the state so delectable in springtime.

✿ **Admission:** Fee.
Garden open: Daily 9:00 A.M. to 6:00 P.M. from May through October, weather permitting.
Directions: Boone is just west of the Blue Ridge Parkway, off U.S. Highway 421, U.S. Highway 321, and the Route 105 extension. Follow the signs to Horn in the West. The entrance is from US 421 or the Route 105 extension.

5. North Carolina Botanical Garden

University of North Carolina, Laurel Hill Road, **Chapel Hill,** NC; (919) 962–0522; www.ncbg.unc.edu

*T*HE UNIVERSITY of North Carolina Botanical Garden is actually made up of two separate sites: the Coker Arboretum—in the center of the campus—and a large woodland and demonstration and research garden complex. Each site is enjoyable in its own way; together they add up to some 600 acres of plantings.

The Coker Arboretum, which is next to the planetarium in the heart of the campus, is an informal setting rather like a good-size city park. Once a pasture, the space was converted by a professor of botany, William Coker, beginning a century ago. Professor Coker wanted an area to preserve North Carolina's native shrubs, trees, and flowers, and that is just what this arboretum does in a charming, rather overgrown way. Don't miss the great wisteria arbor that runs the entire length of one side (see it in spring), the camellia collection, sweet-breath-of-spring, and a variety of other blooms. Amid the nice sandy paths and moss-covered walls are wonderful, very tall trees, including some unusual ones: the dove tree, Chinese fringe tree, Chinese pistachio, Japanese plum yew, as well as the lovely crape myrtle, bald cypress, and Marshall's hawthorn. Pick up a guide to the many trees, each of which is numbered. There are also many, many birds.

The botanical garden on Laurel Hill Road is a research and teaching facility, with a large area of different types of plantings and collections—many of them nicely obscure or unusual—a carnivorous garden, an aquatic collection, a knot garden, and a series of different habitat gardens, among others. You can enjoy these different sites in a variety of ways, and if you are a gardener yourself, you will appreciate the emphasis on learning the ins and outs of gardening (there are numerous events and classes here), from fertilizer to container gardening. But parts of the facility are lovely to look at too.

❀ **Admission:** Free.

Garden open: Daily dawn to dusk.

Directions: From Durham on I–40, exit south to U.S. Highway 15/501 for 1½ miles to a Y. Bear left and continue for 2⁷⁄₁₀ miles. Just past the intersection with Route 54, turn left to the botanical garden entrance. For the Coker Arboretum, return to the Y and bear right. Turn left at the arboretum entrance, which is on Franklin Street.

6. University of North Carolina at Charlotte Botanical Gardens

Mary Alexander Road and Craven Road, **Charlotte,** NC; (704) 687–2364; http://gardens.uncc.edu

*T*HIS NINE-ACRE garden is nearly forty years old, with greenhouses and several specialty gardens. The greenhouses have 4,000 square feet of space. They feature five distinct growing environments, including a rain forest and herbarium, and collections of succulents, orchids, and pitcher plants, among the most popular. The herbarium contains more than 20,000 preserved specimens of native and nonnative plants.

The outdoor specialty gardens are devoted to North Carolina native plants, rhododendron hybrids, hardy ornamentals, and some fifty species of ferns. Of particular charm is the Van Landingham Glen, named for the rhododendron enthusiast who planted it; this is one of the largest collections of rhododendrons in the Southeast, numbering in the thousands. Also of note is the Susie Harwood Garden with its lushly overgrown steps and moon gate. This rather Asian-in-style, three-acre garden has an aquatic section, an area of perennials, and all-season plantings.

Pick up a self-guiding brochure at the greenhouses before you set out on the very beautiful outing through the gardens.

❀ **Admission:** Free.

Garden open: Daily sunrise to sunset. Greenhouses open Monday through Friday 9:00 A.M. to 4:00 P.M., Saturday 10:00 A.M. to 3:00 P.M.

Directions: Take I–85; the university is located at the intersection of I–85 and Route 49. Enter the campus from Route 49 and bear right to Mary Alexander Road. Park in lot 2.

7. Wing Haven Gardens and Bird Sanctuary

248 Ridgewood Avenue, **Charlotte,** NC; (704) 331–0664; www.winghavengardens.com

*S*ITUATED IN an old Charlotte neighborhood, Wing Haven is a three-acre walled delight, densely planted by the owners Elizabeth and Edwin Clarkson starting back in 1927. A tiny wilderness and sanctuary (birds have always loved the spot, and indeed an orphaned bluebird had the run of the house and bathed in the bathroom!), Wing Haven is one of those special gardens with its own ambience. There are birdbaths and fountains among the flowers, a formal garden, a rose garden, woodland shrubs, and pleasantly uneven brick paths and plazas with benches, a sundial, and an oval reflecting pool.

This is an old garden, and it has the great trees (though Hurricane Hugo brought down seventy-five of them—many now replaced), the aged brick, and the statuary and plantings of a

Choosing an Outing in North Carolina

American History
Biltmore Estate
Elizabethan Gardens
Old Salem
Tryon Palace Gardens

*Aquatic Gardens and
Gardens with Water Views*
Greensboro Arboretum
Greensboro Bicentennial Garden
  and Bog Garden
New Hanover County Extension
  Service Arboretum
Orton Plantation Gardens

Arboretums
Campus Arboretum of Haywood
  Community College
Greensboro Arboretum
J. C. Raulston Arboretum
New Hanover County Extension
  Service Arboretum
North Carolina Botanical Garden
Tanglewood Arboretum and Rose
  Garden

Birds and Other Animals
Orton Plantation Gardens
Wing Haven Gardens and Bird
  Sanctuary

Child-Pleasing Gardens
Daniel Boone Native Gardens

Sandhills Horticultural Gardens
Wilkes Community College Gardens
Wing Haven Gardens and Bird
  Sanctuary

Conservatories and Botanic Gardens
Botanical Gardens at Asheville
Cape Fear Botanical Garden
Daniel Boone Native Gardens
Daniel Stowe Botanical Garden
New Hanover County Extension
  Service Arboretum
Reynolda Gardens of Wake Forest
  University
University of North Carolina at
  Charlotte Botanical Garden

Famous Landscape Designer Gardens
Biltmore Estate (Frederick Law
  Olmsted)
Botanical Gardens at Asheville
  (Doan Ogden)
Campus Arboretum of Haywood
  Community College (Doan
  Ogden)
Daniel Boone Native Gardens
  (Doan Ogden)
Sarah P. Duke Gardens
  (Ellen Biddle Shipman)

Formal Gardens
Airlie Gardens
Orton Plantation Gardens

Reynolda Gardens of
Wake Forest University

Historic Houses and Plantations
Orton Plantation Gardens
Tryon Palace Gardens

Informal and English-style Gardens
Airlie Gardens
Biltmore Estate

Italianate Gardens
Biltmore Estate

Medicinal and Herb Gardens
Old Salem
Wing Haven Gardens
and Bird Sanctuary

Romantic Gardens
Airlie Gardens

Rose Gardens
Biltmore Estate
Raleigh Municipal Rose Garden
Tanglewood Arboretum and
Rose Garden

Specialty Gardens
Greenfield Gardens (azaleas)
J. C. Raulston Arboretum
(redbud trees)
Sandhills Horticultural Gardens
(holly)

Urban Settings
North Carolina Botanical
Garden
Raleigh Municipal Rose Garden

Wildflowers and Woodland
Sarah P. Duke Gardens

traditional southern garden. There are tunnels of ivy, wooden arbors, wildflowers, an herb garden with seventy-five different kinds of herbs, boxwood hedges, a camellia collection, ducks who wander through the garden, and wonderful birdcalls throughout. In fact, all the garden elements have the pleasure of birds in mind, from water elements to nesting spots to favorite foods.

A visit here makes you feel like a privileged visitor to a private garden. The brochure for the Wing Haven Foundation (which now runs the gardens) quotes the great garden designer Gertrude Jekyll: "I hold the firm belief that the purpose of a garden is to give happiness and repose of mind." Wing Haven is a perfect case in point.

❖ **Admission:** Free.

Garden open: Tuesday 3:00 to 5:00 P.M., Wednesday 10:00 A.M. to noon, Sunday 2:00 to 5:00 P.M.

Directions: From I–77, which runs north–south through Charlotte, exit east onto Woodlawn Road. Turn left onto Selwyn Avenue and left again onto Ridgewood Avenue.

8. Tanglewood Arboretum and Rose Garden

4061 Clemmons Road (U.S. Highway 158), **Clemmons,** NC; (336) 778–6333; www.ces.ncsu.edu/copubs/garden/027

*L*OCATED IN A large recreational complex called Tanglewood Park, these gardens are just one section of the large entertainment area (racetrack, golf course, campground, etc.). But here you'll find a most unusual arboretum, one that specializes in Piedmont trees, and a fine rose garden near the manor house. The land was left to the public by one of the Reynolds (tobacco) family, and the handiwork of Frank Lustig, a Reynolds family gardener, can be seen in the fine landscaping.

The arboretum features oak and black walnut, flowering native trees (dogwoods, azaleas, rhododendrons), and specimens from around the world. The rose garden has some 800 plants. There is also a hedged fragrance garden and a self-guided nature trail with audio stations for the blind.

❖ **Admission:** Fee to park.

Garden open: Daily 7:00 A.M. to dusk.

Directions: Take I–40 west from Winston-Salem. Take exit 184 (Lewisville–Clemmons Road) and turn left (south). Go about 1 mile to U.S. Highway 158. Turn right onto US 158 and continue for 1 ²⁄₁₀ miles. The garden entrance is just after Harper Road.

9. Campus Arboretum of Haywood Community College

Freedlander Drive, **Clyde,** NC; (828) 627–4500, (828) 627–4640;
www.haywood.edu

*T*HIS fairly new, eighty-acre campus has made a point of turn-ing much of its open space into garden areas. The school hired the noted landscape architect Doan Ogden to create a master landscape plan for the campus, set in what was once a farm, and beautifully located in the Southern Appalachians. (Other North Carolina gardens designed by Ogden are in Boone and Asheville.)

Ogden's accomplishment includes a fine series of flower gardens (such as a dahlia garden, an Oriental garden, and a rose garden), a preserved native forest, a wonderful variety of trees (including a willow walk), and one of the best rhododendron collections in this western region of North Carolina. Don't miss the "tunnel walk" through the laburnum trees or the outdoor circular classroom sur-rounded by boxwoods. There are many more garden delights here, maintained by horticulture students. Western North Carolina is a pretty part of the world—particularly in springtime—and this campus has truly captured the natural beauty of its surroundings.

❋ **Admission:** Free.

Garden open: Monday through Friday 8:00 A.M. to 11:00 P.M., Satur-day 8:00 A.M. to 4:00 P.M.; closed Sunday.

Directions: From Asheville take I–40 toward Clyde. Take exit 27 onto U.S. Highway 19/23. Follow signs to campus.

10. Sarah P. Duke Gardens

Duke University, **Durham,** NC; (919) 684–3698;
www.hr.duke.edu/dukegardens

*O*NE OF the best-known of southern gardens, the Sarah P. Duke Gardens can best be described as grand. Though originally planned for the use of the Duke University community, the impressive gardens were opened to the public, which takes full advantage of them: Some 200,000 visitors come each year. But these fifty-five acres are large enough to accommodate everyone without crowding, and you'll find lots to catch your eye as you walk through the 5 *miles* of carefully marked pathways from one scenic beauty to the next. The gardens are divided into both wooded and formal areas: Twenty acres are developed, and thirty-five are native woodland, mostly pine forest. There are more than 2,000 species of plants in these acres.

We found the most spectacular part of the gardens to be the great hillside Terrace Garden, which was commissioned by Mary Duke Biddle in honor of her mother, Sarah P. Duke, who financed the original gardens. The design was by Ellen Biddle Shipman; her terraced layout has become something of a landmark among eastern and southern gardens. The Terraces, as they are known, are giant—an entire hillside of blooms divided by terracing rock walls. Between the flagstone walls are rows and rows of bulbs and seasonal flowers. From the bottom looking up, you feel as though you are in an amphitheater of blooms, with each flower neatly in place, like an audience! This is truly a sight to see. Among the glories of the Terraces are an octagonal Chinese wisteria pergola at the top and the flowering trees interspersed among the flowers: ornamental cherry, dogwood, redbud, and crab apple. At the bottom of this garden is a naturalistic pool with water lilies and goldfish. Stretching beyond it are open fields.

Major garden areas are devoted to irises, azaleas, peonies, hollies, and in fall 7,000 chrysanthemums. There is a walled, circular rose garden; a garden of native plants (600 species); and a bog garden where you may spot a Venus flytrap. You can visit this site year-round and always find something blooming.

Another extraordinary pleasure of the gardens is the Asiatic Arboretum, a very beautiful twenty-acre area, with water, bamboo, forsythia, rocks, and a general atmosphere of serenity. This large area is particularly quiet and pretty.

If you are looking for small-scale intimacy in garden design, this is not the place for you. Our overall impression was of grandeur and magnificence from the moment we entered the imposing wrought-iron gates and were greeted by a vast formal bed of blooming flowers (hundreds and hundreds of bright tulips when we were there). Students and other members of the university community have a most extraordinary place to study outdoors!

❁ **Admission:** Free.
Garden open: Daily 8:00 A.M. to sunset.
Directions: Sarah P. Duke Gardens are located off Duke University Road and Academy Road, about 1 mile west of downtown Durham, on the western side of the Duke University campus.

11. Cape Fear Botanical Garden

536 North Eastern Boulevard, **Fayetteville**, NC; (910) 486–0221; www.capefearbg.org

*T*HERE ARE eighty-five acres in this botanical garden bordering the Cape Fear River. Ranging from formal plantings to trails through a wilderness, these acres will suit a variety of tastes. There are some terrific views; take the trails to bluffs that overlook the Cape Fear River and a nearby meandering stream called Cross Creek. You will also find a natural amphitheater and a series of well-kept flower gardens. The combining of wilderness trails and formal gardens is increasingly popular in botanical gardens, giving both lovers of cultivated flowers and natural plantings plenty to enjoy.

✿ **Admission:** Fee.
Garden open: Monday through Saturday 10:00 A.M. to 5:00 P.M., Sunday noon to 5:00 P.M.; closed mid-December through mid-February.
Directions: From Interstate 95 take exit 52 onto Route 24 west. Go approximately 5 miles. Turn right onto Route 301N (Eastern Boulevard). Go ⅛ mile. The entrance is on the right.

12. Greensboro Arboretum

West Market Street, **Greensboro,** NC; (336) 297–4162;
www.greensborobeautiful.org/Arboretum.htm

*G*REENSBORO BEAUTIFUL, INC. is an organization that works to beautify its city at three major sites: the Greensboro Arboretum, the Bog Garden, and the Bicentennial Garden (see the gardenwalk description below). The arboretum, though primarily a wooded, seventeen-acre site, also features a number of specialty gardens, including a butterfly garden with fountain, a winter garden, a ground cover garden, a hydrophytic garden (aquatic plants), a vine garden, a rhododendron garden, and many trails through wildflowers both native and exotic. This is a lovely place for a walk!

✿ **Admission:** Free.
Garden open: Daily sunrise to sunset.
Directions: Take I–40 to Greensboro and exit at 217B onto High Point Road. After a little more than a mile, turn right onto Holden Road and continue 2½ miles. Take a right onto Cornwallis Drive and go 1 block to Hobbs Street. Go 1 ⁴⁄₁₀ miles on Hobbs until you reach West Market Street. Turn left to the arboretum entrance on your right.

13. Greensboro Bicentennial Garden and Bog Garden

Hobbs Street, **Greensboro,** NC; (336) 373–2199;
www.greensborobeautiful.org/BiC.htm

*T*HE BICENTENNIAL GARDEN consists of seven and a half acres of year-round formal gardens, with bulb and annual beds, a rose garden, two rock gardens, and a variety of other pleasures, including a fragrance garden for the blind. The spring bulb garden has more than 30,000 plants! One hundred and five varieties of daylilies grow here. There are camellia and azalea collections and an overall ambience of brilliant color and pleasant design. Best viewing is in springtime and summer. You may well spot a wedding being held among the flowers.

Just across the street is the Bog Garden, adjacent to a lake, where you'll discover a wild bog and an elevated wooden walkway that leads you through the marshy land to see its indigenous plants and wildlife. There are stands of bamboos, ferns, wildflowers, and a variety of wild ducks and fish.

The two gardens and arboretum (see previous listing) of Greensboro Beautiful, Inc. can be visited on one outing. They are excellent examples of how a city and its residents can join together to take undeveloped land and maintain public gardens for the enjoyment of all.

❀ **Admission:** Free.

Garden open: Daily sunrise to sunset.

Directions: Take I-40 to Greensboro and exit at 217B onto High Point Road. After just over a mile, turn right onto Holden Road and continue 2½ miles. Turn right onto Cornwallis Drive for 1 block to Hobbs Street to find the parking area.

14. Elizabethan Gardens

U.S. Highway 64/264, **Manteo**, NC; (252) 473–3234;
www.elizabethangardens.org

*I*N OUR myriad visits to gardens, a few stand out as places that
capture an intangible quality of design and history—a delicate
ambience that makes them special. Elizabethan Gardens is truly one
of the most beautiful gardens of all. Located on Roanoke Island, this
ten-acre garden is an artist's dream. The layout centers around a
great empty lawn, but everywhere you find curving, twisting shapes
of tree limbs: crape myrtles and live oaks. Their branches make
sweeping forms reminiscent of those painted by Vincent van Gogh,
a stunning contrast with the formal straight lines of stone
balustrades and parterre gardens of geometric beds outlined neatly
in boxwood. Throughout the gardens are inviting vistas in every
direction, from overlooks of beach and water to arched lookouts to
a sunken garden through a great tightly knit holly allée. You will not
often find a garden that is so imaginatively conceived as this one.

Elizabethan Gardens is on the site of the first English colony
(1587) in the New World, the ill-fated Roanoke colony. The gardens, in a style reminiscent of sixteenth-century English pleasure
gardens, were created in 1951 by two well-known landscape designers, Richard Webel and M. Umberto Innocenti. Gifts from John Hay
Whitney of antique British garden statuary and fountains—some dating from the fifteenth century—added to
the historic nature of the design.

The plans included elements familiar to
Elizabethan gardeners: a sunken garden, a
rose garden, a thatched gazebo with a coni-
cal roof, marble fountains and balustrades,
a mix of culinary and decorative plantings,
an herb garden with Shakespearean quota-
tions, a sundial, and a gatehouse patterned

after a sixteenth-century orangery. A water gate marks the spot where the colonists are thought to have come ashore. Punctuating the entire acreage are great trees (there is an ancient oak from the sixteenth century) and massive shrubs (hibiscus, rhododendrons, camellias) that are stunningly lush in blooming season.

Among our favorite spots was the sunken garden surrounded by a holly allée (some 10 or 11 feet high) with long shady paths surrounding an open garden and a central fountain. Another was the amazing camellia collection, through which one could stroll on pine-needle paths. The crape myrtle trees with their bright pink blossoms and gnarled white branches are an integral part of these gardens, creating a glorious, decorative setting for plants ranging from wildflowers (including wild orchids) to gardenias.

It is nice to imagine this lovely spot as a touch of home for the poor colonists who struggled to survive here, but in any case, it is a reminder of how far back the beauty of English garden design goes. Certainly the Elizabethans knew a great deal about landscape and gardens, both from practical and aesthetic viewpoints. Don't miss this one!

❁ **Admission:** Fee.
Garden open: Daily; closed major holidays; call for hours.
Directions: Take U.S. Highway 64 to Roanoke Island. At the entrance to Fort Raleigh, you'll find the Elizabethan Gardens entrance on the left, just after you cross the bridge.

Garden Shows and Festivals in North Carolina

FEBRUARY
Southern Spring Show, Charlotte; (704) 376–6594

APRIL
Festival of Flowers, Asheville; (800) 543–2961

Spring Historic Homes and Garden Tour, New Bern; (919) 633–6448

15. Tryon Palace Gardens

610 Pollock Street, **New Bern**, NC; (252) 514-4900,
(800) 767-1560; www.tryonpalace.org

A THOROUGH TOUR of Tryon Palace will take you through
a grand historic site—the great building itself, a series of
smaller structures, and all of their gardens. Georgian-style Tryon
Palace sits proudly on the water's edge in the heart of New Bern,
and it has a long and illustrious history as the governor's seat of
power before the Revolution and as a prime example of an "English" colonial estate. The palace's gardens, laid out in the 1770s,
were elegant from the start. The palace and the gardens fell into dis-
repair, but their careful renovation gives us a revitalized mansion
and fourteen acres of landscaping to enjoy.

The gardens at the palace are actually a collection of different
settings, many of them bordered by the brick wings and walls of the
palace. Since no plan remained of the original gardens, they have
been restored in a variety of styles, ranging from the simple colonial
kitchen garden to formal elegance more reminiscent of the Victorian era. But most of today's trees and flowers are known to have
been used in the United States in the eighteenth century, and many
British gardens of the period were studied for the restoration.

The Wooded Outer Banks

The Buxton Woods Nature Trail is a ¾-mile self-guided trail near
Cape Hatteras Lighthouse. This loop walk takes you through
marshes and through one of the few remaining maritime forests.
Signs along the walk explain the fragile ecosystem, while all
around you are songbirds and ocean birds. It's a great place for
bird-watching and enjoying unspoiled nature. You'll find the trail
along Route 12 in Buxton.

High points include the fine brick walls, paths, antique statuary, white marble classical temple, wrought-iron gates, espaliered fruit trees, round topiary forms, and a pretty parterre garden with a series of arabesques of boxwood filled with flowers (hundreds of tulips at our visit). These small garden settings are interspersed with a large open lawn (with water view), a wilderness area, and continuous walkways (where you can occasionally see colonial-dressed employees of the palace going by). The gardens are at their best beginning in April.

❋ **Admission:** Fee.
   Garden open: Monday through Saturday 9:00 A.M. to 4:00 P.M., Sunday 1:00 to 4:00 P.M.; closed some holidays.
   Directions: Take U.S. Highway 17 into New Bern. Turn left onto George Street (at the sign) and you'll see Tryon Palace.

16. Sandhills Horticultural Gardens

2200 Airport Road, **Pinehurst**, NC; (910) 695–3882; www.sandhills.edu

*D*EMONSTRATION GARDENS are part of the horticultural program at Sandhills Community College; they are maintained by the students and faculty of the Landscape Gardening School and the community. High points of the twenty-five-acre landscape are the unusually extensive holly garden (some 350 different cultivars and a real maze—take the kids) and a boardwalk through the wetlands garden. Other specialty gardens include the wonderfully named Sir Walter Raleigh Garden, a rose garden, and a conifer garden. One of the nicest aspects of this site is the use of trellises and other decorative elements like fountains and nicely placed benches, waterfalls, bridges, and pools.

❋ **Admission:** Free.
   Garden open: Daily dawn to dusk.
   Directions: From U.S. Highway 74, head east on U.S. Highway 1 to

Aberdeen. Turn west onto US 15/501 and go 3 7/10 miles. At the traffic circle, take the first right (Route 211) for 1 block. Turn left onto Airport Road for 2 4/10 miles to the campus entrance. The gardens are behind Heutte Hall.

17. J. C. Raulston Arboretum

North Carolina State University, 4301 Beryl Road, **Raleigh**, NC;
(919) 515–3132; www.ncsu.edu/jcraulstonarboretum

*N*ORTH CAROLINA STATE UNIVERSITY has two separate—both interesting—garden areas to visit. This eight-acre arboretum, founded in 1976, is used by the horticultural program at the university as an outdoor classroom and demonstration garden. It was the pet project of Dr. J. C. Raulston, a professor of horticulture, who wanted to expand the vistas of North Carolina gardeners.

In addition to its useful aspects as a research and teaching facility, this large, flat arboretum has a number of specialty gardens that are quite lovely to look at. Our favorite was the Shade House, a slatted-walled garden. This unusual space is quite large, with delicate, flickering sunlight that shines through the thin wooden slatted walls onto 1,500 different plants that thrive in shady climates. There is a somewhat Asian atmosphere here, and it is well worth a visit.

Other specialty areas include gardens devoted to roses and magnolias, a Victorian gazebo, a Zen garden, a paradise garden, a white garden, a reading garden, an edible garden, a fern collection, and a variety of North Carolina trees, including crape myrtle, junipers, dwarf loblolly pine, and the world's largest collection of redbud trees. Some 6,000 different species (from fifty-five countries) are planted here, and just about all of them are labeled.

A perennial garden has thousands of blooms within a 450-foot-long border; the pattern follows the precepts of the great landscape designer Gertrude Jekyll. (It was described by the noted British landscape architect Sir Geoffrey Jellicoe, as "an epic border, a heroic event in landscape architecture.") It is at its best from May to November.

In keeping with its function as a teaching and research facility, there is little overall design tying the arboretum gardens together. But each individual part is well thought out and attractive, and you'll enjoy the variety: It is almost like walking through a garden bazaar. If you are a gardener, this is a very useful spot; material about how to grow the plants you see is available at the entrance.

❀ **Admission:** Free.

Garden open: Daily 8:00 A.M. to sunset.

Directions: Take I–40 to Interstate 440. Exit at Hillsborough Street (exit 3). Turn left onto Hillsborough Street. Go to the first light and turn right on Beryl Road. Go over the railroad tracks (bearing right) and continue about a half mile to the arboretum entrance.

18. Raleigh Municipal Rose Garden

Pogue Street, **Raleigh**, NC; (919) 821–4579

*T*HIS ROSE GARDEN is set on a charming six-and-a-half-acre hilly site behind a theater of North Carolina State University—in fact, the garden shares the dell with an amphitheater. It is unpretentious in design, but its terraced feeling and a variety of delicious plantings make it quite lovely. If you like rose gardens, you'll find this one unusually pleasing. Though it is open year-round and includes some additional types of plants, rose enthusiasts should visit from mid-May until late fall.

❀ **Admission:** Free.

Garden open: Daily.

Directions: Follow the directions to the J. C. Raulston Arboretum (above). Pass the arboretum and turn left on Pogue Street, opposite the NCSU campus. Take Pogue Street to the 300 block, where you'll find the Gaddy-Goodwin Teaching Theater. The rose garden is behind this building.

19. Elizabeth Holmes Hurley Park

Lake Drive, **Salisbury,** NC; (704) 638–5260

*T*HIS IS A fifteen-acre park that was carefully designed not as formal gardens but as a year-round attraction with natural plantings for each season. The park features woodland trails, wildflowers, footbridges over water, and other quiet pleasures. Stroll here in spring for the lovely collection of flowering delights, such as azaleas and magnolias, perennials, and wildflowers dotted throughout the woods. Or visit in winter for its outstanding redberry holly collection. All of the plants are labeled.

❀ **Admission:** Free.

Garden open: Daily sunrise to sunset.

Directions: From I–85 take exit 76B. Go right onto West Innis Street. At 2 ³⁄₁₀ miles, turn right onto Nahaley Avenue, which will become Confederate Avenue. Go 3½ miles to Lake Drive and turn right. The park entrance is on the right.

20. Wilkes Community College Gardens

Collegiate Road, **Wilkesboro,** NC; (336) 838–6100;
www.wilkescc.edu

*T*HIS 140-ACRE campus includes a number of specialty gardens; among them are a rose garden, a native plant garden, a Japanese garden, a wildflower meadow, a victory (vegetable) garden, and a distinctive sensory garden. Kept up with community support, including that of noted bluegrass musician "Doc" Watson, the gardens are the setting for an annual bluegrass festival. The Eddy Merle Watson Memorial Garden for the Senses includes a 70-foot concrete-and-brick wall with carvings to touch, the work of local artist Patricia Turlington. Children will enjoy a nice playground in these gardens.

❀ **Admission:** Free.

Garden open: Daily dawn to dusk.

Directions: From I–40 take exit 188 (US 421 north). In Wilkesboro, at the intersection with Route 268, take the exit marked Wilkes Community College. Go left at the end of the ramp. At ³⁄₁₀ mile, turn left onto Collegiate Road. The parking lot is ½ mile farther.

21. Airlie Gardens

Airlie Road off U.S. Highway 76, **Wilmington,** NC;
(910) 798–7700; www.airliegardens.org

*I*F YOUR taste runs to the old and lush and naturalized in public gardens, visit Airlie Gardens. It is huge (155 acres—though about 50 of them are the primary garden area), gracious, and pre–Civil War in design. It is sometimes described as a paradise on the North Carolina coast.

Airlie's setting and history are both colorful: It sits along Bradley Creek and the Wrightsville Sound, overlooking Money Island, which is thought to be the site of Captain Kidd's buried treasure. In the nineteenth century the estate was owned by wealthy rice plantation owner Pembroke Jones, who named it after his ancestral home in Scotland. It was he who built the thirty-five-room mansion and developed the gardens. Fortunately, its present owners, the Corbetts, have opened their elegant gardens to the public.

The pleasures of Airlie Gardens reflect the overall age and lushness of the landscape. There are azaleas and camellias in abundance (many reflected in the waters of a spring-fed garden lake) and great live oaks draped with Spanish moss. Swans glide under the flowering shrubs that overhang the lake. There are many walking trails, a formal garden called the Spring

Garden, an 1835 rural chapel, a pergola, and other delights. We suggest a visit in spring to see this place at its most breathtaking.

✿ **Admission:** Fee.
Garden open: Daily 9:00 A.M. to 5:00 P.M. from March 1 through October 3.
Directions: From I–40 take U.S. Highway 76 (Oleander Drive) toward Rightsville Beach. Turn left onto Oleander Drive (east), and go 3½ miles. Cross Bradley Creek Bridge. Airlie is ³⁄₁₀ mile on your right.

22. Greenfield Gardens
South Fifth Avenue, **Wilmington,** NC;
(910) 341–7855

*T*HESE GARDENS are part of Greenfield Park in the heart of this coastal city. Once a plantation, the park covers 180 acres; it offers a variety of recreational activities, including boating and a scenic drive around a lake that is graced by a spectacular collection of azaleas said to number in the thousands. (Call for the dates of the azalea festival each spring.) The formal plantings include many specialty areas, such as a fragrance garden, a summer annual garden, and a rose garden, maintained by civic associations. And throughout the park there are nature trails leading the visitor to spectacular examples of bald cypresses dripping with moss, crape myrtles (a personal favorite of ours), flowering trees including dogwoods—and those azaleas. Visit in early spring for this treat.

✿ **Admission:** Free.
Garden open: Daily dawn to dusk.
Directions: Take US 421, which runs through Wilmington and becomes Third Street. Turn east onto Willard. Greenfield Gardens is on South Fifth Avenue at Willard.

23. New Hanover County Extension Service Arboretum

6202 Oleander Drive, **Wilmington,** NC; (910) 452–6393;
www.gardeningnhc.org

*S*ITUATED ON the southeastern coast of North Carolina, this
seven-acre arboretum features plants that are best suited to
the geographical conditions of coastal gardens. Among the thirty-
two different gardens here are several that will be of interest to local
gardeners, a conservatory with exotic plants from other regions,
and even a miniature rain forest. Included in the specialty gardens
are an aquatic garden, a perennial garden, a rose garden, and a shade
garden. You can walk along paved pathways from garden to garden
under the mature live oak trees.

🌼 **Admission:** Free.
Garden open: Daily sunrise to sunset.
Directions: Take I–40 east; it becomes North College Road north of
Wilmington. At the juncture with US 76 (Oleander Drive), turn left.
The garden is on the right, 3 miles along Oleander Drive.

24. Orton Plantation Gardens

9149 Orton Road SE, **Winnabow,** NC; (910) 371–6851;
www.ortongardens.com

*O*NE OF THE few great plantation gardens open to the public in
North Carolina, Orton's magnificent gardens were actually
planted in the twentieth century around the family's historic antebellum home. This former rice plantation along the Cape Fear River
(not far from Wilmington) encompasses thirty acres in a coastal area
more typical of the Deep South than North Carolina. Although its
once-thriving rice production was abandoned in the late nineteenth
century, the owners continued to flood the fields each winter.
Migrating birds and other wildlife are abundant in this wildlife
sanctuary.

In 1910 the first garden terraces were built by James and Luola Sprunt. They planted camellias, azaleas, rhododendrons, and banana shrubs. In the 1930s their son began the extensive landscaping of the estate, laying out the formal (and the natural) gardens that give the landscape its great beauty. Today, twenty of the acres form the well-known gardens. (The plantation house is still lived in by members of the original family and is not open to the public.)

A visit to Orton will take you into a world of lagoons and winding paths, belvederes and great live oaks draped with moss arching overhead, and a series of small, delightful gardens devoted to beautiful plantings—crape myrtles, hydrangeas,  Cherokee roses, wisterias, camellias, oleanders, magnolias, and other southern specialties. Individual gardens are ornamental pleasures; among them are a radial garden, a scroll garden, a sun garden, and a triangle garden. Each of these design-oriented, well-kept sites has its own kinds of flowers and ambience. Of particular note is the shade in this region of searing hot sunlight. The gardens are best from March through September. The first two weeks of April are the high point with a dazzling azalea display, but this garden also offers flowering trees and shrubs throughout the summer months.

The overall atmosphere is created by the juxtaposition of natural wetlands, lagoons, waterfowl, and wildlife with the elegance of formal gardens. (Not for the faint of heart, these gardens' low bridges and walkways are just above water—and alligator—level.) Orton's gardens will make a vivid impression, evoking both the beauty of the Old South with its plantation culture and the bright face and hidden dangers of the tropics. As you stroll among the great oaks or over a Chinese bridge or through the colonial cemetery, or as you watch for waterbirds from a belvedere over a lagoon, you will be transported to another time and place. A great garden can do that.

✿ **Admission:** Fee.

Garden open: Daily 8:00 A.M. to 6:00 P.M. from March through August; daily 10:00 A.M. to 5:00 P.M. from September through November.

Directions: From downtown Wilmington cross the river to Route 133. Go south for about 12 miles, then follow signs to Orton Plantation Gardens.

25. Old Salem

U.S. Highway 52, **Winston-Salem**, NC; (336) 721–7300; www.oldsalem.org

*O*LD SALEM is a restored late eighteenth- and early nineteenth-century community, originally settled by the Moravians, that today includes wonderful old period houses covering a twelve-city-block area. Of particular interest to us are the many restored or re-created gardens, including several kitchen gardens, herb gardens, medicinal gardens, and even beds of rosebushes planted in the early nineteenth century.

Old Salem has eighteen garden sites. (You can get a brochure of garden descriptions at the gate.) The majority are kitchen gardens in fenced areas behind the houses. You'll find everything from perennial borders to fruit trees and beehives, to vegetables and hops (grown for beer and bread), to a wide variety of herbs for both cooking and medicinal use.

Not to be missed: Salt Street, where some of the most interesting gardens are found. For instance, the John Henry Leinbach property features a hilly garden that stretches down to a creek behind the house. You can read Leinbach's gardening diary at the site. He terraced the land with a series of rock walls, planted potatoes and other vegetables, grew apples, and made honey, among many other gardening endeavors. His wife planted rosebushes in 1823 and they are still blooming atop the terrace. Also on Salt Street are gardens displaying medicinal herbs, a cherry orchard, and another garden of hops. Be sure to visit the Cape Fear Bank garden and the 1759 Triebel garden.

If you enjoy historic settings with their antique ambience, you will like these small, unpretentious Moravian plots with their combination of prettiness and usefulness. The people who have restored Old Salem have tried to retain the original flavor of each garden, and you can well imagine yourself back in time, tending to the plantings.

❈ **Admission:** Free (garden).
Garden open: Tuesday through Sunday; call for hours and details and fees to visit the houses.
Directions: Old Salem is located southwest of the intersection of Business Route 40 and U.S. Highway 52, within sight of downtown Winston-Salem. The visitor center is at 900 Old Salem Road.

26. Reynolda Gardens of Wake Forest University

100 Reynolda Village, **Winston-Salem,** NC; (336) 758–5593; www.wfu.edu/gardens

REYNOLDA GARDENS, which cover 130 acres, were created in the early twentieth century by the noted Philadelphia architect Thomas Sears for the R. J. Reynolds tobacco family. The lovely garden features include four acres of meticulous, geometrically laid-out formal gardens; demonstration gardens; a three-section greenhouse; huge open lawns and meadows; and daffodil- and log-lined nature trails through 130 acres of woodland, streams, ponds, and waterfalls. (You should take a map for the nature walk, as the trails are mostly unmarked.)

The great formal gardens are divided into northern and southern sections. A highlight is the All-America Rose Garden (visit in June or July), but there are many other attractions in these boxwood-edged, rectangular flower beds. A wisteria pergola, several arbors, and a reflecting pool accent the design. There are peonies, phlox, magnolias, flowering crab apples, weeping cherries in rows, and a group of stately Japanese cedars leading to the Lord and Burnham Greenhouse, a well-cared-for facility used for research by the university but open for the enjoyment of the public as well. Collections of orchids, bromeliads, and other tropical plants are centerpieces of the collection within.

Over the near century of this garden's existence, many of the trees and shrubs have grown so big that original designs for the formal gardens are sometimes no longer visible. But the resulting profusion of flowers and trees makes this combination of formal arrangements and natural landscape just right for a long walk (particularly if you head away from the traffic sounds), and there are

Wildflowers and Waterfalls

In May, Crabtree Meadows Recreation Area is a meadowland park filled with the pink blossoms of dozens of flowering trees and with the delicate blooms of dwarf irises, lady's slippers, and even orchids. For the adventurous, this jewel-like scenic area also offers a 2½-mile hiking trail that takes you to the beautiful Crabtree Falls. You'll find Crabtree Meadows at milepost 339.5 on the Blue Ridge Parkway.

beautifully placed, white-painted benches surrounded by colon-
nades along the way.

✿ **Admission:** Free.

Garden open: Daily. Greenhouse open Monday through Friday 10:00
A.M. to 4:00 P.M.

Directions: Take Business I-40 and exit onto Silas Creek Parkway
north. Go 4 ²⁄₁₀ miles and exit right onto Reynolda Road. The entrance
is on your left.

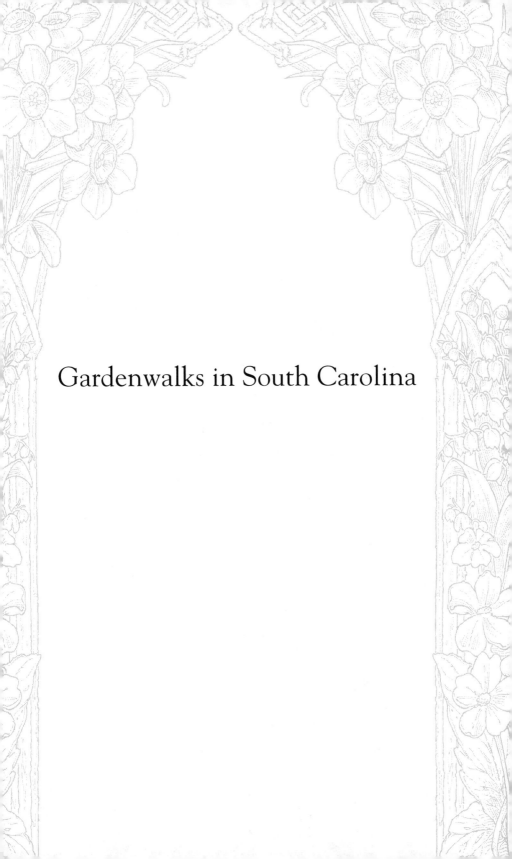

Gardenwalks in South Carolina

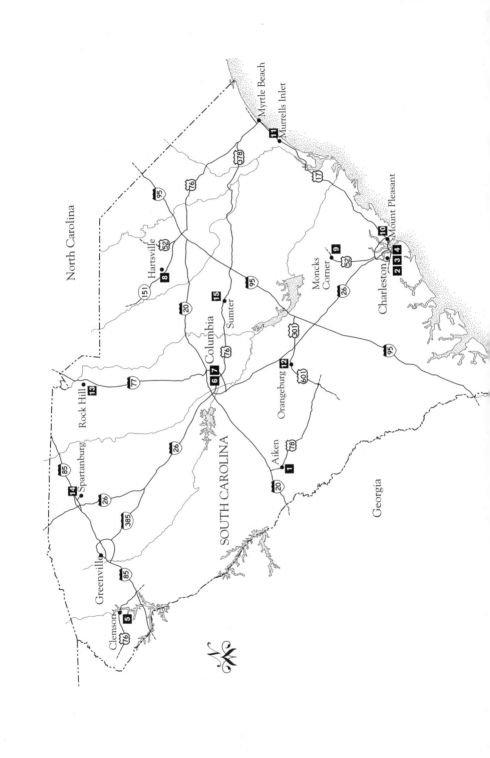

1. Aiken: Hopeland Gardens and Rye Patch
2. Charleston: Hampton Park
3. Charleston: Magnolia Plantation and Gardens
4. Charleston: Middleton Place
5. Clemson: South Carolina Botanical Garden
6. Columbia: Boylston Gardens
7. Columbia: Robert Mills House
8. Hartsville: Kalmia Gardens of Coker College
9. Moncks Corner: Cypress Gardens
10. Mount Pleasant: Boone Hall Plantation and Gardens
11. Murrells Inlet: Brookgreen Gardens
12. Orangeburg: Edisto Memorial Gardens
13. Rock Hill: Glencairn Garden
14. Spartanburg: Hatcher Gardens
15. Sumter: Swan Lake Iris Gardens

1. Hopeland Gardens and Rye Patch

Whiskey Road and Dupree Place, **Aiken,** SC; (803) 642–7630

*I*T IS ALWAYS a pleasure to visit the fourteen-acre Hopeland Gardens, even on the hottest of summer days, for they are shaded by gazebos, willows, ancient live oaks, towering magnolias, and deodar cedars and are cooled by fountains and pools. There are colorful blossoms to enjoy year-round; fragrant spring roses; crape myrtle blooms in summer; and camellias, azaleas, wisterias, magnolias, lilies, and dogwoods throughout the growing season.

A scenic walk takes you past reflecting pools with statuary and fountains and two small lakes surrounded by weeping willows and spring bulbs. Other highlights at Hopeland include a Touch and Scent Trail for the visually impaired and the thoroughbred Racing Hall of Fame, appropriately located in what used to be a carriage house.

Hopeland Gardens and the adjoining estate, Rye Patch, were once the winter homes of the Iselin and Rogers families. Hope Goddard Iselin and her neighbor, Dorothy Knox Rogers, loved gardens and horses, passions that are reflected in both properties. Hopeland, the Iselin estate, is now a garden dotted with a few remaining structures (the house no longer exists): among them, the carriage house and a very large dollhouse, now used as the Garden Club Council Center. The smaller property, Rye Patch, features the residence of the Rogers as well as stables, a carriage house, and a memorial rose garden. When Mrs. Iselin died in 1970 (at age 102), her property was bequeathed to the city of Aiken and the gardens were redesigned for public use. In 1982 Rye Patch also opened to the public.

Hopeland Gardens and Rye Patch are connected via meandering paths and a small footbridge over wetlands. Everything at both sites is free, except for a small fee to visit Rye Patch House, which will give you a taste of what life was once like for South Carolina's gentry.

✿ **Admission:** Free.

Garden open: Daily dawn to dusk.

Directions: Take Interstate 20 to exit 18 and go south on Route 19 (Laurens Street). Turn left onto Richland Avenue (still called Route 19), and go east 2 blocks. Turn right onto Chesterfield Street and go south for about a mile. Turn right onto Dupree Place, and the parking lot will be on the left.

2. Hampton Park

30 Mary Murray Drive, **Charleston,** SC; (843) 724–7321

*T*HIS PRETTY city park, bordered by avenues of ancient oaks, is especially known for its formal rose walk. Here you can enjoy more than a hundred varieties of roses, along with groupings of camellias, azaleas, magnolias, crape myrtles, and many perennials. Also featured are a picturesque fountain and Victorian bandstand where concerts are held during the summer.

Early in the twentieth century these grounds were part of a much larger tract of land slated to become a park designed by the Olmsted Brothers of Boston. The illustrious plan was never realized, for half of the property was given over to constructing the Citadel instead. Despite its reduced size, the existing sixty-five-acre park is a spacious and pleasant place for a gardenwalk.

✿ **Admission:** Free.

Garden open: Daily dawn to dusk.

Directions: The park is looped by Mary Murray Drive, adjacent to the campus of the Citadel. From Interstate 26 eastbound take the Rutledge Avenue exit (219A). Follow Rutledge Avenue 1 ⁷⁄₁₀ miles, then turn right on Moultrie Street. Hampton Park is on your right.

3. Magnolia Plantation and Gardens

Route 61 (Ashley River Road), **Charleston**, SC; (843) 571–1266;
www.magnoliaplantation.com

ATING FROM the 1680s, these are among America's oldest and most beautiful gardens. And among its most famous. Indeed, at the turn of the twentieth century, they were considered among its premier attractions, along with Grand Canyon and Niagara Falls. Picturesquely set along the Ashley River about 10 miles from Charleston and endowed with a magnificent landscape of ancient live oaks, tall cypress trees, haunting waterways, enchanting forests, and countless blossoms, Magnolia Plantation offers the essence of the southern plantation garden.

The present fifty acres of gardens are within a vast wildlife refuge. They began in the seventeenth century as ten acres of English-style flower beds and landscaped lawns. Over the years, under the care of successive family heirs (from the very beginning the site has been—and continues to be—owned and operated by the Drayton family), the gardens have grown and evolved into a more naturalistic mode. Lakes and pathways have been added, as have countless colorful plantings along the water, in forests, and in meadows.

The gardens combine romantic landscapes—dark pools reflecting lush vegetation, fields of wildflowers, enchanting waterside vistas —with more formal areas. Among the highlights are a camellia maze, a biblical garden, a topiary garden featuring animals shaped from fig vines, an eighteenth-century herb garden, and the Barbados Tropical Garden, an enormous glass conservatory filled with exotic plants from the Drayton family's Caribbean origins.

If all these attractions weren't enough, there are yet more: a 125-acre wildlife refuge that can be enjoyed on foot or by rented bike or canoe; an observation tower, from which you can view 170 species of birds and waterfowl; and the nearby Audubon Swamp Garden, an atmospheric sixty-acre tupelo and cypress swamp dotted with palmettos, wildflowers, and ferns as well as herons, osprey, egrets, and even occasional alligators. (The site was named after John J. Audubon, who once came to visit the Draytons and study waterbirds.) Don't miss the plantation house, a historic landmark and museum featuring memorabilia and photos of early plantation life.

Magnolia Gardens are a wonder at any time of year. Bear in mind that the spring azaleas are among the best in the East; the rich camellia collection (900 varieties) is at its height between November and March; and summertime brings forth blooming hydrangeas, oleanders, roses, gardenias, crape myrtles, mimosas, and more.

❀ **Admission:** Fee.
Garden open: Daily 8:00 A.M. to 5:30 P.M.
Directions: From downtown Charleston take U.S. Highway 17 south over the Ashley River Bridge. Take the first exit to the right off the bridge onto Route 61 north. Follow Route 61 north all the way to Magnolia, approximately 10 miles. Magnolia Plantation is on the right.

4. Middleton Place

4300 Ashley River Road, **Charleston,** SC; (843) 556–6020; www.middletonplace.org

*M*IDDLETON PLACE is a celebration of nature at its most sublime. With its majestic vistas overlooking the serene Ashley River, its vast lawns and landscaped terraces, peaceful lakes, and magnificent

Choosing an Outing in South Carolina

American History
Boone Hall Plantation and Gardens
Middleton Place

Aquatic Gardens and Gardens with Water Views
Edisto Memorial Gardens
Hopeland Gardens and Rye Patch
Magnolia Plantation and Gardens
Middleton Place
Swan Lake Iris Gardens

Art in the Garden
Brookgreen Gardens

Asian Gardens
Swan Lake Iris Gardens

Child-Pleasing Gardens
Brookgreen Gardens

Formal Gardens
Glencairn Garden
Middleton Place

Historic Houses and Plantations
Boone Hall Plantation and Gardens
Boylston Gardens
Magnolia Plantation and Gardens
Robert Mills House

Informal and English-style Gardens
Brookgreen Gardens
Hatcher Gardens
Magnolia Plantation and Gardens

Notable Americans' Gardens
Brookgreen Gardens
  (Anna Hyatt Huntington
  and Archer Huntington)
Middleton Place (Henry Middleton)

Romantic Gardens
Glencairn Garden
Middleton Place

Rose Gardens
Edisto Memorial Gardens

Specialty Gardens
Glencairn Garden (azaleas)
Kalmia Gardens of Coker College
  (mountain laurel)
Swan Lake Iris Gardens
  (Japanese iris)

Topiary Gardens
Magnolia Plantation and Gardens

Tropical, Subtropical, and Swamp Gardens
Cypress Gardens
Magnolia Plantation and Gardens

Urban Settings
Boylston Gardens
Hampton Park

Wildflowers and Woodland
Brookgreen Gardens
Hatcher Gardens

old trees, this is truly a site not to be missed. Believed to be the oldest formal landscaped garden in the country, Middleton Place reflects the grand symmetrical style of European gardens of the seventeenth and eighteenth centuries, particularly those of the French master André Le Nôtre.

The gardens, arranged around a main axis in the French tradition, were laid out in 1741 by Henry Middleton, an influential social and political figure who eventually became president of the Continental Congress. For his magnificent estate he selected an unusually picturesque site along the shores of the Ashley River (where many other prominent Carolina families lived), on a bluff about 20 miles downstream of Charleston. The gardens, cut out of the tidewater wilderness, required the labors of one hundred slaves for almost ten uninterrupted years.

The landscape is a delight to explore at the leisurely pace that such an idyllic spot demands. You'll need plenty of time to contemplate the many views. Among the many sights to savor are the sculptured, gently undulating grass terraces descending gracefully to water's edge; a pair of matching artificial lakes shaped like butterfly wings, separated by a grassy walkway; rectangular parterres of boxwood and crape myrtle surrounded by elegant walkways and shaded allées; and many, many blossoms that add charm to the southern plantation ambience—azaleas, dogwoods, magnolias, and camellias, just to name a few. The first four camellias in America were planted here in 1786; incredibly, three of these still exist, having grown to enormous size.

One of the garden highlights is the Middleton Oak, a magnificent 90-foot-tall specimen reputed to be a thousand years old. You will find it in a picture-postcard setting overlooking the river. Other delights are the sunken octagonal garden, sundial garden, and two secret gardens—enclosed, intimate, and perfect for a quiet conversation.

Now designated a National Historic Site, Middleton Place still includes traditional plantation features that give you a sense of what life was like here: farmyards, sugarcane works, stables, a blacksmith shop, even a few farm animals—cows and sheep that can be seen grazing on the vast front lawn. You can also visit the plantation house (the original one was burned to the ground during the Civil War, but the present one is quite grand!), which displays eighteenth- and nineteenth-century family furnishings and artifacts.

❀ **Admission:** Fee.

Garden open: Daily 9:00 A.M. to 5:00 P.M.

Directions: From downtown Charleston take US 17 south across the Ashley River Bridge and stay in the right lane. Take the Route 61 north exit just after the bridge. Follow Route 61 north (which is Ashley River Road) for approximately 14 miles. Middleton Place will be on the right.

5. South Carolina Botanical Garden

Clemson University Department of Horticulture,
Perimeter Road, **Clemson,** SC; (864) 656–3405;
www.clemson.edu/scbg

*L*OCATED ON the eastern side of Clemson University on land that was once the plantation of statesman John C. Calhoun, this garden has had several names. Originally known as the Horticultural Gardens of Clemson University, it later became the Clemson University Botanical Garden, and in 1992 the South Carolina Botanical Garden (the first botanical garden in the state).

Within these 270 leafy acres is a rich collection of plants, more than 2,000 varieties in all. In addition to the typical azaleas, rhododendrons, and camellias, there are a wildflower garden, bog and marsh habitat, fern garden, flower and turf garden, dwarf conifer garden, a braille trail for the visually impaired, and a garden of meditation—with picturesque glade, waterfalls, and pagoda. You will also find a demonstration vegetable and herb garden and pioneer complex, complete with log cabins, gristmill, and farm implements from colonial times.

The garden offers trails for hikers and bird-watchers, guided nature walks, horticultural lectures, and a popular annual daffodil festival.

❀ **Admission:** Free.

Garden open: Daily dawn to dusk.

Directions: Take Interstate 85 south from Greenville to exit 19B. At the end of the exit ramp, turn right onto U.S. Highway 76 and go about 11 miles. Turn left onto Perimeter Road (Silas Pearman Boulevard). The garden is on the east end of the Clemson University campus. The main entrance is located off Silas Pearman Boulevard, at the intersection with US 76.

6. Boylston Gardens

Governor's Mansion, 800 Richland Street, **Columbia,** SC; (803) 737–1710; www.scgovernorsmansion.org

*T*HESE HISTORIC GARDENS are situated on a nine-acre site that includes three mansions dating from the mid-nineteenth century: the Governor's Mansion, Caldwell-Boylston House, and Lace House. The restored gardens consist of elegant tree-lined paths leading to secluded areas, flower beds in colorful patterns, boxwood hedges, a rose garden, and statuary and fountains. There is also a very popular wedding garden, which is as lovely as you might expect.

The original gardens, located behind Caldwell-Boylston House, were planted by Sarah Smith Boylston, a gifted horticulturist. Although there is no fee to visit the gardens, you must make a reservation to tour the complex, allowing a good two hours to savor it all.

❀ **Admission:** Free.

Garden open: Monday through Friday 9:30 A.M. to 4:30 P.M.

Directions: Take Interstate 126/US 76 east, which becomes Elmwood Avenue. After 3 8/10 miles, turn right onto Lincoln Street. Go 2 blocks to Richland Street. The gardens are on the corner.

7. Robert Mills House

1616 Blanding Street, **Columbia,** SC; (803) 252–1770;
www.historiccolumbia.org

*T*HIS FOUR-ACRE GARDEN adorns one of Columbia's most beautiful historic houses. The Robert Mills House was named after the man who designed it in 1823, but he was most famous for designing the Washington Monument. Originally a private home, it was later owned by the Presbyterian Church, and it became a decorative arts museum in the 1960s.

The grounds showcase the Founder's Garden, a formal parterre of clipped boxwood hedges with roses, crape myrtles, native plants, and magnolia trees. Elegant urns and statuary are found amid the plantings. Beyond are broad expanses of lawn. Now restored to its former glory, the garden is a graceful extension of one of several historic houses that is worth visiting in the Columbia area.

❁ **Admission:** Free (fee for house tour).
Garden open: Daily dawn to dusk. House open Tuesday through Saturday 10:00 A.M. to 3:00 P.M., Sunday 1:00 to 4:00 P.M.
Directions: Take I–126/US 76 east, which becomes Elmwood Avenue. Go 4½ miles, and turn right onto Assembly Street. After 4 blocks you'll come to Blanding Street. Turn left to the entrance.

8. Kalmia Gardens of Coker College

1624 West Carolina Avenue, **Hartsville,** SC; (843) 383–8145;
www.coker.edu/kalmia

*T*HE MOUNTAIN LAUREL (*Kalmia latifolia*), the featured plant here, gives the gardens its unusual name. Growing wild along the Black Creek, these white-blossomed shrubs are complemented by profusions of azaleas and camellias.

The thirty-three-acre Kalmia Gardens are a naturalistic wonder of woodland, streams, laurel thickets, and black swamp. You can stroll beneath the welcoming shade of pine, oak, and holly trees and enjoy inviting walking trails—the Camellia Trail, Bluff Trail, and Bog Garden Trail among them. New boardwalks have been added, as well as sensory and memorial gardens.

Located on a site that was once Laurel Land, the eighteenth-century plantation of Capt. Thomas E. Hart, the gardens were developed during the 1930s under the guidance of a determined lady named May Roper Coker. "Miss May's Folly," as the project was described by some skeptics during those difficult Depression years, opened its doors to the public in 1935. (Miss May has been more than vindicated since then with the resulting woodland paradise.) In the mid-1960s the gardens were donated to Coker College.

Although open year-round, Kalmia Gardens are especially spectacular during May, when the mountain laurels are in full bloom.

❀ **Admission:** Free.

Garden open: Daily dawn to dusk.

Directions: From Interstate 95 take exit 164 to U.S. Highway 52 north, to Route 151 to Hartsville. The gardens are located 2 ⁶⁄₁₀ miles west of downtown Hartsville on Business 151 (West Carolina Avenue).

9. Cypress Gardens

3030 Cypress Gardens Road, **Moncks Corner,** SC; (843) 553–0515;
www.cypressgardens.org

*C*YPRESS GARDENS is a mysterious forest of moss-covered cypress emerging from dark swampland. The peaceful lakes, blackened by the acid from the trees, mirror the surrounding lush vegetation—thousands of azaleas and other flowering plants, not to mention the great trees themselves standing in the smooth waters.

The swamp gardens' 163 acres were once part of a riverside rice plantation endowed with natural lakes. In the late 1920s, years after the site had reverted to a wilderness, its owner, Benjamin Kittredge, decided to create a garden. An army of workers was hired to rid the lakes of debris; wisterias, azaleas, daffodils, and lilies were planted along the shore; and paths were cleared deep into the forest. The gardens opened to the public in 1963.

Today you can visit these atmospheric gardens on foot along 4 ½ miles of woodsy footpaths or, for a fascinating glimpse into a world rarely seen from the shore, by flat-bottomed boat. The many horticultural offerings include the azalea garden, camellia garden, woodland garden, butterfly garden, and garden of memories. Two new gazebos are the latest additions. The best time to see the forest come alive with its thousands of bulbs and flowering plants is from February through the summer months.

❊ **Admission:** Fee.

Garden open: Daily 9:00 A.M. to 4:00 P.M.

Directions: Cypress Gardens is located approximately 24 miles north of Charleston. From Charleston take I–26 west to exit 208 to US 52 west going into Goose Creek. After about 6 miles, watch for signs on the right to Cypress Gardens.

10. Boone Hall Plantation and Gardens

1235 Long Point Road, **Mount Pleasant,** SC; (843) 884–4371;
www.boonehallplantation.com

ITH 738 ACRES of property, Boone Hall is a very grand plantation by any standard, but its most imposing feature by far
(and well worth the price of admission) is its entrance, a half-mile
live oak allée leading to the manor house. This is one of the fabled
images of the southern plantation that has been immortalized in the
collective imagination (it was the model for *Gone with the Wind*),
and this particular avenue of ancient trees laced with dripping moss
is the quintessential plantation sight.

The existing garden surrounding the plantation manor was
designed early in the twentieth century. Among its delights are the
graceful formal gardens of camellias and azaleas that surround brick
walkways in front of the house, the variety of tulips and other spring
bulbs scattered about the grounds, and the large collection of roses
—some centuries old, dating from the earliest settlement. And of course a tour of the manor (a 1936 replica of the original eighteenth-century house), restored cotton-gin houses, and nine remaining slave cabins (built in 1743 and listed in the National Register of Historic Places) is also highly rec-ommended.

Boone Hall Plantation was named after Maj. John Boone, one of the original settlers of Charles Town in the late seventeenth cen-tury. At first a prosperous cotton plantation, it eventually became

Garden Shows and Festivals in South Carolina

FEBRUARY
Spring Bulbwalk, Murrells Inlet;
(803) 237–4218

MARCH AND APRIL
Historic Charleston Annual
Festival of Houses and Gardens;
(803) 723–1623

APRIL
South Carolina Festival of Roses,
Orangeburg; (803) 534–6376

known for its handcrafted bricks and tiles, which were used in many historic homes in the area. In the early part of this century the plantation also contained the world's largest pecan groves, many still productive today.

🌼 **Admission:** Fee.

Garden open: Monday through Saturday 8:30 A.M. to 6:30 P.M. and Sunday 1:00 to 5:00 P.M. from April 1 through Labor Day; Monday through Saturday 9:00 A.M. to 5:00 P.M., and Sunday 1:00 to 4:00 P.M. during the rest of the year; closed Thanksgiving and Christmas.

Directions: From downtown Charleston take US 17 north toward Mount Pleasant, about 7 miles. Turn left onto Long Point Road. Follow Long Point Road and you'll see signs for Boone Hall Plantation; the entrance to the site will be on the right.

11. Brookgreen Gardens

1931 Brookgreen Gardens Drive (U.S. Highway 17),
Murrells Inlet, SC; (843) 235–6000; www.brookgreen.org

*B*ROOKGREEN GARDENS is a quiet joining of hands between science and art. . . ." With these words, Archer M. Huntington, who with his wife, noted sculptor Anna Hyatt Huntington, created this site in 1931, described the mission of the gardens. The land surrounding their home was not only to be an outdoor gallery for the works of great sculptors (including Anna Huntington herself) but also to be a nature sanctuary, to perpetuate the land's natural beauty and provide a safe haven for its wildlife. In fact, Brookgreen is a remarkable 300-acre garden with sculpture, as well as plants, surrounded by a 9,000-acre preserve. The new Lowcountry Center is devoted to the rice culture.

The art collection contains about 550 works by some 250 noted sculptors—largely American—magnificently set amid terraces, pools, fountains, and the lush plantings typical of the region. Here you will see works by such artists as Frederic Remington, Carl Milles,

Daniel Chester French, and Paul Manship, not to mention Anna Hyatt Huntington (among her works on display is her *Fighting Stallions*, the largest sculpture ever cast in aluminum).

But the gardens are hardly secondary to the art; they are well worth a visit in their own right. Anna Hyatt Huntington was not only a highly regarded sculptor but also a masterful gardener. She herself drew up the basic garden design for Brookgreen. A beautiful 250-year-old live oak allée leads to connecting informal gardens, whose pathways wind around in the shape of an enormous butterfly.

More Wildflowers and Flora

You can see wildflowers and woodland in the gardenwalks at Brookgreen Gardens and Hatcher Gardens. But if you wish to enjoy more wildflower and native flora tours, consider these sites.

Aiken State Park
Located off Route 78 in Aiken, this park offers wildflower tours in spring. You can also explore a jungle nature trail of about 3 miles. Native trees, birding, and ponds in a pleasant environment make this a good place for an outing with kids in tow.

Columbia Museum of Art Garden
At the back of this lovely museum on 1519 Senate Street in Columbia, you'll find a small garden filled to the brim with a vast collection of native flora. More than fifty species represent South Carolina's lowcountry, upcountry, and midlands.

Carolina Sandhills National Wildlife Refuge
Spring wildflower tours are just one of the events at this nature preserve located off U.S. Highway 1 between McBee and Patrick. One hundred and ninety species of birds can be observed in its wildlife habitats, which include areas of wildflowers and great trees.

The gardens are planted with azaleas, dogwoods, magnolias, and other flowering specimens that create vibrant color, especially in spring. In addition, 2,000 native wildflowers and plants add their natural beauty to the grounds.

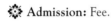

Nature lovers won't want to miss the wildlife park, adjacent to the sculpture gardens. Included are a walk-through cypress bird sanctuary, otter pond, alligator swamp, fox and raccoon glade, deer savannah, and other delights.

✿ **Admission:** Fee.

Garden open: June through September: Wednesday through Friday 9:30 A.M. to 9:00 P.M., Saturday through Tuesday 9:30 A.M. to 5:00 P.M. October through May: daily 9:30 A.M. to 5:00 P.M.

Directions: Located on the Atlantic coast, Brookgreen is 18 miles south of Myrtle Beach on Pawleys Island. Take US 17 toward Litchfield Beach and follow signs.

12. Edisto Memorial Gardens

U.S. Highway 301 South, **Orangeburg,** SC; (800) 545–6153

*I*T IS easy to understand why Edisto Memorial Gardens receives so many visitors each year. Idyllically set along the Edisto River, the longest black-water river in the world, it combines rich plantings of azaleas, dogwoods, and roses with majestic and towering oaks and cypress trees.

The garden presently features more than 150 acres, including a newer 6-acre wetlands accessible by boardwalk. It began modestly as a small city park with a few azaleas plantings. In 1951 a rose garden was added; it is now a major highlight of Edisto. Endowed with fifty-plus beds and featuring more than 4,000 roses, from miniatures to tall climbing specimens, this specialty garden has been designated an All-America Rose Selection display garden. Each year, during the last week of April, it is featured in the South Carolina Festival of Roses. A butterfly garden and sensory garden are among the treats here.

On the grounds also is a fountain commemorating the soldiers who died, giving the garden its name.

❁ **Admission:** Free.

Garden open: Daily dawn to dusk.

Directions: From I–95 or I–26, take U.S. Highway 301 south to Orangeburg. The gardens are on US 301 (John C. Calhoun Drive) behind the Orangeburg Chamber of Commerce.

13. Glencairn Garden

Charlotte Avenue and Crest Street, **Rock Hill,** SC; (803) 329–5620

*A*ZALEAS—thousands of them—and flowering trees abound on these lush grounds. From mid- to late April especially, the many magnolias, dogwoods, redbuds, crape myrtles, and wisterias are a sight to see and are the main draw for Rock Hill's weeklong Come See Me festival.

Once private (it was named after the owners' ancestral home in Scotland), Glencairn was opened to the public in 1940. This formal seven-and-one-half-acre garden is a harmonious combination of terraced lawns, a fountain gently cascading down stone tiers to a water-lily pond, a Japanese footbridge, and flower beds of summer annuals. Winding paths meander throughout, past the colorful banks of azaleas, grape hyacinths, daffodils, and other garden delights.

Glencairn is perfect for strolling and nature watching. It also provides a romantic setting for art shows, concerts, and of course weddings.

❁ **Admission:** Free.

Garden open: Daily dawn to dusk.

Directions: Rock Hill is located at the intersection of Interstate 77 and

U.S. Highway 21. The gardens are in the center of the city at the corner of Crest Street and Charlotte Avenue.

14. Hatcher Gardens

820 John B. White Sr. Boulevard (Reidville Road),
Spartanburg, SC; (864) 582–0138; www.hatchergarden.org

*H*AROLD HATCHER created this naturalistic seven-acre garden that bears his name. In 1969 he began to transform an overgrown urban eyesore into a lush garden. Gradually acquiring more property, he and his wife almost single-handedly cleared and reshaped the landscape, planting thousands of native varieties. In the late 1980s they donated this sanctuary to the city so that others could learn more about plants and be inspired to preserve the environment.

The garden is an inviting landscape of tall trees, shrubs, wildflowers, picturesque ponds, and wildlife. Some of the plants you will likely spot from an observation deck or the walking trails are red buckeye, witch hazel, pawpaw, magnolia, jack-in-the-pulpit, deutzia, beauty bush, winter daphne, and Virginia bluebell. Blossom season is from early spring to late fall, so plan accordingly.

❀ **Admission:** Free.
Garden open: Daily 9:00 A.M. to dusk.
Directions: From I–26 take exit 22 (Route 296/Reidville Road) and go east on John B. White Sr. Boulevard. Travel 2 miles; the garden is on the left.

15. Swan Lake Iris Gardens

822 West Liberty Street, **Sumter,** SC; (800) 688–4748;
www.sumtertourism.com

*T*HIS DREAM GARDEN could be straight out of an impressionist painting. The scene shows a peaceful lake dotted with little islands, black and white swans, water lilies, and lotuses. The dark waters reflect the colors of the surrounding foliage: pale pinks, creamy yellows, soft lavenders, and deep, deep purples. Masses of azaleas, camellias, magnolias, wisterias, and—most notably—irises are framed by towering oaks and cypress.

The incredible Japanese iris collection shares center stage with the eight species of swans, gathered from around the world, that float languidly amid lily pads and wander about the gardens. There are millions of irises (apparently six million!) in a rainbow of colors, an unforgettable sight during blooming season in May.

The gardens began in a serendipitous fashion. When Hamilton Carr Bland, a local businessman and amateur gardener, was unsuccessful in growing irises in his own backyard, he disposed of the uprooted flowers, carelessly tossing them on the banks of a nearby swamp. Unexpectedly, the plants thrived there, indicating to him that these wetlands were the ideal site for the iris garden he had always wanted. With the addition of a large piece of wooded land and much imaginative planting, Swan Lake Iris Gardens were launched. In the late 1940s they were opened to an enthusiastic public.

Since then the 150-acre gardens have been embellished with more landscaped areas, lawns, rustic bridges, and shaded pathways. To make the site even more pleasurable to families, park amenities such as picnic tables and tennis courts have been added.

✺ **Admission:** Free.
Garden open: Daily dawn to dusk.
Directions: Take US 76 to Sumter and pick up U.S. Highway 378 south (Broad Street). It becomes Washington Street. At Liberty Street, turn right. The gardens will be on your right.

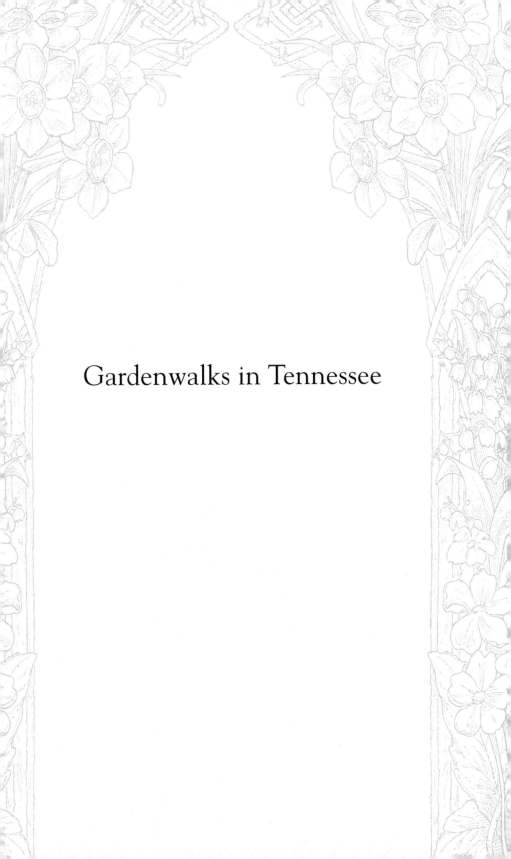

Gardenwalks in Tennessee

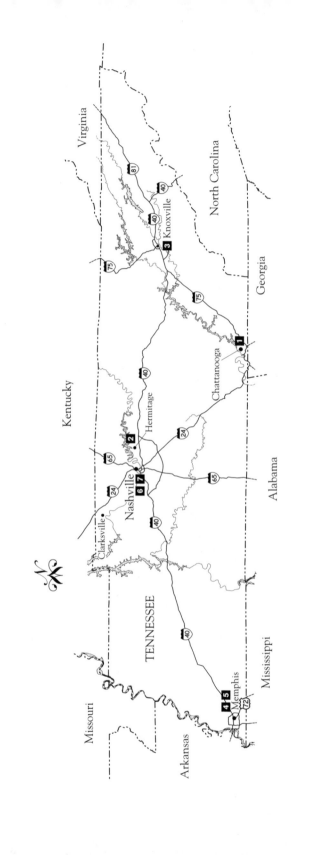

1. Reflection Riding

Chattanooga Nature Center,

400 Garden Road, **Chattanooga, TN;** (423) 821–1160,

(423) 821–9582; ww.reflectionriding.org

*T*HIS VAST 300-acre nature preserve/botanical garden is yet another reason to visit Chattanooga, a city known for its Civil War battlefields and many museums. At Reflection Riding you can view on foot or from your car a wide variety of wildflowers set amid flowering shrubs and trees in a design reminiscent of a romantic English landscape. Vividly colorful azaleas, rhododendrons, asters, mountain laurels, and other plantings can be enjoyed from spring into autumn, although the park is open in the winter too. A nature center offers educational programs, workshops, and displays geared to all ages.

✿ **Admission:** Fee.

Garden open: Monday through Saturday 9:00 A.M. to 5:00 P.M., Sunday 1:00 to 5:00 P.M.

Directions: Reflection Riding is located about ten minutes from downtown Chattanooga. Take Interstate 24 west toward Nashville/Birmingham. Exit at Brown's Ferry Road and make a left at the traffic light, heading toward Lookout Mountain. At the next traffic light (Cummings Highway), turn left. Go a little less than a mile and take the first right, following the signs for Reflection Riding and the Chattanooga Nature Center.

2. The Hermitage

4580 Rachel's Lane, **Hermitage,** TN; (615) 889–2941;
www.thehermitage.com

*H*ERE IS A small garden—only one acre in all—but a historically important one. Set within the vast and hilly 625-acre estate of President Andrew Jackson, it is known as Rachel's Garden. His wife, Rachel Jackson, was an avid amateur horticulturist. A visitor to the Jackson home once remarked he had never met anyone who loved flowers as much as she. After Rachel died in 1828, her devoted husband not only had her buried amid her beloved flowers but he took special care that the garden would always be perfectly maintained in her memory.

The history of the Hermitage is fascinating. Some years after buying this property in 1804, the Jacksons decided to create a residence more in keeping with their increased national prominence (they had been living in a small log cabin on the premises). Apparently they were inspired by such elegant Virginia plantations as Mount Vernon. They engaged a well-regarded Philadelphia landscape designer, William Frost, for the grounds. Rachel worked closely with him in designing the small formal garden right next to the mansion, and until her premature death ten years later, she helped maintain it.

Even though the garden was always considered an integral part of the quite grand estate, it was not—and is not—pretentious (today's garden may be a bit fancier and more manicured than the

Choosing an Outing in Tennessee

American History
Blount Mansion

*Aquatic Gardens and
Gardens with Water Views*
Opryland USA

Art in the Garden
Cheekwood
Dixon Gallery and Gardens

Asian Gardens
Cheekwood
Memphis Botanic Garden

Conservatories and Botanic Gardens
Memphis Botanic Garden
Reflection Riding
Opryland USA

Formal Gardens
Dixon Gallery and Gardens

Informal and English-style Gardens
The Hermitage

Notable Americans' Gardens
Blount Mansion (William Blount)
The Hermitage (Andrew Jackson)

Specialty Gardens
Cheekwood (trillium)

*Tropical, Subtropical,
and Swamp Gardens*
Opryland USA

Wildflowers and Woodland
Reflection Riding

original). English in style, it includes a group of rectangular and circular flower beds at the center, contained by unusual bricks and pebbled pathways. Surrounding them are four large grassy squares bordered with flowers and herbs. (During the time of the Jacksons there was also an abundance of vegetables.) Among the many varieties of flowering plants are hickory and magnolia trees planted during the Jacksons' lifetime. The garden is now enclosed by a white picket fence.

The Ladies' Hermitage Association, which took over the upkeep of the property in the late 1880s and maintains it impeccably to this day, has restored much of Rachel's Garden over the years.

Although the plantings today are purely ornamental (except for a few herbs) and do not include Andrew Jackson's much-loved vegetables, they reflect the love and care of flowers that were essential to Rachel.

❁ **Admission:** Fee.

Garden open: Daily 9:00 A.M. to 5:00 P.M.; closed the third week of January, Thanksgiving, and Christmas.

Directions: The Hermitage is located 12 miles east of downtown Nashville; from Interstate 40 take exit 221A (the Hermitage exit). Or from Interstate 65 north take exit 92 (Old Hickory Boulevard South).

3. Blount Mansion

200 West Hill Avenue, **Knoxville**, TN; (865) 525–2375; www.blountmansion.org

*S*URROUNDING a late-eighteenth-century manor house is this colorful colonial-style garden. The garden may remind you of some at Colonial Williamsburg; it was redesigned in 1960 by landscape architects from that historic site. An unusually long boxwood walkway sets off formal beds of wildflowers, annuals, perennials, and herbs. In spring it is featured as part of the area's annual Dogwood Arts Festival.

History buffs will want to visit the 1792 frame house (locally referred to as the "mansion"), a Registered National Historic Landmark. It was here that William Blount (governor of the territory south of the Ohio River and a delegate to the Federal Constitutional Convention) and his associates planned the admission of Tennessee as the nation's sixteenth state in 1796.

❁ **Admission:** Fee.

Garden open: Monday through Saturday 9:30 A.M. to 5:00 P.M., Sunday 1:00 to 5:00 P.M. from April to December; weekdays 9:30 A.M. to 5:00 P.M. during winter months.

Directions: Blount Mansion is located on Hill Avenue between Gay

Street and State Street in downtown Knoxville. From I–40 take exit 388A, the James White Parkway. On the parkway, veer left when the road splits into Neyland Drive. Take the first exit after the split, Hill Avenue. Turn right at the top of the exit. Go through the traffic signal at Hall of Fame Drive and cross the Hill Avenue viaduct. At the end of the viaduct, turn left into Blount Mansion's driveway. Free visitor parking is located behind the mansion.

4. Dixon Gallery and Gardens

4339 Park Avenue, **Memphis,** TN; (901) 761–2409; www.dixon.org

*J*UST MINUTES from Memphis's lively downtown you'll discover a delightful oasis of shade, tranquillity, and quiet beauty. Dixon Gallery and Gardens offers naturalistic woodland; a collection of carefully designed formal, intimate gardens; and grassy terraces with vistas in an English parklike landscape. Once the private estate of Margaret and Hugo Dixon—she was from Mississippi, he from England, and they shared a great love of nature—it includes a seventeen-acre garden surrounding an elegant Georgian house, now a gallery of impressionist and postimpressionist painting.

The Dixons traveled around the country and throughout Europe visiting gardens. They bought a small untamed property in 1939 (it was much expanded as the years went by) and, with the help of Hugo's sister, Hope Crutchfield, began to design the grounds. Fortunately they carefully preserved most of the majestic old trees that

Garden Shows and Festivals in Tennessee

APRIL
National Daffodil Show,
Nashville; (513) 248–9137

Spring Wildflower Festival,
Chattanooga; (615) 821–1160

MAY
National Rose Show, Nashville;
(615) 352–5310

MAY AND JUNE
Good Earth Festival, Memphis;
(901) 685–1566

now give the garden its cathedral-like aura—not to mention its particularly inviting shaded walkways. Beneath stately canopies of oaks and hickories they added to the indigenous dogwoods and hemlocks and planted azaleas and boxwood. And they created connecting garden rooms, featuring colorful flower beds to provide visual interest year-round.

The gardens are landscaped around two main axes: the north–south axis includes the house on one end and an impressive sculpture of Europa and the Bull at the other; the east–west axis, an elegant avenue of azaleas and evergreens, is called the Venus allée for its 1960s statue of Venus (on its other end is a swimming pool).

Brick paths lead to a group of formal gardens graced with an abundance of flowers. Margaret Dixon chose to have white flowers next to the house, with bright colors beyond.

You won't want to miss the extraordinary camellia collection: More than 200 plants are on display in an enclosed setting from November to March, with February the peak month. Behind the camellia house is a charming cutting garden, featuring narcissi and tulips in spring and phlox, hydrangeas, daisies, and other old-fashioned blossoms in summer. Throughout the garden you'll find small park benches, carefully framed with wildflowers or ferns or mosses.

Dixon Gardens is especially lovely in spring, when its azaleas and wildflowers are truly breathtaking. But this is a place for all seasons, offering visual pleasure throughout the year.

❀ **Admission:** Fee.

Garden open: Tuesday through Saturday 10:00 A.M. to 5:00 P.M., Sunday 1:00 to 5:00 P.M.

Directions: Take U.S. Highway 72 (Poplar Street) east from downtown Memphis about 6 miles. Dixon Gardens is across from Audubon Park, on Park Avenue between Getwell Road and Perkins Road.

5. Memphis Botanic Garden

750 Cherry Road, **Memphis,** TN; (901) 685-1566;
www.memphisbotanicgarden.com

*W*ITHIN THIS flower-loving, green city of urban parks and garden areas is the ninety-six-acre Memphis Botanic Garden, famous for its lovely and extensive displays in twenty-three unique gardens. Among its many offerings are the four-acre Japanese Garden of Tranquility surrounding Lake Biwa (stocked with thousands of goldfish); the outstanding seven-acre Tennessee Bicentennial Iris Garden with hundreds of varieties that bloom over a six-week period; the Four Seasons Water Garden; the Rose Garden; Daffodil Hill; the Little Garden Club Sensory Garden; the Azalea Trail of brilliant colors; and many wildflowers.

A conservatory contains noteworthy tropical plant collections, a camellia house, and seasonal displays. In the garden center is an elegant courtyard water garden. Oriental in style, it features fountains trickling into a reflecting pool bordered by evergreens. The center also contains a library, gift shop, and meeting rooms for educational programs, garden clubs, and plant societies.

❀ **Admission:** Fee.

Garden open: Monday through Saturday 9:00 A.M. to 4:30 P.M. and

A Stagecoach Inn Garden

The largest extant log structure in Tennessee, Wynnewood was built in 1828 as a stagecoach inn and mineral springs resort. Today the inn is restored and open to the public, as is its charming nineteenth-century garden. The sulphur springs still flow too. Wynnewood State Historic Area is located at 210 Old Highway 25 in Castalian Springs, 7 miles east of Gallatin. For information call (615) 452-5463.

Sunday 11:00 A.M. to 4:00 P.M. from November through February; Monday through Saturday 9:00 A.M. to 6:00 P.M. and Sunday 11:00 A.M. to 6:00 P.M. from March through October.

Directions: Located in Audubon Park, the gardens are between Park and Southern Avenues, just east of Memphis State University, about 6 miles east of downtown Memphis. From Interstate 240 take exit 20B (Getwell Road North exit) approximately 2½ miles to Park Avenue. Turn right and proceed to the second traffic light. Turn left onto Cherry Road. The garden is on your right.

6. Cheekwood

1200 Forrest Park Drive, **Nashville**, TN; (615) 353-2148;
www.cheekwood.org

WITH ITS imposing hilltop Georgian-style mansion surrounded by handsome gardens and grounds, Cheekwood is reminiscent of a grand English estate. It was the home of Leslie and Mabel Cheek, who had a particular fondness for eighteenth-century-style English houses and gardens. They had visited a number of traditional country estates during their frequent travels abroad in the 1920s; inspired by these, they created Cheekwood on their newly purchased property just southwest of Nashville.

Today this fifty-five-acre site is a combination botanical garden and fine arts museum (in the 1950s the then-owners donated the house and about half of their land for this cultural purpose).

The splendid grounds offer a wide range of gardens—both formal and woodsy—from the English flower gardens and boxwood hedges designed by the Cheeks and their gardeners to more recent additions. You'll find a Japanese tea garden complete with bamboo gate, dry streambed of pebbles, and dwarf conifers; a scent and taste garden for the visually impaired; a trillium collection, reputed to be the largest of its kind in the Southeast; a fine iris collection (particularly apt, since the iris is Tennessee's state flower); a color garden; a water garden; and daffodil, herb, rose, and peony gardens. Along woodland paths are azaleas, dogwoods, and wildflowers, all spectacular in spring. You can enjoy garden statuary, ponds, fountains, and broad vistas throughout the gardens and from the house and surrounding hillside.

Adding to these pleasures are greenhouses featuring orchids, camellias, and species native to the cloud forests of Central America. Next to the mansion is a romantic wrought-iron arbor with wisteria, as well as reflecting pools (with water lilies in summer), fountains, and some of the earliest of the boxwood collection.

Don't miss the Cheek house itself, with its permanent collection of nineteenth- and twentieth-century American artists and special exhibits.

❀ **Admission:** Fee.

Garden open: Tuesday through Saturday 9:30 A.M. to 4:30 P.M., Sunday 11:00 A.M. to 4:30 P.M.; closed holidays.

Directions: Cheekwood is about 8½ miles southwest of downtown Nashville. From downtown take Broadway south and continue southbound as it becomes West End Avenue and then Harding Road. At Belle Meade Boulevard turn left and travel approximately 2½ miles. Turn right onto Page Road, then take the first left onto Forrest Park Drive.

7. Opryland USA

2800 Opryland Drive, **Nashville,** TN;
(615) 889–1000;
www.gaylordhotels.com/gaylordopryland

*T*HE NAME "Opryland" brings to mind country-and-western music and other lively entertainments. But gardens? Surprisingly, within the enormous resort called the Opryland Hotel are extensive indoor conservatory gardens that are quite remarkable and well worth a visit.

Occupying nine acres (and thus requiring a longish walk), the conservatories feature winding walkways perched high above dramatic botanic displays. Hundreds of tropical and subtropical plants—brilliant flowers and exotic trees—are set amid ravines, rocky coves, waterfalls, fountains, and terraces. One of these glass-roofed gardens, perhaps the boldest and most Disneyesque in concept, includes three massive waterfalls spilling down an artificial 40-foot "mountain" surrounded by thousands of brightly colored plants. The newest atrium garden, the Delta, occupies four and one-half acres and even includes a river!

This fanciful slice of botanic Americana should engage just about anyone, from young children to serious garden lovers to foreign visitors. The gardens at Opryland are in fact an entertainment as well as a garden experience.

❀ **Admission:** Free.

Garden open: Daily.

Directions: Opryland is northeast of downtown Nashville. Go east through Nashville on I-40 to exit 215 and take Briley Parkway/Route 155 north to exit 12. Turn left off the exit ramp onto McGavock Pike. Turn left at the first intersection into the Opryland complex.

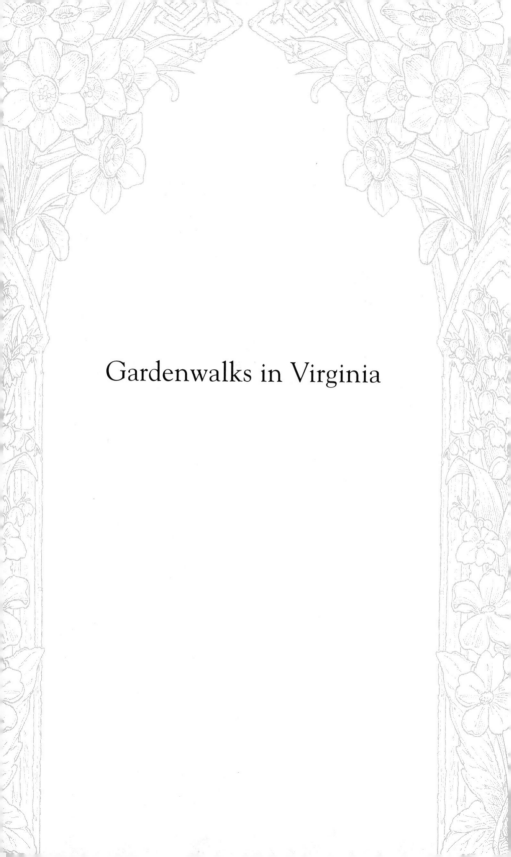

Gardenwalks in Virginia

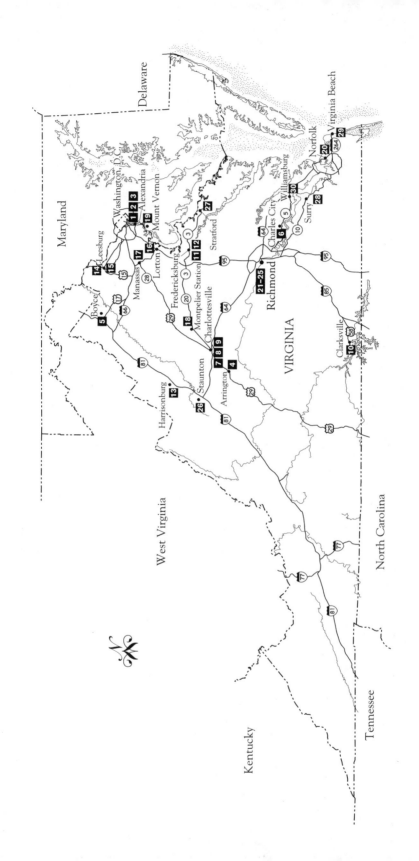

1. Alexandria: Green Spring Gardens
2. Alexandria: River Farm
3. Alexandria: Woodlawn Plantation
4. Arrington: Oak Ridge Estate
5. Boyce: State Aboretum of Virginia at Blandy Experimental Farm
6. Charles City: Berkeley Plantation
7. Charlottesville: Ash Lawn–Highland
8. Charlottesville: Monticello
9. Charlottesville: Pavilion Gardens
10. Clarksville: Prestwould Plantation
11. Fredericksburg: Kenmore
12. Fredericksburg: Mary Washington House and Garden
13. Harrisonburg: The Arboretum at James Madison University
14. Leesburg: Morven Park
15. Leesburg: Oatlands Plantation
16. Lorton: Gunston Hall Plantation
17. Manassas: Ben Lomond Manor House
18. Montpelier Station: Montpelier
19. Mount Vernon: Mount Vernon
20. Norfolk: Norfolk Botanical Garden
21. Richmond: Agecroft Hall
22. Richmond: Bryan Park Azalea Gardens
23. Richmond: Lewis Ginter Botanical Garden
24. Richmond: Maymont
25. Richmond: Virginia House
26. Staunton: Woodrow Wilson Birthplace and Gardens
27. Stratford: Stratford Hall Plantation
28. Surry: Bacon's Castle
29. Virginia Beach: Adam Thoroughgood House
30. Williamsburg: Colonial Gardens of Williamsburg

1. Green Spring Gardens

4603 Green Spring Road,
Alexandria, VA; (703) 642–5173;
www.greenspring.org

*N*o LESS than two dozen different gardens are presented here on this twenty-seven-acre former farm with an eighteenth-century manor house. These gardens take horticulture seriously; there is a greenhouse and there are many classes and research facilities and garden events. The gardens themselves, which are comparatively new, surround a large circular lawn. No matter what your horticultural interests are, you are sure to find a garden here at any time of year to capture your attention: a children's garden, a family garden, an iris garden, a mixed border garden, a roses and companions garden, a witch hazel collection, a Virginia native plant garden, and a pond area.

❀ **Admission:** Free.

Garden open: Daily dawn to dusk.

Directions: From Interstate 495 take exit 52B (Little River Turnpike east). Travel 3½ miles. Turn left onto Braddock Road. Drive ²⁄₁₀ mile and turn right onto Witch Hazel Road and the garden entrance. Or from Interstate 395 take exit 3B (Little River Turnpike west). Travel 1¼ miles. Turn right onto Braddock Road. Drive ²⁄₁₀ mile and turn right onto Witch Hazel Road and the garden entrance.

2. River Farm

7931 East Boulevard Drive, **Alexandria,** VA;
(703) 768–5700, (800) 777–7931;
www.ahs.org

*G*EORGE WASHINGTON purchased this farm above the Potomac River (and just minutes from Mount Vernon) in 1760. Though he never lived on the farm, he planted wheat, rye, and corn there, and he is thought to have planted the walnut trees in the meadow. Now the headquarters for the American Horticultural Society, River Farm naturally has extensive and very pretty gardens.

River Farm is perched at the top of a hill overlooking the Potomac and its curious meandering shores. The large elegant house and series of various garden areas befit a horticultural society. You'll find many types of garden settings, ranging from the more traditional rose garden and perennial plantings to America's Front Yard Garden, a children's garden, a wildlife garden, and even that English necessity, a ha-ha. Many are trial gardens run by the society; the dahlia beds are one of seven such trial sites in the nation, and there are more than one hundred types of daylilies in another spot. Some of the garden features go back in history: The boxwood hedges, for example, were planted in Lincoln's time.

Each of the display gardens is extensive, luxuriant in season, and obviously well worth visiting, for these gardeners are definitely

Garden Shows and Festivals in Virginia

APRIL
Historic Garden Week at Ash Lawn–Highland, Charlottesville;
(434) 293–9539

Spotswood Garden Club Daffodil Show, Harrisonburg;
(703) 434–8587

Tulipmania, Richmond;
(804) 353–4241

MAY
Annual Rose Garden Tea,
Mount Vernon (703) 780–4000

experts. For instance, the herb garden, designed by a specialist from the United States Botanic Garden, has herbs for aromatherapy, flavor, habitat, and health surrounded by unusual trees like the silver weeping peach. Spring shrubs are well represented. The dogwood collection has many rare species, as does the azalea garden, which is maintained by the Azalea Society of America. Both gardens are particularly dazzling in April and May. The garden for children is a particular pleasure, and we recommend it—it offers a bat cave, an alphabet garden, and even a garden that displays all the ingredients found on the average pizza! Kids will love this spot.

For the traditionalist, the flower-filled spaces behind the house are lovely. Under a series of brick arches and surrounded by brick walls, these beds include All-America Selections (labeled) of every kind of bloom beloved by home gardeners.

❁ **Admission:** Fee.

Garden open: Daily in season.

Directions: In Alexandria take Washington Street, which becomes the George Washington Parkway, toward Mount Vernon. Go 1½ miles. Pass under the overpass and make a left turn onto East Boulevard Drive, where a sign directs you to the American Horticultural Society at River Farm.

3. Woodlawn Plantation

9000 Richmond Highway, **Alexandria**, VA; (703) 780–4000; www.woodlawn1805.org

*T*HIS PRETTY ESTATE overlooking the Potomac was given by George Washington to his step-granddaughter Nelly as a wedding present. The fine house was designed by Dr. William Thornton, the first architect of the U.S. Capitol. Unfortunately, Woodlawn and its land (originally 2,000 acres) had a checkered history through the nineteenth and twentieth centuries, including serious storm damage, tree cutting, subdividing, and near decay and ruin (sixty cats lived there at one time). In 1951 the National Trust took charge, and today there are twenty acres of restored gardens, with a particular emphasis on parterre gardens with boxwood hedges and roses. If rose gardens are your special interest, don't miss Woodlawn. The gardens border an irregular lawn with informal clusters of trees and shrubs. The restoration has been accomplished using old descriptions and records as much as possible. Visit in late spring and early summer.

❀ **Admission:** Fee.
Garden open: Tuesday through Sunday 10:00 A.M. to 5:00 P.M.
Directions: From Interstate 95 take exit 166A (Fairfax County Parkway). Proceed on the parkway until you dead-end at Richmond Highway/U.S. Highway 1. Turn left and continue north to the fourth light at the intersection of US 1 and Route 235. Turn left into the Woodlawn entrance.

4. Oak Ridge Estate

2300 Oak Ridge Road, **Arrington,** VA; (434) 263–8676;
www.oakridgeestate.com

*W*E APPROACHED Oak Ridge on a narrow drive through what seemed like miles of picturesque rural scenery—and in fact, a lot of it belongs to this amazing estate: some 4,000 acres. When we finally reached the fine white mansion and gardens, we were struck by the overwhelming sense of the past. Everything about Oak Ridge is old, and a lot of it somewhat decayed, in the nicest sense. A reconstruction is taking place here, and we can only hope that the current owners retain the evocative air of faded elegance and eccentricity.

If your idea of a plantation estate is a spiffy reconstruction complete with costumed docents, this is not the place for you. On the other hand, if you respond to a decidedly southern ambience with a grand old mansion set in a lovely green landscape with great oak trees (one is 350 years old), winding paths, the haunting skeleton of a conservatory, and ancient statues and overgrown gardens, this is certainly the place to come. The sweeping panorama of Oak Ridge is a taste of the Deep South in rural Virginia, only a short drive from sophisticated Charlottesville. Unlike most southern open-to-the-public plantations, Oak Ridge's major period of elegance came well after the antebellum period.

The original estate dates to the eighteenth century. The mansion, influenced by Thomas Jefferson's designs, was constructed in 1802 by a tobacco planter named Robert Rives. Its owners included his unmarried daughter, who successfully ran the plantation herself, and a number of notable Virginians, including a Confederate congressman. When Thomas Fortune Ryan took possession in 1901, Oak Ridge's glory days began. Ryan, a Virginian who was a poor orphan as a child, became one of the nation's richest men, and Oak Ridge was to become his showplace—his own personal city. Like the Vanderbilts in New York, Ryan traveled about on his own train car; one of the delights of this visit is seeing his private station and the tracks and gilded railroad gate that bisect his vast property. Don't fail to walk down through the sloping grounds to this piece of Americana and to visit the iron-fenced gravesites.

Ryan employed 300 people at Oak Ridge, among them a legion of gardeners, lawn keepers, beekeepers, and an estate florist. He had Italianate formal gardens installed and a large rose garden put in. The great conservatory, modeled after London's famous domed greenhouse, the Crystal Palace, was built near the house. Today you can see the structure in its evocative, grass-filled, ruined state. Behind the mansion the formal gardens are terraced and outlined in boxwood. Statues and ornaments and an old well cover adorn the gardens and accent the geometric patterns of the plantings. Some of the statues are purported to date from the Renaissance. There is also an artistic waterfall designed by Mrs. Ryan, called Crabtree

Falls Cascade. At Oak Ridge, the gentle decay and ancient trees are metaphors for the passage of time.

✿ **Admission:** Fee.

Garden open: Tuesday through Thursday 10:00 A.M. to 3:00 P.M. in summer; phone for additional times.

Directions: Oak Ridge Estate is located between Charlottesville and Lynchburg (approximately 35 miles from both). Take U.S. Highway 29 south to Route 653 (also Oak Ridge Road). Proceed 2 4/10 miles on Oak Ridge Road to the driveway entrance on the right (marked by an open gate and an Oak Ridge sign).

5. State Arboretum of Virginia at Blandy Experimental Farm

U.S. Highway 50, **Boyce,** VA; (540) 837–1758; www.virginia.edu/blandy

*T*HIS IS A most unusual arboretum, with a specialty of box-wood. In fact, this is the largest collection of boxwood in the nation. The arboretum also features fully half of the world's pine species and a grove of 350 ginkgo trees. As for gardens, you'll find a native Virginia plant trail and collections of azaleas, perennials, daylilies, and herbs. You can walk here or take a 3-mile driving loop.

✿ **Admission:** Free.

Garden open: Daily dawn to dusk.

Directions: From Washington, D.C., the arboretum is about 70 miles. Take Interstate 66 west to U.S. Highway 17 north (exit 23, Dela-plane/Paris). Follow US 17 north to its junction with U.S. Highway 50 west at a traffic light. Turn left onto US 50/17; the arboretum is approximately 7 miles on the left, about 3 miles past the Shenandoah River.

6. Berkeley Plantation

12602 Harrison Landing Road (Route 5), **Charles City,** VA;
(804) 829–6018; www.berkeleyplantation.com

*T*HIS IS THE quintessential James River plantation to visit. It
has history, charm, and lovely gardens. Berkeley was the
home that Benjamin Harrison IV and his wife, Anne, built in 1726;
the Georgian mansion is said to be the oldest three-story brick house
in Virginia. The plantation boasts of many historical highlights. It
was the site of the first Thanksgiving in America. It was the birthplace of a signer of the Declaration of Independence as well as of
the ninth president of the United States, William Henry Harrison.
George Washington and nine succeeding presidents visited the
plantation. Berkeley was the site of a Civil War encampment of
140,000 northern troops reviewed by President Lincoln in 1862
(*Taps* was written there at the same time). It might also be noted
that the first bourbon in America was distilled at Berkeley.

With such an illustrious history, it is no wonder that Berkeley
is a much-visited site. Its gardens are among its notable attractions.
Formal, terraced, boxwood gardens—interspersed with flowers—
and a large green lawn cover ten acres, extending a quarter of a mile
down to the banks of the James River. A charming gazebo (known
as the Tea and Mint Julep House) ornaments the landscape. Great
trees surround the house. If you are at nearby Williamsburg, this is
an easy detour to make, and certainly a pleasant one.

❀ **Admission:** Fee.

Garden open: Daily 8:00 A.M. to 5:00 P.M.

Directions: Berkeley Plantation is 18 miles west of Williamsburg and
35 miles east of Richmond on Route 5, the John Tyler Memorial
Highway. The plantation is 3 miles east of the Charles City County
Courthouse.

Choosing an Outing in Virgina

American History
Adam Thoroughgood House
Agecroft Hall
Bacon's Castle
Berkeley Plantation
Colonial Gardens of Williamsburg
Gunston Hall Plantation
Kenmore
Mary Washington
    House and Garden
Monticello
Montpelier
Mount Vernon
Oatlands Plantation
Pavilion Gardens
Prestwould Plantation
Stratford Hall Plantation
Woodlawn Plantation

Aquatic Gardens and Gardens with Water Views
Norfolk Botanical Garden
Virginia House

Arboretums
The Arboretum at James Madison
    University
State Arboretum of Virginia at
    Blandy Experimental Farm

Asian Gardens
Lewis Ginter Botanical Garden
Maymont

Child-Pleasing Gardens
Agecroft Hall
Maymont
Mount Vernon
Norfolk Botanical Garden

Conservatories and Botanic Gardens
Agecroft Hall
Green Spring Gardens
Lewis Ginter Botanical Garden
Norfolk Botanical Garden

Famous Landscape Designer Gardens
Monticello (Thomas Jefferson)
Norfolk Botanical Garden
    (Charles Gillette)
Pavilion Gardens (Thomas Jefferson)
Virginia House (Gertrude Jekyll)
Woodrow Wilson Birthplace and
    Gardens (Charles Gillette)

Formal Gardens
Gunston Hall Plantation
Maymont
Morven Park

Garden Rooms
Agecroft Hall
Virginia House

Historic Houses and Plantations
Berkeley Plantation
Monticello
Mount Vernon

Oak Ridge Estate
Oatlands Plantation
Prestwould Plantation
Stratford Hall Plantation
Woodlawn Plantation

*Informal and
English-style Gardens*
Virginia House

Italianate Gardens
Maymont
Norfolk Botanical Garden

Medicinal and Herb Gardens
Agecroft Hall
Colonial Gardens of Williamsburg
River Farm

Notable Americans' Gardens
Ash Lawn–Highland
   (James Monroe)
Gunston Hall Plantation
   (George Mason)
Kenmore (Col. Fielding Lewis)
Monticello (Thomas Jefferson)
Montpelier (James Madison)
Mount Vernon
   (George Washington)
Oak Ridge Estate
   (Thomas Fortune Ryan)
Pavilion Gardens
   (Thomas Jefferson)
Stratford Hall Plantation
   (Robert E. Lee)

Woodrow Wilson Birthplace and
   Gardens (Woodrow Wilson)

Rock Gardens
The Arboretum at James Madison
   University

Romantic Gardens
Oak Ridge Estate
River Farm

Rose Gardens
Ben Lomond Manor House
Norfolk Botanical Garden
Woodlawn Plantation

Specialty Gardens
Bryan Park Azalea Gardens
Gunston Hall Plantation (boxwood)
Norfolk Botanical Garden
   (camellias)
State Arboretum of Virginia at
   Blandy Experimental Farm
   (boxwood)

Topiary Gardens
Adam Thoroughgood House
Gunston Hall Plantation
Colonial Gardens of Williamsburg

Wildflowers and Woodland
The Arboretum at James Madison
   University
Morven Park
Norfolk Botanical Garden
Prestwould Plantation

7. Ash Lawn–Highland

James Monroe Parkway, **Charlottesville**, VA; (434) 293-9539;
www.ashlawnhighland.org

*T*HIS PRETTY ESTATE was the home of President James Monroe
from 1799 to 1823. Monroe built the Charlottesville house
so as to be close to Jefferson at Monticello (and you will find visiting both gardens convenient as well). The house and gardens have
been tastefully restored. This garden will particularly interest those
with a taste for old-fashioned boxwood gardens; these are filled with
specimen plants that bloom profusely throughout a long season.
There is a fine herb garden. And you may find peacocks strolling
through the scenic landscape.

❀ **Admission:** Fee.
Garden open: April through October: daily 9:00 A.M. to 6:00 P.M.
November through March: daily 11:00 A.M. to 5:00 P.M.
Directions: From Interstate 64, take exit 121 (from the east) or 121A
(from the west). Turn onto Route 20 south. Go through one stoplight.
Take an immediate left onto Route 53, and follow the signs to Ash
Lawn–Highland. You will pass Monticello on the left. Continue on
Route 53 to the intersection with County Road 795. Turn right onto
CR 795, and Ash Lawn–Highland will be on your right about ½ mile
down CR 795.

8. Monticello

Route 53, **Charlottesville**, VA; (434) 984-9822; www.monticello.org

*E*VERY INCH of this beautiful place built and landscaped by
Thomas Jefferson is so deeply connected with history and significance that it's hard to separate and describe just the gardens. If
your only interest is the flower gardens, you'll have to block out a
fascinating collection of extraneous material on your tour, for each
corner of Monticello has something to capture your attention.
Monticello is one of the nation's most worthy and delightful historic

estates, the physical representation of Jefferson's genius. He was a gardener par excellence, as well as an architect and statesman, and here at Monticello you'll find many of his ideas about gardens and nature and economy that were put into practice in the early nineteenth century.

The gardens, elegantly restored by the Garden Club of Virginia using Jefferson's own notes and drawings and correspondence, were an abiding interest of the president's. "No occupation," he wrote, "is so delightful to me as the culture of the earth, and no culture comparable to that of the garden. . . . But though an old man, I am but a young gardener."

There are 2 miles of trails throughout this ninety-five-acre estate. They skirt three lakes, hills, forest, orchards, and flower gardens. Along the walk are seasonal plantings and flowering trees of all types. The flower gardens themselves are at the four corners of the house: Twenty oval-shaped beds with a winding gravel walk through them are especially pretty in spring and early summer. The serpentine walk and surrounding lawn are bordered with flowers, and everything is labeled. Among the great varieties of blooms here are not just the familiar spring bulbs but also such rarities as twinleaf, or *Jeffersonia diphylla* (named of course for the master), and Columbian lily (a discovery of Lewis and Clark).

Among the interesting sights are a 1,000-foot-long terraced vegetable garden, which features delightful patterns and climbing varieties, including some of the twenty types of peas Jefferson grew—peas were apparently Jefferson's favorite vegetable. He grew more than 250 types of vegetables and herbs. The garden, which is divided into twenty-seven growing beds, has a stone wall with a reconstructed pavilion where Jefferson sat to read among the vegetables. (A research facility now at Monticello studies propagation and historic plants; you can purchase historic seeds too.)

To appreciate fully the grand plan of Monticello's gardens requires understanding Jefferson's goals and preoccupations, and the visitor center, guides, and printed material are fully prepared to help you. But you can also walk around and enjoy this elegant and historic site with a minimum of knowledge and the greatest of aesthetic pleasure. Spring and summer are the best times for gardenwalks.

❀ **Admission:** Fee.

Garden open: Daily 8:00 A.M. to 5:00 P.M. from March through October, 9:00 A.M. to 4:30 P.M. from November through February. The gardens near the house are easily seen on a tour of the estate; tours devoted primarily to the garden (including the more distant landscape) are given on Saturday morning.

Directions: Monticello is located a few minutes from downtown Charlottesville. From Charlottesville take I–64 to Route 20. (Here you'll find the visitor center.) To get to the house, turn left onto Route 53 and continue 1 $^6/_{10}$ miles to the entrance on the left.

Heirloom Plants

The Thomas Jefferson Center for Historic Plants, established at Monticello in 1987, documents, collects, and distributes heirloom plants. The greater part of the collection consists of varieties grown by Jefferson. (He grew 250 varieties of herbs and vegetables, not counting the plants in his flower gardens, vineyards, and orchards.) The center offers workshops, lectures, and special tours in addition to selling plants and historic seed. For more information, visit www.monticello.org.

9. Pavilion Gardens

University of Virginia, **Charlottesville,** VA; (434) 924–7969;
www.virginia.edu/uvatours/gardens

*T*HOMAS JEFFERSON'S campus at the university is a graceful,
green wonder; its beautifully aged brick walls and white pillars
harmonize completely with the landscape. In addition to the architectural delights, set amid the lovely landscape with its grand,
imposing trees, are the pavilion gardens that the master statesman,
architect, and gardener included in his plan. Though Jefferson did
not himself lay out each of these ten gardens, his original design
included the serpentine garden walls and the concept of the individual gardens in conjunction with the groves of academe. The pavilions are behind each of the old brick houses; their object was to
provide members of the academic village with a place for contemplation and study.

You can take a formal tour, or you can pick up a brochure
describing each pavilion garden and walk unescorted from one to
the next through little white connecting doors here and there. The
high walls provide privacy that makes entering each garden a new
experience. The gardens are divided into two sections matching the
two facing rows of arcades that border the great lawn and the
Rotunda. Behind these original buildings you'll find the five East
Pavilion Gardens and the five West Pavilion Gardens. Each is different; those on the west side are predominantly flat, while the east gardens are hilly and terraced. The overall sense of each of the gardens
is of Jefferson's time, and experts have managed to re-create the
eighteenth century in both the geometric designs and the plantings.

If you begin your walk on the west side with Pavilion Garden
I, you'll find a geometrically patterned garden with a serpentine walk
reflecting the curving walls and small oval flower beds. A center
stone was an attempt by Jefferson to carve capitols for the Rotunda
from local stone. Pavilion Garden III, next door, has raised oval

flower beds and unusually pretty trees, among them a silver bell and a golden rain. Next door in Garden V are two of Jefferson's favorite apple trees, set in the center of a series of squares with parterres and gravel walks. This garden is divided into upper and lower sections; the higher part includes a formal boxwood garden and lovely crape myrtle trees. Garden VII is characterized by benches along curving walks bordered by roses. Garden IX also has a two-part design; its lower part is cool and shady with large trees and pomegranate shrubs, while the upper garden features a four-part formal arrangement of viburnums, peonies, and lilacs.

On the east side of the great lawn is Pavilion Garden II, which is divided into three sections, with great trees, including an umbrella magnolia and a pecan tree, as well as a grape arbor and many fruit trees. Next door in Garden IV there is a combination of formality in a boxwood garden and informality in flower beds in natural settings. Garden VI is one of the best known. Here the Merton Spire (given by Oxford University) is in the center of a naturalistic rhododendron and laurel garden. Garden VIII is a summer garden, with profusely blooming shrubs and an aerial hedge of golden rain trees. The final, and one of the largest, is Garden X. Its design is actually based on the Monticello gardens, with an oval lawn flanked by two smaller ovals (called elephant ears) and a romantic setting of benches amid Kentucky coffee trees. These thumbnail descriptions cannot begin to describe the atmosphere in these gardens, particularly in springtime. You'll seldom see prettier or more historic campus gardens.

✿ **Admission:** Free.
Garden open: Year-round, but the gardens are at their best from mid-April through summer. There are additional gardens at various sites on campus; for full details pick up a flyer at the information center.
Directions: The university is located in Charlottesville; take US 29 south and follow signs for university information.

10. Prestwould Plantation

U.S. Highway 15, Clarksville, VA; (434) 374-8672

*O*NE OF THE most interesting things about a visit to Prestwould is that you can see both the reconstructed gardens and the model of the original garden on display in the octagonal summer-house. The Prestwould house was built in 1795. The gardens, outlined with original ancient boxwoods that are as much as 30 feet in diameter, are described as an interpretative restoration based on detailed plans and extensive records made by Lady Jean Skipwith. She was the wife of Sir Peyton Skipwith—the only baron born in Virginia—who won the 10,000-acre estate gambling with William Byrd III of Westover. In any case, Lady Jean was a great gardener, and her records, kept over a twenty-year period, are among the earliest known listings of native plantings; Lady Jean is considered the most important woman gardener in eighteenth- or early nineteenth-century America.

The setting of Prestwould's gardens was an unusual one—a virtual island between two rivers. The house was on the hilly terrain above, with apparently a well-landscaped slope down. Lady Skipwith's garden included orchards and native wildflowers that could be seen from the house on the hill. She combined agriculture and landscape design in an unusually sophisticated fashion. She also relished the native plants of the Virginia wilderness, describing her island garden as "a cabinet of curiosities." The reconstruction has followed her notes as faithfully as possible, both in the plantings and in the trellises and arbors of the charming setting. If your interests tend toward early American garden design and indigenous plants—as well as lovely garden vistas—this visit should capture your imagination.

❀ **Admission:** Fee.

Garden open: Daily 1:30 to 4:30 P.M. from June through September; Monday through Friday 1:30 to 4:30 P.M. from October through May.

Directions: Prestwould is located 2 miles north of Clarksville on U.S. Highway 15 in south-central Virginia. Take Interstate 85 to U.S. Highway 58 west, then turn onto US 15 north.

11. Kenmore

1200 Washington Avenue, **Fredericksburg,** VA; (540) 373-3381; www.kenmore.org

*I*T IS NOT surprising that many visitors are particularly drawn to Kenmore, one of the many historic houses that grace the region. A picture-perfect eighteenth-century estate set on four acres of broad lawns with gardens and stately trees, it combines classic simplicity with a touch of formality. The house is a Georgian manor whose unpretentious facade belies an elaborate interior of magnificently decorated rooms; some consider it to hold some of the most beautiful period rooms in America. It was built in the mid-eighteenth century by Col. Fielding Lewis, George Washington's brother-in-law. Washington, a frequent visitor, is reported to have designed some of the ornate interior plasterwork himself. The house was surrounded by a 13,000-acre plantation; today, just five acres of gardens remain, but what lovely, serene gardens they are!

Kenmore's restoration began in the 1920s after a somewhat turbulent history, including war and inevitable neglect. In 1929 the Garden Club of Virginia decided it was high time to do something about the unkempt grounds. To accomplish a full-scale renovation, the club initiated Historic Garden Week (a fund-raising event that has since benefited many other gardens throughout the South). Mindful of the historic significance of the estate, the club members introduced plantings in keeping with its setting and period.

The gardens have undergone yet another renovation since then, and today they are a harmonious blend of graceful formality and natural beauty. Within the grounds are restful expanses of grass shaded by venerable hardwood trees, a wilderness area laced with wildflowers, and many beautifully tended plantings. Among the specialties here are a colorful cutting garden and flowering trees and shrubs, including rhododendrons, boxwoods, camellias, and dogwoods. A magical time to visit Kenmore is during the height of dogwood season, when the grounds look like a fairyland of delicate white blooms.

❀ **Admission:** Free; fee for house visit.
Garden open: March through December: daily 10:00 A.M. to 4:00 P.M. January and February: weekends only 10:00 A.M. to 4:00 P.M. Closed certain holidays.
Directions: From I-95 take exit 130 and head east on Route 3. Pass several strip malls and at the bottom of a long hill, move to the left lane as you pass under a bridge (US 1). Turn left onto Route 3 Business (William Street). Follow William Street through three traffic lights. After you pass through the third light, look for the brick-walled cemetery on your left. At the end of the cemetery, turn left onto Washington Avenue. Two blocks later, Washington becomes a divided street—make a short jog to the right onto Lewis Street then left back onto Washington. Kenmore is on your right.

12. Mary Washington House and Garden

1200 Charles Street, **Fredericksburg,** VA; (540) 373-1569

*I*N 1772 George Washington purchased this house and garden for his mother "to make her more comfortable and free from care." He often visited her there (though he apparently heard many complaints from her about her expenses in maintaining it). Today the restored house and garden are charming; Mrs. Washington's garden is in a typically eighteenth-century style. There are boxwood-lined brick walkways, a sundial, and a vegetable garden separated from a flower garden in the English style. Nearby are an apothecary shop and a historic tavern. This site is not far from Kenmore.

Admission: Fee.

Garden open: March through November: Monday through Saturday 9:00 A.M. to 5:00 P.M., Sunday 11:00 A.M. to 5:00 P.M.; December through February: Monday through Saturday 10:00 A.M. to 4:00 P.M., Sunday noon to 4:00 P.M.

Directions: From I–95 take Route 3 (exit 130) toward downtown Fredericksburg. Take Business Route 3 (William Street), then turn left onto Charles Street.

13. The Arboretum at James Madison University

Off University Boulevard, **Harrisonburg**, VA; (540) 568–3194; www.jmu.edu/arboretum

*T*HE UNIVERSITY has turned 125 acres of oak-hickory forest into an arboretum with many walking trails and a series of gardens and natural habitats. There are several striking gardens here; the most extraordinary in spring is one of the state's largest wildflower collections. You'll also see rhododendrons, ferns, and a bog garden. In April the daffodils—more than fifty varieties of them—and the perennial bulb garden make a great display. In the pond area there are aquatic plants and wildlife to be seen, and another section features a rock garden and herb collection.

Admission: Free.

Garden open: Daily dawn to dusk.

Directions: James Madison University is alongside Interstate 81 in Harrisonburg. From I–81 take exit 245, go east on Port Republic Road, turn left onto Forest Hills Drive, and proceed to University Boulevard. The arboretum is located on JMU's East Campus, near the Convocation Center, along University Boulevard.

14. Morven Park

17263 Southern Planter Lane, **Leesburg,** VA; (703) 777-2414;
www.morvenpark.org

*M*ORVEN PARK is still a working farm with a 1780 Greek
revival mansion and significant gardens. Two noted governors lived here in the nineteenth and early twentieth centuries; the wife of Virginia Governor Westmoreland Davis planted the gardens. Covering seven acres, the gardens are noted for their enormous boxwood parterre patterns. Called the Marguerite Davis Boxwood Gardens, these formal settings include an elegant reflecting pool and a wide variety of flowers: spring bulbs, June dahlias, and summer annuals. There are notable trees here too: flowering dogwood, crab apple, crape myrtle, Japanese cherry, and magnolia. There are two self-guided nature trails as well, where you'll see more informal settings with wildflowers.

❀ **Admission:** Free.
Garden open: Friday through Monday noon to 4:00 P.M. from April through October.
Directions: From Route 7 west take the Route 7 Business exit in Leesburg, and turn right onto Market Street. Turn left onto Fairview Street, then left onto Old Waterford Road. Turn right onto Southern Planter Lane to the park.

15. Oatlands Plantation

20850 Oatlands Plantation Lane, **Leesburg,** VA; (703) 777-3174;
www.oatlands.org

*S*ITUATED IN the quiet hills of Virginia's hunt country, Oatlands Plantation is a grand federal-style, columned mansion surrounded by acres of magnificent terraced gardens overlooking open meadows. The estate—a National Trust for Historic Preservation property—is among the jewels of the Piedmont area, offering historic perspectives on life from the early 1800s through the 1930s, along with one of the most enchanting gardens in the region. Here you can enjoy elaborate interior decors reflecting different styles and periods at the mansion, as well as such garden pleasures as impeccably groomed boxwood parterres, flower gardens, reflecting pools, and elegant statuary.

The site reflects two basically different historic periods and styles: Oatlands as a working plantation in its early days, and Oatlands as a pleasure country retreat in the twentieth century. In 1803 George Carter, a great-grandson of Robert "King" Carter, a wealthy Virginia land baron, designed and built Oatlands House and its gardens on his large property. As with other plantations, the gardens were set near the house to shelter them from the wind. Carter installed a complex series of descending terraces connected by stone and brick stairways. On the terraces he planted fruit trees, vegetables, herbs, flowers, and shrubs. Several acres were dedicated to magnificent English boxwood gardens. To the standard plantation structures—sawmill, gristmill, blacksmith shop, store—he added a large greenhouse, today considered to be one of the oldest in the East.

After the Civil War, Oatlands became a refuge for the homeless, then a summer boardinghouse. At the turn of the twentieth century, the Carter family, whose fortune had been steadily withering, was forced to sell the property, by then sadly in shambles. The new owners, the Eustis family, were well-connected Washingtonians who used Oatlands as a retreat to pursue their interests (his for foxhunting, hers for gardening). History buffs as well, they restored both house and gardens to their former splendor, infusing new design ideas in the process. Mrs. Eustis refurbished Carter's gardens, planting new boxwood hedges, a lovely boxwood allée, and flower beds with peonies, tulips, irises, and lilies. She also added parterres, statues, a teahouse, a bowling green, a rose garden, and a reflecting pool—all still there as part of her legacy.

In the 1980s the National Trust hired Alfredo Siani (a former airline executive with horticultural gifts, who is responsible for a number of Virginia garden restorations). He was given the task of restoring the gardens to their heyday in the 1930s. Carefully researching the Carter and Eustis records, he refurbished garden walls, boxwoods, the rose garden, and flower beds (mindful of the pink, blue, and white color schemes favored by Mrs. Eustis). He designed a formal herb garden and a memorial garden too. The newest restoration is the oldest greenhouse in the nation (1810).

When visiting Oatlands, allow enough time to give both house and its four-and-one-half-acre gardens their due. Before starting out on your gardenwalk, look over the elegant balustrade for a breath-taking view of the gardens as a whole. From this vantage point, with descriptive leaflet in hand (available at the entrance), you can iden-tify terraces, parterres, flower gardens, and many other delights.

❀ **Admission:** Fee.
Garden open: Monday through Saturday 10:00 A.M. to 4:00 P.M., Sunday 1:00 to 4:00 P.M., from April to December.
Directions: Oatlands is 6 miles south of Leesburg on US 15, approxi-mately 40 minutes from Washington, D.C.

16. Gunston Hall Plantation

Route 242, **Lorton,** VA; (703) 550–9220; www.gunstonhall.org

*T*HE DIGNITY and eminence of George Mason, author of the Virginia Declaration of Independence and a framer of the United States Constitution, are reflected in Gunston Hall Planta-tion, his estate for many years. The beautiful brick manor and its surrounding garden—both of which the great statesman designed for himself—are impressive without being in the least showy or pretentious. In its recent restoration, the house is a sparkling tribute to classic eighteenth-century style and taste.

Mason began building the house in 1755, on his 5,000-acre tobacco and grain plantation on the shores of the Potomac River. Like much of the colonial tidewater architecture, the house has a simple facade, in contrast with its more elaborate interior, which features baroque carvings and other high-style decorative elements. Mason also had a keen interest in plants, much like his neighbor George Washington at Mount Vernon. He oversaw the management of his plantation himself. Clearly, he was partial to English boxwood, for it is found everywhere at Gunston Hall—including some of the original plants.

The formal gardens include extensive parterres, boxwood hedges, and a magnificent 200-foot-long boxwood allée. Now almost 250 years old and 12 feet high, this green avenue is the most historic garden feature here. Gunston Hall is considered to have among the best boxwood green gardens anywhere, England included. Portions of the garden are temporarily dug up for archaeological research, and some of the box has been moved to lower sections of the garden, but the remarkable boxwood allée still stands.

The gardens are set within the remaining 550 acres that comprise the plantation. Leading to the house and its surrounding meadows is the welcoming Magnolia Avenue, a double line of magnolias and cedars. Beyond are a deer park and a woodsy nature trail profuse with spring wildflowers, mountain laurels, and dogwoods. The trail leads to the Potomac, about half a mile away, where, back in the old days, George Mason's crops would be loaded onto sailing ships for the long voyage to Europe. From this spot you can still enjoy views of water and birds.

✿ **Admission:** Fee.

Garden open: Daily 9:30 A.M. to 5:00 P.M.; closed some holidays.

Directions: Gunston Hall is located 20 miles south of Washington,

D.C., on the Potomac River. Take I–95 to exit 163. Turn left onto Lorton Road. Turn right onto Armistead Road. At the light turn right onto US 1 south. At the third light turn left onto Gunston Road (Route 242). The Gunston Hall entrance is 3½ miles on the left.

17. Ben Lomond Manor House

10311 Sudley Manor Drive, **Manassas,** VA; (703) 368–8784; www.benlomondmanorhouse.org

*Y*OU MAY BE visiting this famous Civil War site to see the battlefield; if you are also a rose enthusiast, make a detour here. This site features a different sort of history: It is a garden devoted to ancient roses. This antique rose collection was amassed by a noted rose grower named Jim Syring; it was replanted here and dedicated in 1996. There are some 160 varieties of roses that were grown between the 1400s and 1867, a truly astounding bit of horticultural history.

❀ **Admission:** Free.
Garden open: Daily dawn to dusk.
Directions: The site is about 30 miles outside of Washington, D.C. From I–66 west take exit 47A onto Business Route 234. Take a left onto Sudley Manor Drive and go past two traffic lights. The manor house will be on the right.

18. Montpelier

11407 Constitution Highway (Route 20), **Montpelier Station,** VA; (540) 672–2728; www.montpelier.org

*T*HE ELEGANT Georgian home of President James Madison here stands on a 2,700-acre estate, some of which was patented in 1723. Its long history includes an eighty-year period as a duPont family residence and its acquisition as a National Trust Historic Site. It was the duPont family who laid out the two-acre formal gardens (on the site of earlier gardens), and now the duPont gardens have been beautifully re-created. Without original plans, the Garden Club of Virginia undertook to create a typical turn-of-the-twentieth-century garden. By 1992 twenty different beds had been restored, redesigned, and replenished with spring bulbs; the layout includes the original terraced design of President Madison's time, with a flower-bordered brick entrance wall and gate and large, crescent-shaped borders.

This is also a place to enjoy unusual trees. There is a self-guided walk with more than forty varieties of native and nonnative trees, including such specimens as cedar of Lebanon, tulip poplar, and black walnut. Two hundred additional acres have been established as a natural landmark.

❋ **Admission:** Fee

Garden open: April through October: daily 9:30 A.M. to 5:00 P.M. November through March: daily 9:30 A.M. to 4:00 P.M. Closed Thanksgiving and Christmas.

Directions: Montpelier is about 45 minutes from Charlottesville. From Charlottesville take US 29 north to Ruckersville, take a right onto U.S. Highway 33 east. At Barboursville take a left onto Route 20 north toward Orange. Go about 8 miles; the Montpelier visitor center is on the left.

The Garden Club of Virginia

This organization has been involved in the reconstruction of dozens of gardens in the state, including several of the garden-walks featured in this chapter: Monticello, Montpelier, Kenmore in Fredericksburg, Gunston Hall Plantation in Lorton, the Woodrow Wilson Gardens in Staunton, and Bacon's Castle in Surry. To learn more about the club's works in progress—all gardens that are worthy of visits—go to the Web site www .gcvirginia.org.

19. Mount Vernon

3200 George Washington Memorial Parkway, **Mount Vernon,** VA; (703) 780–2000; www.mountvernon.org

*M*OUNT VERNON, the legendary home of George Washington, is a serenely green and spacious eighteenth-century plantation overlooking the Potomac. This picturesque site has an elegant aura of history, with its imposing, columned mansion, period exhibits, and scrupulously restored colonial gardens (largely based on Washington's diaries and letters). Not surprisingly, it draws more than a million visitors a year, from schoolchildren to foreign tourists to history buffs and—yes—garden lovers. Here you can get a taste of the gracious plantation life of the time and catch a glimpse of the private world of Washington as gentleman farmer and assiduous botanist. Because the grounds are so vast—including some 500 landscaped acres within an extensive property easily four times that size—the crowds are not necessarily intrusive, and a self-guided gardenwalk here, amid flowers and fruit trees and herbs and boxwood, is highly recommended.

Largely responsible for the gardens' preservation has been the Mount Vernon Ladies' Association. The oldest preservation society in the country, it purchased the badly neglected property in 1858, maintaining it to this day in as strict accordance with Washington's original plans as possible.

Washington's legacy as a gifted gardener and horticulturist and even landscape designer lives on at this homesite. The president himself laid out the bowling green, flanked on either side by specimen trees (some of which still exist), serpentine walks, and symmetrical gardens. In keeping with the ideas of balance and perspective embodied in eighteenth-century garden design, the bowling green is aligned with both river and mansion. On one side of the expansive green is the large Upper Garden, a formal composition of flowers, blooming shrubs and trees, and boxwood. Among the flowers (unspecified in Washington's writings) are a typical eighteenth-century mix, including heliotrope, foxglove, pansies, bloodroot, larkspur, and Canterbury bells, set in alternating patterns with vegetables. Espaliered fruit trees against brick walls and boxwood hedges, both favorites of Washington's, are found here. (Some of the boxwood was actually rooted by Washington himself and has been carefully nurtured ever since.) A dwarf box parterre features a fleur-de-lis pattern, a popular design in many eighteenth-century French gardens.

The Lower Garden, entered through a boxwood arch from the south side of the bowling green, is a less formal kitchen garden. Here on two terraced levels surrounded by brick walls are herb-bordered geometric vegetable beds (featuring more than thirty varieties) and yet more espaliered trees—figs, apples, pears, peaches, and of course cherries. A deliciously heady aroma emanates from all of these herbs and fruits. There is also a picturesque bee house based on early designs.

A third restored garden area is the Botanical Garden. This spot was used for experimenting on imported seeds and plants; if you're interested in botany you will find it intriguing. In addition to these gardens, Mount Vernon offers numerous lovely walks among the beauties of the landscape overlooking the river.

❀ **Admission:** Fee (except on Washington's Birthday holiday).
Garden open: March through October: daily 9:00 A.M. to 5:00 P.M. November through February: daily 9:00 A.M. to 4:00 P.M. There are no

formal guided tours, but interpretive guides are stationed in the house and gardens to answer questions.

Directions: From Old Town Alexandria take George Washington Memorial Parkway south for about 8 miles. Mount Vernon is clearly signposted.

20. Norfolk Botanical Garden

Azalea Garden Road, **Norfolk,** VA;
(757) 441–5830; www.norfolkbotanicalgarden.org

*T*HIS IS one of the most satisfying public gardens we have visited. Not only is the overall arrangement graceful, spacious, and inviting in all its many parts, but it is in each particular well designed and lovely to walk through. From the long row of artistic statuary surrounding a great mowed lawn bordered with flowers, to the wooded gardens of rhododendrons and camellias, to the lovely lines of flowering fruit trees—this is truly a pleasure garden. It has been ranked by the American Automobile Association as one of the ten best gardens in the country.

The gardens are situated near the water, overlooking a daffodil-bordered canal (which is home to many waterfowl) and two pretty lakes, Lake Whitehurst and Mirror Lake near the Norfolk waterfront. The site was once known as Gardens by the Sea, and there is a definite sea breeze above the shorelines. The nearby airport is almost adjacent; if you bring your children here, you can show them striking views in addition to the gardens. You can also ride on a "trackless" train or a canal boat through the gardens.

This botanical garden with about 155 acres of plants was originally a WPA Project. It began with 4,000 azalea bushes in 1938, and those flowering beauties now number a quarter of a million. Over the years the garden developed into twenty distinct theme areas, but the overall impression is woodsy throughout. The hand of Charles Gillette, the noted garden designer, can be seen in the care taken here.

Among our favorite features is the Renaissance Court. This spacious garden has several different levels, with ornamental walls and balustrades on each, and a semicircular reflecting pool. It is a masterpiece of garden design, representing the style of Italian Renaissance gardens of the late sixteenth century. Adjacent is another unusually lovely spot, the Statuary Vista. Two long rows of tall evergreen hedge with flower beds below are punctuated by a series of nineteenth-century marble statues by Sir Moses Ezekiel, representing the great European artists. You will seldom see a more enchanting combination of art and nature.

Other specialty gardens include a bog garden, a Japanese garden, a flowering arboretum, a historic garden, a native plant garden, an award-winning rose garden, a colonial herb garden, a hydrangea collection, a butterfly garden, a wildflower meadow, and a healing garden that includes shade plants with healing properties. When we visited in spring, the dazzling azaleas and rhododendrons (150 varieties) were fully abloom. It's no wonder that the International Azalea Festival honoring NATO has been held here since the 1950s. And of course there are perennials galore, plus 25,000 tulips in spring and more than 50,000 annuals flowering in summer. More than 300 varieties of camellias bloom in the woodsy landscape during fall and winter months, and a vast holly collection adds winter interest too. There are 12 miles of trails, a gazebo, terraces, and occasional benches for reflection. No matter what your garden interest, you won't be disappointed.

❀ **Admission:** Fee.

Garden open: Mid-April through mid-October: daily 9:00 A.M. to 7:00 P.M. Open daily 9:00 A.M. to 5:00 P.M. rest of year.

Directions: Norfolk Botanical Garden is next to Norfolk International Airport. From I-64, take exit 279 (Norview Avenue). Follow Norview for 1 mile and turn left onto Azalea Garden Road. The garden entrance is on the right.

21. Agecroft Hall

4305 Sulgrave Road, **Richmond,** VA; (804) 353–4241; www.agecrofthall.com

*T*HIS HOUSE and garden truly seem to carry the visitor back in time—not just to colonial propriety or to the nineteenth-century "gardenesque," but to Tudor and Stuart times in an England transposed to Virginia. Every stone of the late-fifteenth-century house, Agecroft Hall, was rescued from wrecking in Lancashire, England, and brought to this pretty setting by a Virginia business-man named T. C. Richards. The elegant manor was reconstructed on this picturesque riverfront of Richmond in 1928.

The twenty-three-acre gardens, at the house level and on a sloping hillside down to the James River, were designed to maintain the Tudor atmosphere. There are picture-perfect grounds, green hillside lawns, elms and magnolias, and, best of all, a set of semi-formal gardens and walkways that are both charming and curious. These pleasure gardens are especially inviting in springtime; each garden room is outlined in boxwood hedge and accented with small statuary and seasonal flowers.

Agecroft's gardens represent an era when gardening was done for pleasure and with purpose. You begin your tour in an almost fully enclosed courtyard equipped with seventeenth-century tools used for farming and other Tudor chores. The first of the pleasure garden rooms is a fragrance garden—the nearest to the house, so that its sweet odors presumably would waft through the open leaded win-dows. Among the many (identified) flowers whose scent and very names are intriguing are pheasant's eye narcissis, heliotrope, and gillyflower. Next is the sunken garden with a raised pond, a replica of the pond garden at England's Hampton Court, and truly a pleas-ure garden both in design and color. Lilies and irises are planted here and there, giving a sense of perfect harmony in this enclosed gar-den room.

A particularly intriguing walkway, bordered by fifty-year-old crape myrtle trees with their gnarled and graceful branches, edges the similarly pale-colored path. Tudor-style shelters from the sun add charm to this odd and pleasing connecting link to the knot garden. This traditional part of early gardens is a formal, enclosed area in which patterns are created by the plantings themselves. This is undoubtedly one of the best knot gardens we've visited; radishes, lettuce, and cabbages crisscross through one bed. In another, various herbs form the patterns. Colored stone and crimson barberry create color contrast. What an amusing way to grow food!

Another highlight is the garden named for John Tradescant the Younger (an English botanist who first came to Virginia in 1637 to collect American plant specimens) in which many rare and exotic plants are surrounded by walls with espaliered pear trees. Bordering this garden is the herb garden, where some eighty-five types of herbs used for medicine or cooking grow. Nearby are a still house where the herbs were dried and several beehives woven of rye, bulrush, and cattails. You can almost imagine yourself puttering about in the seventeenth century, a recipe book of herbs and honey in hand.

The six garden rooms form the formal part of the grounds. You'll also find a cutting garden and a serpentine path through a sloping landscape dotted with flowers, ferns, and woodland, which takes you finally to the riverbank.

❀ **Admission:** Fee.

Garden open: Tuesday through Saturday 10:00 A.M. to 4:00 P.M., Sunday 12:30 to 5:00 P.M. The entrance tour includes a house tour; garden tours are self-guided.

Directions: From I–95 into Richmond, exit onto Interstate 195 (southwest), and then turn right onto Cary Street, which is also Route 147. Make a quick left at the light onto Canterbury Road, which will merge with Sulgrave Road. The entrance will be on your left.

22. Bryan Park Azalea Gardens

Hermitage Road and Bellevue Avenue, **Richmond,** VA;
(804) 358–7166; www.friendsofbryanpark.com/azaleas.htm

*F*IFTY THOUSAND azalea plants on twenty acres and some 600
white dogwoods are the major attractions here. Needless to
say, this is a place to see in springtime. We recommend telephon-
ing in advance to find out the perfect week to visit—generally
between mid-April and mid-May. (Some 200,000 visitors are
expected each year.) Among the most popular features is a huge, 35-
foot red and white azalea cross, and about fifty species of azaleas
bloom at the same time. The rest of the park is quite pretty, with
camellias, magnolias, crab apples, American hollies, and many other
types of flowering plants. But if it's azaleas and dogwoods you particularly want to see, plan accordingly.

✿ **Admission:** Free.

Garden open: Daily dawn to dusk.

Directions: The azalea gardens are in the southeastern corner of Bryan
Park, which is bordered along its southern edge by I–95 and I–64 and
along its northern border by Bryan Park Avenue.

23. Lewis Ginter Botanical Garden

1800 Lakeside Avenue, **Richmond,** VA; (804) 262–9887;
www.lewisginter.org

*T*HIS FORTY-ACRE botanical garden bordering a small lake
was begun in 1984. There are a number of imposing buildings, including a recently constructed greenhouse featuring worldwide plants and some 200 orchids. You'll find lots of water here,
many bright pink stone and brick paths, and a series of individual
gardens rather than an overall design. Its most impressive area is the
Asian garden, with water running gently over rocks and a nice Japanese teahouse. Numerous additional areas include an interactive
one-and-one-half-acre children's educational garden with a new

accessible treehouse, daylily collections, and more than 850 varieties of daffodils. Great care has been taken throughout to label all
plants, and many educational programs are offered.

❀ **Admission:** Fee.
Garden open: Daily 9:00 A.M. to 5:00 P.M. Call for visitor center hours.
Directions: From downtown Richmond take I–95 north to exit 80, the
Lakeside Avenue exit. Keep to the right and take the right at the first
light onto Lakeside Avenue. (You will see a sign for the Lewis garden.)
Follow Lakeside; the garden entrance is just past the intersection of
Lakeside Avenue and Hilliard Road.

24. Maymont

1700 Hampton Street, **Richmond,** VA; (804) 358–7166;
www.maymont.org

*L*UCKY Richmond residents have this very beautiful one-
hundred-acre park with extensive gardens to visit year-
round at no charge. Maymont is indeed a treasure, with both a large
and inviting park and a series of exquisite gardens. Its Italianate garden is surely one of the most inviting such formal gardens anywhere
in the East, with its natural setting on a cliff above a stream, and
there's an equally enchanting Japanese garden and, just beyond, the
James River.

Maymont was a dairy farm when purchased by Maj. and Mrs.
James Dooley. The elaborate Victorian Romanesque mansion they
built was finished in 1893; it took thirty years to complete the magnificent gardens. Having traveled abroad extensively, the Dooleys
had clear ideas about what they wanted, and when Maymont's gardens were finished, the estate became a noted showplace. For here
were many of the best worldwide garden features re-created—and
in a natural setting of uncommon beauty.

The Italianate garden, completed in 1910, is the pièce de résistance. With its natural setting atop a cliff, it has several levels with

a 200-foot-long antique-columned, wisteria-covered pergola, parterres and terraces, fountains, and Renaissance statuary. In between these formal divisions, a profusion of flowers (tulips, candytuft, roses, osmanthus, and many, many perennials and annuals) is surrounded by clipped evergreens. This is a place to spend precious hours—whether exploring the horticultural or antique aspects, or merely enjoying the picturesque design or the dramatic view of the deep ravine below.

This entire site has a sense of the garden as part of its overall environment, not just as a formal work of art. Each garden fits into its setting in such a natural way that it is hard to imagine what was already growing and what was planted specifically for the site. This is particularly true where the steep rocky hillside descends to the six-acre Japanese Stroll Garden. Taking a delightful, very steep, winding stone staircase down, the visitor comes upon the serpentine stream and stepping-stones and raked sand of the formal Asian garden. This lovely spot has a tree-shaded teahouse amid small koi ponds and a spectacular high point—a 42-foot-high waterfall.

Other pleasures include the recently added Via Florum walkway from the house to the gardens; the European grotto, with its mysterious rocky setting; a collection of more than one hundred varieties of daylilies; an herb garden; and an extensive arboretum with more than 200 trees, including rare and exotic species planted by the Dooleys nearly a century ago. You can wander vast fields and lawns and stony bluffs and visit the house, a carriage house, and a children's farm too. Don't visit Richmond without seeing Maymont!

❀ **Admission:** Free.
Garden open: Tuesday through Sunday noon to 5:00 P.M.
Directions: Maymont has several entrances: The nature and visitor center is located at 2201 Shields Lake Drive in Byrd Park. From I–64 or I–95 take exit 78 (Boulevard/Route 161). Go south on the Boulevard (Route 161) for 2 miles to the Columbus statue. Turn right onto Grant

Street/Blanton Avenue (Route 161) and go ³⁄₁₀ mile to the Carillon monument. Turn left onto Park Drive (Route 161) and go ³⁄₁₀ mile. Turn left onto Shirley Lane and go 1 block (past the children's farm entrance); bear left (not the hard left onto Westover Road) and go 1 block into Byrd Park. Turn right at Shields Lake Drive and continue around the lake to the nature and visitor center parking lot on the right. The Hampton Street Entrance is located at 1700 Hampton Street and provides the easiest access to Maymont House, the herb garden and the Italian garden. From I–64 and I–95, take exit 78 (Boulevard/Route 161). Go south on the Boulevard (Route 161) for 2 miles. Turn left onto Cary Street (Route 147) and go ½ mile. Turn right onto Meadow Street and go 1 mile. Turn right onto Pennsylvania Avenue and go 1 block to the parking lot.

25. Virginia House

4301 Sulgrave Road, **Richmond,** VA; (804) 353-4251; www.vahistorical.org

*T*HIS GARDEN fairly takes your breath away. Not just because of the heady aroma of thousands of blooms, among them a glorious rose garden, but because it is so aesthetically lovely. A big, rather gloomy mansion reconstructed stone by stone in 1925 from its English incarnation as a twelfth-century priory called St. Sepulchre, Virginia House is virtually surrounded by gardens of contrastingly bright, light, colorful flowers. These are divided into garden rooms, called "pleasances," mostly walled, and one more delightful than the next.

Everything here is pale lavender and pink, rose and jasmine. We were truly enchanted by the variety and design; the creators of these gardens (landscape architect Charles Gillette, known for his designs in the picturesque style, and Virginia Weddell) had a real eye for color, proportion, and line as well as an interest in rare plants and exotic trees. More modern additions retain a similar style. Gillette is sometimes called the Interpreter of Southern Gardens, and he certainly created one here that is quintessentially southern in its old-world charm. Take your time; anyone who ever planned a garden will appreciate the sleight of hand demonstrated at this site.

Your tour of the garden (on your own with map in hand or with a guide) begins at the terrace behind the house. From this spot you'll have an expansive view of the estate and the water beyond, and you'll get a feeling for the overall design. The alignment of a distant pergola, a canal, pools, and a sundial with garden walls and planting demonstrates the strong east–west axis (in contrast with the north–south axis of the staircase to the house and the downhill path). This carefully planned arrangement suggests the European stylistic origins of Virginia House's landscape.

The first garden we visit is the water garden. This enchanting spot is fashioned after one designed by Gertrude Jekyll and Edwin Lutyens in Berkshire, England. The use of water—running in an east-to-west canal—is one of the most appealing of any water garden we've seen. Instead of the ubiquitous floating water lilies in still ponds found in so many water gardens, this garden includes a rectangular court enclosed by boxwood and a low brick wall; within the water are clumps of Japanese iris, sagittaria, and pink and white lotus flowers, all blooming successively. The effect is breathtaking, for the combination of geometric design, small statues, and free-form plantings is both graceful and poetic—seemingly cut off from the world.

And speaking of walls, each pleasance has its own wall surrounding it, and no two are the same. Varied designs are built into them, here and there dotted by statuary, small fountains, a sundial, and antique vases. These walls, like fine frames on great paintings, add to rather than detract from the composition within.

The next two gardens are devoted to perennial beds featuring mixtures of blooming shrubs, flowers, and clinging vines, and a four seasons bed. The latter includes little statues of the seasons, and in spring the unusual combination of waving tulips in a sea of forget-me-nots is original and thoroughly delightful. This is a Victorian garden in the best sense. Next you'll find azalea and laurel collections surrounding a fifteenth-century bird bath, and a rose garden with several espaliered varieties, enclosed with special openwork walls so that the air can circulate.

Below the many formal gardens are the wildflower meadow and the bog garden, where some 125 species of plants grow in wetlands poetically set beneath a weeping willow. Beyond is a woodland walk, and then the riverbank. This is one of the outstanding gardens in our book. Don't miss it!

❁ **Admission:** Fee.

Garden open: Friday and Saturday 10:00 A.M. to 4:00 P.M., Sunday 12:30 to 5:00 P.M., or by appointment.

Directions: At the intersection of Malvern Avenue and Cary Street, as Malvern crosses Cary, Malvern becomes Canterbury Road. Follow Canterbury to the yellow sign for Virginia House, bear left, and Canterbury will merge with Sulgrave Road. Virginia House will be on the left.

26. Woodrow Wilson Birthplace and Gardens

18-24 North Coalter Street, **Staunton,** VA; (540) 885–0897; www.woodrowwilson.org

*S*INCE NOTED Richmond landscape designer Charles Gillette restored these gardens in 1933, you can be sure they are well worth a visit. Often known as the Interpreter of Southern Gardens, Gillette turned his hand to the elegant estate where President Wilson was born. There is now a complex of four buildings on-site, including a museum. The gardens are set in an intricate system of terraces and courts, with the center focus on a bowknot parterre garden outlined in boxwood. Work here by the Garden Club of Virginia has created one of the loveliest gardens in Virginia.

❁ **Admission:** Fee.

Garden open: March through October: Monday through Saturday 9:00

A.M. to 5:00 P.M., Sunday noon to 5:00 P.M. November through February: Monday through Saturday 10:00 A.M. to 4:00 P.M., Sunday noon to 4:00 P.M. Closed Thanksgiving, Christmas, and New Year's Day. **Directions:** The Woodrow Wilson birthplace is five minutes from I–81 and twenty minutes from the Blue Ridge Parkway and Skyline Drive. Follow signs from all approaches.

27. Stratford Hall Plantation

Route 214, **Stratford,** VA; (804) 493–8038; www.stratfordhall.org

A VISIT TO Stratford Hall Plantation is a step back in history, both as a house museum (the ancestral home of two signers of the Declaration and Robert E. Lee's birthplace), and as thoroughly researched and restored gardens. The Great House, built by Thomas Lee in about 1738, is considered one of the finest examples of early Georgian architecture in the country and its Great Hall one of the most beautiful rooms in America. Today the 1,600-acre site is maintained as an authentic example of a colonial plantation, with spinning and weaving in process, fields cultivated, and a gristmill in operation. The site of this plantation overlooking the Potomac River in the distance (a mile-long vista) is very grand.

The elegant house has two formal gardens, one to each side. Its gardens were reconstructed by two well-known landscape architects in the 1930s: Morley Williams and Arthur Shurcliff. The brick-walled East Garden is based on site archaeology and is one of the most authentic early American gardens around; you'll find a boxwood maze and delightful flower parterres that have no fewer than 3,200 boxwoods. The West Garden has eighteenth-century herbs, a kitchen garden, and an orderly arrangement of flowers.

Stratford offers wildflowers, formal plantings (a rose garden, espaliered fruit trees, spring and summer annuals, and other seasonal delights), and great trees—crape myrtles, flowering dogwoods, and old hickory trees that have seen a lot of history at this site.

✿ **Admission:** Fee.

Garden open: Daily 9:30 A.M. to 4:00 P.M.

Directions: From Washington, D.C. take I–95 south to exit 130A (Route 3 east) in Fredericksburg. Follow Route 3 for about 45 miles, then take a left onto Route 214 at Lerty. Follow Route 214 for 2 miles. Stratford's gate is on the left.

28. Bacon's Castle

County Road 617, **Surry,** VA; (757) 357–5976;
www.apva.org/apva/bacons_castle.php

*B*ACON'S CASTLE features one of the oldest restored gardens in the nation. The garden is authentically restored to the 1680s, based on archeological evidence. The "Castle" was built in 1665 by an Englishman named Arthur Allen, and it is the oldest documented brick house in English North America. The Jacobean mansion is of architectural interest because it is built in an unusual cruciform style with a porch tower in the front, a medieval stair tower in the rear, and curious Flemish-style gables. Its three massive chimneys were a symbol of status. It became known as Bacon's Castle because a group of Nathaniel Bacon's supporters barricaded themselves within for three months during Bacon's Rebellion in 1665.

The garden, originally laid out by Allen's son, has been restored by the Garden Club of Virginia. It is described as "the oldest, largest, most sophisticated, and best preserved seventeenth-century garden in America." Archeological evidence shows that Allen took a certain interest in the garden's design as well as its functionality, for the design includes some ornamental touches as well as the geometric plainness typical of the time. A large, rectangular growing area, bounded by a brick wall southwest of the house, holds long, raised planting beds. This area is dissected by white sand walkways. Archeological evidence suggests that other growing areas had curving borders and perhaps little brick seats for viewing the garden.

Shurcliff Gardens

Landscape designer Arthur Shurcliff reconstructed many historic American gardens, including Stratford Hall Plantation in Stratford and two gardens in Surry. While you are visiting Bacon's Castle, make a detour to see the Rolfe-Warren House and Smith's Fort Plantation. The layout of walks and fencing—as well as the plantings of perennials, shrubs, and herbs—were based on archaeological research and were reconstructed by Shurcliff in the 1930s.

The restored garden includes a combination of flower and vegetable sections; border beds are filled with fruits, shrubs, and flowers. Other features are a forcing wall, starting beds, and extensive vegetable plots. This is an interesting and informative place to visit, particularly if you like history and its horticultural discoveries.

❀ **Admission:** Fee.
Garden open: April through October: Tuesday through Saturday 10:00 A.M. to 4:00 P.M., Sunday noon to 4:00 P.M. February, March, and November: weekends only, or by appointment.
Directions: Bacon's Castle is located on County Road 617, just north of the intersection of CR 617 and Route 10.

29. Adam Thoroughgood House

1636 Parish Road, **Virginia Beach,** VA; (757) 431–4000;
www.vbgov.com/dept/arts/adam_thoroughgood

*T*HIS TINY, charming spot is tucked away in a quiet neighborhood. The small brick farmhouse was built in the 1680s by Adam Thoroughgood (the descendant of an indentured servant) on land granted by the British crown. The restored house and garden are typical of late seventeenth-century English cottage style and show the simplicity of Tidewater life at the time.

The small, but fine, four-and-a-half-acre Tudor-style garden behind the house is divided into two distinct parterre gardens with topiaries in the center of each. Arbors, espaliered fruit trees, topiary shrubs, and flowers are sprinkled throughout the precise geometric design. There are 5,000 bulbs planted here as well as an herb garden; of particular note are the daylily blooms in June.

❀ **Admission:** Fee.
Garden open: Tuesday through Saturday 10:00 A.M. to 5:00 P.M., Sunday 1:00 to 5:00 P.M.
Directions: From Virginia Beach Boulevard (US 58), go north on Independence Boulevard, and right on Pleasure House Road. At the large sign for the Thoroughgood neighborhood, go right. Turn left onto Thoroughgood Drive and follow it all the way to Parish Road, where you'll turn left.

30. Colonial Gardens of Williamsburg

Williamsburg, VA; (757) 229–1000; www.colonialwilliamsburg.com

*C*OLONIAL WILLIAMSBURG is the most famous living restoration of eighteenth-century Virginia. Though you may know it for its careful re-creation of colonial life, landscape architects and horticulturists prize it for its fine gardens. Like the well-maintained houses and streets of its 175 acres, the 90 acres of greens and gardens in Williamsburg are historically restored—delightfully so. The numerous gardens range from intimate, neat, colonial-style flower beds behind the townhouses, to the elegant grounds of Governor's Palace, to the charming plantings in the graveyard behind the Bruton Parish Church. For anyone with an interest in eighteenth-century garden design and an appreciation for Virginia's glorious flowering season, Williamsburg is an enthusiast's pleasure. There are no fewer than ninety residential gardens, of which twenty-five are open to the public daily, with the others visitable by appointment or tour. Be sure to pick up a map at the center before you start.

The colonial gardener had a small, English-style formal layout on the half-acre lots assigned by the laws of colonial settlement. In contrast to the frightening wilderness surrounding their colonial towns, the settlers favored carefully planned, rigorously neat gardens. These small plots typically featured bright flower beds, vegetable gardens, and fruit-tree areas that were part of the overall architecture of the colonial property, including the dependencies and service areas. (Here you will see the espaliered and dwarf fruit trees that look so charming, but that saved space by growing against the fences.)

The bright flower beds are outlined by English boxwood hedges in geometric patterns. Topiary circles and squares ornament the hedges in some of the gardens, while one can even see an adventurous hen-shaped topiary (in the Bryan Garden across from the Bruton Parish Church); you'll also see dwarf and tree boxwood here. One of the best of these geometric gardens is the formal boxwood design at Wythe House. Typically, the flowers in these town gardens included such English favorites as larkspur, hollyhock, traditional roses, phlox, foxglove, and the colonial specialty—tulips. One of the best tulip gardens is at the Ludwell-Paradise House. But these familiar English flowers were also interspersed with native American plants like dogwood, coreopsis, black-eyed Susan, and redbud. Among the best flower gardens are those behind Carter's Grove Plantation, where 700 acres contain many types of blooms, vegetables, and herbs.

Don't miss the trees in Williamsburg, many as old as the colony. Some were introduced from abroad: the horse chestnut in 1736, the lovely crape myrtle from China in 1747, and the paper mulberry from the Orient in the mid-eighteenth century. The Carter-Sanders House has a number of notable trees. Flowering shrubs, both native and imported, are everywhere; the Ludwell-Paradise House is noted for its summer-blooming shrubs.

The grounds of the Governor's Palace, in contrast to the more modest gardens, show us the elegance of the Dutch-English traditional style introduced by William and Mary. The landscape gardens here are said to have matched the elegance of the great European estates of the time (to the displeasure of some democratically minded colonists). Designed in 1713 for Alexander Spotswood, this landscape will make you imagine you are at a great house in England. Here you'll see a holly maze (bring the kids!), evergreen parterres, a pleached hornbeam allée, espaliered fruit trees, and the spectacular formal garden of sixteen boxwood diamonds accented with topiary cones at each corner. This setting is ornamented with urns and benches as well as spots of color: scilla, periwinkle, daffodil, and hyacinth in spring. Beyond are fields, vegetable and herb plots, a wooded area for deer, a fish pond, and "Falling Gardens."

A pleasant anachronism at Williamsburg is the formal contemporary garden called the Lila Acheson Wallace Garden at the southwest corner of the historic area. Opened in 1986, it has an oblong reflecting pool with perennial borders, statuary, holly in containers, and a lovely pergola.

❄ **Admission:** Fee.
Garden open: Daily 9:00 A.M. to 5:00 P.M.
Directions: Colonial Williamsburg is midway between Richmond and Norfolk on I–64 (exit 238). After exiting, look for signs for the visitor center.

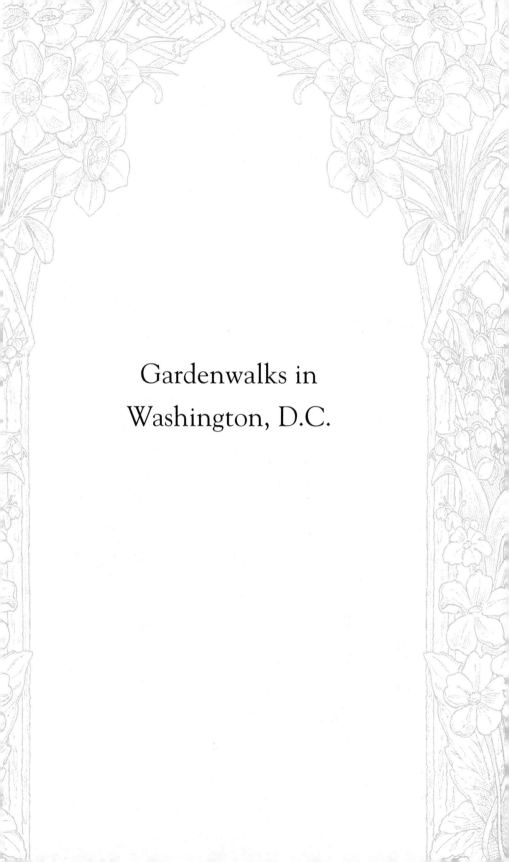

Gardenwalks in
Washington, D.C.

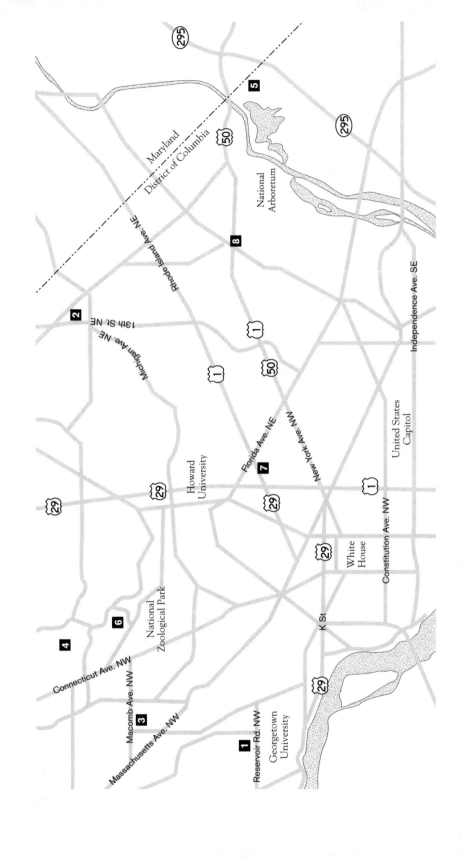

1. Dumbarton Oaks Gardens
2. Franciscan Monastery Garden
3. Gardens of the Washington
   National Cathedral
4. Hillwood Museum

5. Kenilworth Aquatic Gardens
6. Old Stone House Garden
7. United States Botanic Garden
8. United States National
   Arboretum

1. Dumbarton Oaks Gardens

1703 Thirty-second Street NW, **Washington**, DC; (202) 339–6401;
www.doaks.org

*I*N 1921 Robert and Mildred Bliss commissioned the noted landscape gardener Beatrix Farrand to create gardens for their newly purchased mansion, and a masterpiece of American garden design was conceived. The inspired Farrand/Bliss collaboration, based on a mutual admiration of European garden tradition, resulted in the Dumbarton Oaks Gardens. Representing a unique blend of English, French, and Italian styles within an American landscape, the gardens combine classicism with naturalism in a unique and contemporary—and nonderivative—manner.

The well-traveled and cultivated Farrand had learned her craft through trips to Europe and intense training at Boston's Arnold Arboretum under Charles Sprague Sargent. But her inspirations came in large part from her aunt, the novelist Edith Wharton, herself a garden enthusiast and author of the widely regarded *Italian Villas and Gardens,* and the illustrious English landscape gardener Gertrude Jekyll. From Wharton, a key figure in the revival of Italianate gardens in America, Farrand acquired her love of classical gardens; from Jekyll came the emphasis on horticulture over architecture and the idea of garden rooms, a recurring twentieth-century theme.

Farrand believed that the success of professional garden design required a close working relationship with the client. She found an ideal partner in Mildred Bliss, an imaginative gardener in her own right and a talented designer who, among other things, created

Choosing an Outing in Washington, D.C.

American History
Old Stone House Garden

Aquatic Gardens and
Gardens with Water Views
Kenilworth Aquatic Gardens

Arboretums
United States National Arboretum

Art in the Garden
Hillwood Museum

Asian Gardens
United States National Arboretum

Conservatories and Botanic Gardens
Hillwood Museum
United States Botanic Garden

Famous Landscape Designer Gardens
Dumbarton Oaks Garden (Beatrix
  Farrand)
Gardens of the Washington National
  Cathedral (Beatrix Farrand)
United States National Arboretum
  (Russell Page)

Formal Gardens
Dumbarton Oaks Gardens
Franciscan Monastery Garden
Gardens of the Washington National
  Cathedral

Garden Rooms
Dumbarton Oaks Gardens

Informal and
English-style Gardens
Dumbarton Oaks Gardens
Franciscan Monastery Garden
Gardens of the Washington
  National Cathedral

Italianate Gardens
Dumbarton Oaks Gardens

Notable Americans' Gardens
Hillwood Museum (Marjorie
  Merriweather Post)

Romantic Gardens
Dumbarton Oaks Gardens

Rose Gardens
Dumbarton Oaks Gardens

Specialty Gardens
United States National Arboretum
  (bonsai and conifers)

Tropical, Subtropical,
and Swamp Gardens
Kenilworth Aquatic Gardens

Urban Settings
Gardens of the Washington
  National Cathedral
Old Stone House Garden

Wildflowers and Woodland
Franciscan Monastery Garden

some of the ironwork motifs found throughout the grounds. Together they sought a balance between the traditions of formal European gardens (to which Bliss was partial) and the natural landscape, a challenging fifty-acre property with steeply sloping terrain. Their goals were that plants be chosen for beauty and year-round visual pleasure (there is a high proportion of evergreens and ground covers); that the design take advantage of the dramatic site with terracing, flights of steps, and vantage points from which to enjoy garden vistas and the landscape beyond; and that architectural features—pergolas, paths, walls, statues, urns, fountains, pools—be included, as Mildred Bliss had a collection of European garden ornaments that she was anxious to display. The gardens were also to provide living spaces and enclosed areas for recreation. In addition to a swimming pool and tennis court, the garden included a small amphitheater, in the tradition of seventeenth- and eighteenth-century European gardens.

Farrand ingeniously devised a scheme of successive formal and naturalistic terraces and enclosures that would allow for distinctive garden segments, each with different design characteristics, planting styles, architectural ornament, and degrees of formality. The gardens flow from one to the next in a seamless transition, from very formal next to the house to informal down below. With two main axes extending at right angles from the house, symmetrical fountains, elegant stairways and ornamentation, and broad vistas, they evoke the Renaissance gardens so admired by Bliss. They also represent the garden as horticultural delight, focusing on plant colors, shapes, and patterns in the English tradition. Farrand was detail oriented. She carefully planned such elements as patterns of mosaics and stone paths; brick steps with broad, grass landings; shapes of garden beds (some are rectangular, other romantically arabesque); even garden furniture, some of which she designed herself. Because of her primary interest in horticulture, she kept track in meticulous detail of each and every planting throughout the grounds. (In *The Plant Book* for Dumbarton Oaks she tells it all.)

The ten-acre gardens were completed between 1921 and 1941, with a few additions later. In 1940 the Blisses donated sixteen acres (including the mansion and gardens) to Harvard University to create the Dumbarton Oaks Research Library and Collection. The remaining twenty-seven acres became a park operated by the National Park Service. In 1944 Dumbarton Oaks was the site for internationally attended meetings that formulated the basic principles of the United Nations. Today both the gardens and the museum (a treasure in itself with noted Byzantine, Pre-Columbian and European art collections and rare books) are open to the public.

At the garden entrance you will be given a carefully prepared and descriptive self-guided walking tour brochure, which identifies eighteen stops of particular interest. You will want to discover and savor each garden room, walkway, and vista at your own pace, lingering at the remarkable views and marveling at the cascades of tumbling forsythia, the romantic wisteria arbors, the graceful courtyards and allées and winding steps, the glorious plantings—more than we can describe here.

Some highlights: the Orangerie, a winter garden featuring a climbing fig from the nineteenth century and clusters of potted plants; the Green Garden, affording magnificent views of formal gardens just below; the Beech Terrace, the setting of one of the grandest American beeches we have ever seen, its roots covered with flowering bulbs; the Urn Terrace, with its beautiful curved pebble mosaic designs; the Rose Garden, a favorite of the Blisses, with its 1,000 plants in geometric beds; the Fountain Terrace, its enchanting classical cupid fountains and grassy lawn bordered with colorful bulbs and perennials; Melisande's Allée and Lover's Lane pool, site of the Roman-style amphitheater; the glorious English-style herbaceous border and vegetable garden, a feast of color combinations in true Jekyllian tradition; the Ellipse, a group of formally clipped ironwood trees (squared off in the French manner) around a small pool with iris; and the magnificent Pebble Garden, an enclosed parterre featuring pebble mosaics in intricate designs and shapes similar to the raised beds of ground cover next to them. The North Vista, a succession of four graceful grass terraces, connected with very gradual brick-and-grass steps, leads back to the mansion. On your walk you will have gone up and down the contoured slope on carefully designed (and beautifully kept) pathways of stone, brick, or grass.

At the end of her long career, Beatrix Farrand stated that Dumbarton Oaks was outstanding among her many gardens, "the best and most deeply felt of a fifty-year career." You will come away feeling that you have experienced a rare aesthetic and horticultural treat.

✿ **Admission:** Fee from March 15 through October 31.

Garden open: March 15 through October 31: Tuesday through Sunday 2:00 to 6:00 P.M. November 1 through March 14: Tuesday through Sunday 2:00 to 5:00 P.M. Closed major holidays. The museum and shop are closed for renovation until 2007.

Directions: In Washington, D.C., make your way to Wisconsin Avenue in Georgetown; approaching from M Street in central Washington, D.C., turn right onto Wisconsin, and again right on R Street. The garden entrance is on the corner of R and Thirty-first Streets, 1 block east of Wisconsin Avenue.

2. Franciscan Monastery Garden

1400 Quincy Street NE, **Washington**, DC; (202) 526–6800

*I*N A SECLUDED hilltop setting within some forty-five wooded acres, this serene garden embellishes the impressive and grand Franciscan Monastery. The fifteen acres of well-tended gardens are in two parts: Next to the church and cloister are formal flower gardens; below, amid a naturalistic setting, native shrubs, flowers, trees, and boulders are evocative re-creations of famous religious shrines from the Holy Land.

The commanding yellow brick main church, Rosary Portico, and cloister—all with graceful, rounded arches in an architectural style reminiscent of Spanish colonial—date from 1899, but it was not until 1920 that the landscaped gardens were open to the public. Beautiful rose parterres (with 2,000 plants) ornament the cloister, along with perennial borders, a small Asian garden near the chapel, and a collection of religious statues (including Saint Francis, of course!) framed by geraniums and other blossoms. From these enclosed formal gardens you take a somewhat steep, shaded path that winds around to the quiet valley below. Along the way, in the cool of the deep woods, you'll find the Stations of the Cross enhanced by tall evergreens, magnolias, ferns, ivies, and masses of azaleas and rhododendrons. (In spring profusions of blooming bulbs and dogwoods add a touch of color.) The path leads to faithful replicas of such spiritual sites as the Grotto of Lourdes, the Grotto of Gethsemane, and the Tomb of Mary, with imposing rock formations and trickling fountains adding to the

Garden Shows and Festivals in Washington, D.C.

MARCH
Washington Flower and Garden Show; (703) 569–7141

MAY
Herb Festival at the United States National Arboretum; (202) 475–4815

Potomac Valley Society Rhododendron Flower Show; (202) 475–4815

JULY
Annual Water Lily and Conservation Festival, Kenilworth Aquatic Gardens; (202) 426–6905

DECEMBER
Poinsettia Show at the United States Botanic Garden; (202) 226–4082

mysterious ambience. From a pretty little brick shrine to Saint Anne at the bottom of the hill, you can enjoy a panorama of meadows with weeping willows, cedars, and magnolias—hardly what you would expect in an urban setting. You will find a visit to these gardens a peaceful and reflective experience.

❀ **Admission:** Free.

Garden open: Daily 8:00 A.M. to dusk. Hourly tours (9:00 A.M. to 4:00 P.M. daily) of the church and catacombs are available; you can walk through the gardens on your own.

Directions: Take Fourteenth Street in northeast Washington. The garden is between Michigan Avenue and Fourteenth Street.

3. Gardens of the Washington National Cathedral

Massachusetts and Wisconsin Avenues NW, **Washington,** DC; (202) 537–6200; www.cathedral.org/cathedral

*A*NY VISITOR to the nation's capital won't want to miss the imposing National Cathedral, a true Washington landmark, and its famous historic gardens. Consistent with the fourteenth-century-style Gothic cathedral (started in 1900 and completed in 1990), the gardens were designed under the guidance of Frederick Law Olmsted Jr. and Beatrix Farrand, among others, to contain "plants of historical interest, plants of the Bible and Christian legends, and native plants." The formal and informal enclosed gardens are a living museum of biblical and medieval European gardening history.

Before embarking on your gardenwalk, pick up the excellent self-guided tour brochure available at the Herb Cottage (which serves as a visitor center). You will be surprised to discover that these intimate gardens are much more complex than you might think at first glance. Combining unusual architectural features—such as authentic medieval archways, bas reliefs, gates, sculpture with perennial borders, herbaceous plantings in intricate patterns, a rose garden, and flowering shrubs and trees of particular significance (such as cedars and figs)—they are a study in symbolism. Among the most evocative is the Bishop's Garden, a medieval garden made up of several tiny parts; it was created by Olmsted for the bishop's private use. You'll find a yew walk (symbolizing immortality), a lower perennial border, a hortulus (small geometric raised beds planted with herbs used in Charlemagne's time), a rose garden (with fragrant floribundas), an herb bed of aromatic and culinary varieties, an old English sundial, a small pool in the shape of a primitive cross, and a stone wall with fifteenth-century bas reliefs of martyrs and saints. Each of these areas invites careful scrutiny. You walk from one garden room to the next, along small brick pathways edged with boxwood, its delicate scent permeating the air.

Other garden sites to visit include the Herb Cottage Garden, the woodland pathway bordered with native wildflowers, and the Cloister Garden, featuring a dramatic contemporary bronze fountain. To the west of the cathedral, next to the West Portal Court entrance, is a grove of stately trees, lawns, plantings, walkways, and benches in a parklike setting typical of Olmsted's landscapes. Throughout the grounds are dogwoods, hollies, camellias, azaleas, and other flowering shrubs. There is also a greenhouse specializing in herbs, shade perennials, cacti, and seasonal annuals.

❀ **Admission:** Free.

Garden open: Daily dawn to dusk. Herb Cottage open Monday through Saturday 9:30 A.M. to 5:00 P.M., Sunday 10:00 A.M. to 5:00 P.M.
Directions: The cathedral is located at the intersection of Massachusetts and Wisconsin Avenues in northwest Washington, D.C. From downtown Washington take Massachusetts Avenue north to Wisconsin Avenue. Turn right onto Wisconsin Avenue. The cathedral is on your immediate right.

4. Hillwood Museum

4155 Linnean Avenue NW, **Washington,** DC; (202) 686–8500;
www.hillwoodmuseum.org

*T*HIS BEAUTIFULLY landscaped site surrounded by deep woods features the elegant mansion and grounds of noted heiress Marjorie Merriweather Post. The Georgian-style house (1920s) contains Post's impressive collection of eighteenth- and nineteenth-century French and Russian fine and decorative arts. It became a public museum in 1977, shortly after her death. One glance at the mansion and meticulously groomed gardens, both formal and informal, will tell you that Marjorie Post knew how to live.

Among the garden pleasures are an elegant and formal French parterre with a central pool and fountains; an enchanting rose garden (designed in consultation with landscape architect Perry Wheeler, who also contributed to the White House Rose Garden); a Japanese garden with stream, rocks, pools, and picturesque arched bridges; and a 1930s greenhouse with an important orchid collection. More naturalistic and native plantings include azalea, rhododendron, dogwood, boxwood, and clusters of trees, some very tall and stately. You can walk around the grounds on your own, though reservations are required for the two-hour house tour.

❁ **Admission:** Free; fee for house.

Garden open: Tuesday through Saturday 10:00 A.M. to 5:00 P.M.; closed in January.

Directions: From the Capital Beltway (Interstate 495), take the Connecticut Avenue (Route 185) exit south. Proceed about 5 miles on Connecticut and turn left onto Tilden Street. Take the second left onto Linnean Avenue. The entrance to the estate will be on the right. From downtown Washington, D.C., take Connecticut Avenue north and turn right onto Tilden Street. Take the second left onto Linnean Avenue. The entrance to the estate will be on the right.

5. Kenilworth Aquatic Gardens

1550 Anacostia Avenue NE, **Washington**, DC; (202) 426–6905;
www.nps.gov/kepa

*P*EACEFULLY SET amid forty-four acres of tidal marsh of the
Anacostia River, just a stone's throw from urban bustle,
these twelve-acre gardens provide a wonderfully naturalistic ambience in which to view aquatic plants. Maintained by the National
Park Service, the specialty gardens feature dozens of ponds filled to
capacity with water lilies and lotuses (especially spectacular in June,
July, and August) as well as cattails, irises, water primroses, and
hyacinths. Grassy (and sometimes muddy) paths circle the ponds,
where you might also see turtles, snakes, frogs, migratory waterfowl,
and other birds. With walking guide in hand (available at the
entrance) you can identify each site. A boardwalk into the marsh
was recently added.

The Gardens of the White House

Yes, you can visit the famous Rose Garden, where every president
and First Lady speaks to the press and invited guests. Four times
a year the White House gardens are open to the public. You can
take an interior tour and see the beautiful roses for yourself from
within the White House. The Rose Garden was installed in 1913
under the guidance of Ellen Wilson, the first wife of Woodrow
Wilson. President John F. Kennedy had the Rose Garden, located
just outside of the Oval Office, redesigned for use as a venue for
outdoor ceremonies. Depending upon when you visit, you may see
tulips, hyacinths, and chrysanthemums in the East Garden and
magnolia trees, Katherine crab apple trees, and of course roses in
the Rose Garden. Garden tour tickets are first-come, first-served
and are distributed at the Ellipse Visitor Pavilion on each tour day
beginning at 7:30 A.M. For more information, call (202) 208–1631.

This national park was once the private waterside garden of Civil War veteran Walter Shaw, who decided to plant water lilies to remind him of his native Maine. From a few specimens the gardens grew and grew, as his daughter Helen traveled around the world in search of more exotic varieties. When the property was threatened by a dredging plan along the river, it was sold to the government for preservation. Since 1957 the Kenilworth Aquatic Gardens have been dedicated to the propagation of water plants, both native and exotic, and to the preservation of the last natural tidal marsh in Washington. Note that water blossoms are best seen in mornings, when day blossoms open and before night blossoms close. Don't miss the wildflower meadow and pretty views from the banks of the river.

❀ **Admission:** Free.
Garden open: Daily 7:00 A.M. to 4:00 P.M.; closed Thanksgiving, Christmas, and New Year's Day.
Directions: Kenilworth Aquatic Gardens is located in northeast Washington, D.C., near the Maryland boundary, along the Anacostia River. The entrance is just west of Route 295 (Kenilworth Avenue), between Quarles and Douglas Streets, on Anacostia Avenue.

6. Old Stone House Garden

3051 M Street NW, **Washington,** DC; (202) 426–6851

*B*EHIND THIS charming 1764 fieldstone house, Washington's only surviving pre-Revolutionary building, is a very pretty, old-fashioned garden. The terraced property is graced with fruit trees, perennial flower beds in great masses, wild roses, curving lawns, and brick stone paths. A walk on these intimate grounds is a real pleasure!

You can visit the garden (which is partly visible from the road) and the house, featuring colonial furnishings and artifacts, on your own; costumed guides are on hand to answer questions.

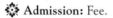 **Admission:** Fee.

Garden open: Daily 9:00 A.M. to 4:00 P.M.

Directions: Old Stone House is accessible from M Street in George-town, between Thirtieth and Thirty-first streets.

7. United States Botanic Garden

245 First Street SW, **Washington,** DC; (202) 225–8333;
www.usbg.gov

*T*HE UNITED STATES BOTANIC GARDEN describes itself as a living museum. It is, in fact, surrounded by the capital's world-famous museums up and down the Mall. But it hardly seems like a museum when you visit it, because you are surrounded by living things; riotous color, delicate shapes, exotic blooms.

The present conservatory was built in 1933 and was renovated in 2001. Major attractions include a desert garden, a primeval gar-den, a wonderful orchid collection, a medicinal house, a garden of rare and endangered species, and a jungle garden. There are outdoor plantings across Independence Avenue from the conservatory in Frederic Auguste Bartholdi Park. Named for the famous sculptor, whose historic fountain is the centerpiece, the park features seasonal displays.

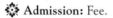 **Admission:** Free.

Garden open: Daily 10:00 A.M. to 5:00 P.M. Bartholdi Park is open daily dawn to dusk.

Directions: The conservatory main entrance is located at 100 Mary-land Avenue SW. Visitors can access Bartholdi Park from any of the three bordering streets: Independence Avenue, Washington Avenue, or First Street.

8. United States National Arboretum

3501 New York Avenue NE, **Washington**, DC, (202) 245-2726; www.usna.usda.gov

*T*HE UNITED STATES National Arboretum is much more than a collection of trees. Amid 444 acres of rolling parkland, you'll find magnificent specialty gardens, many of which are among the best of their kind in the country. The mission of this vast facility, the only federally funded arboretum in the country, is "to conduct research, provide education, conserve and display trees, shrubs, and other plants to enhance the environment." It includes thirty-seven sites that can be visited (preferably traveling from one to the next by car, given the distances), all labeled and identified. You will drive (or walk, if you choose) in a landscape of remarkable trees, ponds, and vistas, seeing important collections of Asian plants, dwarf conifers, azaleas, hollies, crab apples, wildflowers, woodland plants, and some spectacular formal gardens.

This is an enormous place; before you start out, stop at the administration center and information/gift shop to pick up a map numbered according to the suggested route. The administration center itself contains a huge herbarium with more than 600,000 pressed varieties of herbs from all over the world. Follow the small sign pointing to the National Bonsai and Penjing Collections and National Herb Garden, without doubt among the most remarkable displays in the arboretum.

The bonsai compound contains the largest and most complete collection in North America. Here, amid shaded stone and gravel walkways, moon gates, and enchanting little interior gardens, are the fine exhibits, housed in various pavilions and greenhouses. The bonsai on display in the airy Japanese pavilion include fifty-three that were presented as a bicentennial gift to the American people. These rare and precious treasures, representing one of Japan's most revered art forms, can reach a venerable old age—one is apparently already more than 360 years old!

The Chinese pavilion displays its Penjing collection, which features plants that have been dwarfed using a different technique from the bonsai; here too are Chinese artifacts, such as large watering jars and stone lanterns, as well as the craggy symbolic rocks and tiny arched bridges and stone paths traditionally found in Chinese gardens.

Directly across the street from the bonsai collection is the wonderful National Herb Garden, the largest designed herb garden in the world. You enter through a walkway of fragrant boxwood; once inside you will want to linger in this ordered world of clipped hedges, graceful trellises, fountains, and plants in intricate patterns. Beyond is a grand panorama reminiscent of an English romantic landscape, with a broad expanse of meadow framing a group of great columns soaring in the distance. Known as the National Capitol Columns, they were once part of the U.S. Capitol and were salvaged when the building was renovated after the Civil War; in the 1980s they were placed in the arboretum under the personal supervision of the noted landscape designer Russell Page, who added a fountain, water stair, and reflecting pool to enhance them.

The herb garden is made up of three separate gardens: the Knot Garden, Historic Rose Garden, and the oval specialty gardens. The first is a formal arrangement of dwarf evergreens in interlocking designs surrounding a circular brick terrace and fountain; on each side are arbors covered with clematis and grapevines. The rose garden contains specimens of historic interest, many quite rare and of ancient origins; they come from various parts of the world and are all identified. The tiny specialty gardens are thematic and herbal.

Contained within a one-acre grassy oval, they include a garden dedicated to plants listed by the ancient Greeks; a dye garden planted with specimens used in the dyeing of fabric; an early American garden in the colonial tradition; an American Indian garden with herbs used by Native Americans for beverages, medicines, and crafts; a medicinal garden; a culinary garden; a wild-bird garden; an industrial garden containing plants of economic value (rubber, flax, hops, etc.); a fragrance garden; an Oriental garden; and a beverage garden.

There are many other garden sites to enjoy in the arboretum, perhaps too many for one visit. If you have limited time, we especially recommend Fern Valley and the Gotelli Dwarf and Slow-Growing Conifer Collection. The first is a naturalistic wonder with a gentle stream and meadow garden in a valley of deep woods, tall evergreens, century-old beeches, oaks, and tulips. The Gotelli Conifer Collection is a rare experience, considered one of the finest such gardens in the world. Magnificent varieties of fir, cedar, juniper, pine, hemlock, spruce, and other specimens are set on five hillside acres with views of downtown Washington in the distance. It offers a fascinating assortment of plants in different shapes, textures, and sizes set in well-tended, rounded gravel beds, separated by grassy pathways. Surrounding them are ornamental grasses and bulbs, all carefully identified.

❀ **Admission:** Free.

Garden open: Weekdays 8:00 A.M. to 5:00 P.M., weekends 10:00 A.M. to 5:00 P.M.; bonsai collection hours are shorter; closed Christmas.

Directions: The National Arboretum is located in the northeast section of Washington, D.C., approximately ten minutes from the Capitol Building. There are two entrances: one at 3501 New York Avenue NE and the other at Twenty-fourth & R Streets NE off Bladensburg Road. From northwest Washington follow New York Avenue east to the intersection of Bladensburg Road. Turn right (south) onto Bladensburg Road and go 4 blocks to R Street. Make a left onto R Street and continue 2 blocks to the arboretum gates.

Glossary

allée: A stately tree-lined avenue.

arboretum: A place where an extensive variety of trees are cultivated for scientific, educational, or ornamental purposes.

belvedere: A structure such as a summerhouse situated to command a view.

bosquet: A small grove or thicket.

botanical garden: A place where plants are cultivated for scientific, educational, or ornamental purposes.

butterfly garden: A garden in which flowers are specially chosen to attract butterflies.

classical garden: A formal garden whose aesthetic attitudes and values are embodied in ancient Greek and Roman design.

colonial (or plantation) garden: A garden designed or reconstructed in the colonial American style, with separate sections for flowers, fruit trees, vegetables, herbs, and various outbuildings.

conservatory: A greenhouse in which plants are arranged for aesthetic display and in carefully controlled climatic conditions.

cottage garden: A small, unpretentious garden featuring flowers and vegetables in a casual arrangement.

cup garden: A garden in the ancient Chinese tradition, in which an object is framed by its surroundings.

demonstration garden: A garden whose purpose is horticultural education.

English garden: A naturalistic garden style first developed in eighteenth-century England, as compared with the more formal French style.

espalier: A fruit tree or shrub trained to grow flat against a wall, often in a symmetrical pattern.

folly: A whimsical garden structure that is decorative rather than useful.

formal garden: A garden in which nature is trained to adhere to geometric or other formal decorative principles.

gardenesque: A deliberately near-chaotic approach to landscape.

garden rooms: Individual, self-contained, and separately designed sections of a larger garden.

gazebo: A free-standing roofed structure, usually with open sides, that provides a shady resting place in a garden.

grotto: A small cave or cavern or an artificial structure made to resemble one.

ha-ha: A sunken hedge or moat that serves as a fence without impairing the view.

hydrophytic garden: An aquatic garden.

Italianate garden: A garden in the Italian style, often featuring classical elements, statuary, and fountains.

knot garden: An elaborate planting of greenery, usually thyme or boxwood, following the patterns of knots.

maze: A garden labyrinth: an intricate, deliberately confusing, patterned network of hedges and pathways, designed to entertain.

naturalistic garden: A garden in which the design attempts to imitate nature in its free form, rather than to impose form upon it.

orangerie: A sheltered place, such as a greenhouse, used particularly in cold climates to grow oranges.

parterre: An ornamental flower garden whose beds and paths form a pattern.

pergola: An arbor or passageway with a roof or trellis on which climbing plants are trained to grow.

pleasure garden: A garden such as a flower garden or park, designed purely for enjoyment.

promenade: A place for strolling in a garden.

rock garden: A garden in which rocks and plants are arranged in a carefully designed, decorative scheme, often featuring alpine plants.

shade garden: A garden featuring plants that grow best in little or no sun.

topiary garden: A garden in which live trees and shrubs are clipped into fanciful shapes.

water garden: A garden in which ponds, streams, and other water elements, as well as plants that grow at water sites, are an integral part of the overall design.

wildflower garden: Usually a preserve in which flowering plants grow in a natural, uncultivated state.

winter garden: A conservatory or other indoor garden that can be enjoyed all year.

xeriscape: A dry garden, one that makes use of water-conserving techniques and drought-tolerant plants.

Zen garden: A garden in the Japanese tradition, designed for beauty and contemplation.

Index of Gardens

L

Lewis Ginter Botanical Garden (Richmond, VA), 255

Lexington Cemetery (Lexington, KY), 121

Lockerly Arboretum (Milledgeville, GA), 104

Longue Vue Gardens (New Orleans, LA), 134

Louisville Nature Center and Beargrass Creek State Nature Preserve (Louisville, KY), 123

M

Magnolia Plantation and Gardens (Charleston, SC), 191

Marie Selby Botanical Gardens (Sarasota, FL), 71

Mary Washington House and Garden (Fredericksburg, VA), 241

Massee Lane Gardens (Fort Valley, GA), 97

Maymont (Richmond, VA), 256

McKee Botanical Garden (Vero Beach, FL), 76

Memphis Botanic Garden (Memphis, TN), 217

Middleton Place (Charleston, SC), 192

Mobile Botanical Gardens (Mobile, AL), 41

Monmouth Plantation (Natchez, MS), 146

Monticello (Charlottesville, VA), 234

Montpelier (Montpelier Station, VA), 247

Morikami Park (Delray Beach, FL), 51

Morven Park (Leesburg, VA), 243

Mount Vernon (Mount Vernon, VA), 249

Mounts Botanical Garden (West Palm Beach, FL), 77

Mynelle Gardens (Jackson, MS), 144

N

New Hanover County Extension Service Arboretum (Wilmington, NC), 179

New Orleans Botanical Garden (New Orleans, LA), 135

Noccalula Falls Botanical Gardens (Gadsden, AL), 40

Norfolk Botanical Garden (Norfolk, VA), 251

North Carolina Botanical Garden (Chapel Hill, NC), 159

O

Oak Hill at the Martha Berry Museum (Mount Berry, GA), 104

Oak Ridge Estate (Arrington, VA), 228

Oatlands Plantation (Leesburg, VA), 243

Okefenokee Swamp Park (Waycross, GA), 112

Old Salem (Winston-Salem, NC), 181

Old Stone House Garden (Washington, DC), 281

Old Ursuline Convent (New Orleans, LA), 136

Opryland USA (Nashville, TN), 219